Social Problems in India

About the Editors

Dr. Bhola Nath Ghosh obtained M.A. (Sociology) from Kalyani University and Ph.D. in Social Science and also awarded a certificate from the University of East Anglia, Norwich, United Kingdom for participating in the course, entitled, "Course on Monitoring, Evaluation and project Analysis" and currently an Associate Professor, Head in Sociology, Indian Statistical Institute, Kolkata. He presented several papers in National and International Conferences which was held in India and abroad (United Kingdom, Bangladesh, France, Germany, Hungary, Sweden and Malayasia), Austria. He published several articles in National and International reputed journals. He authored several books'.

Professor Himansu S. Ghosh, Ph.D., joined Bishnupur Ramananda College in 1972 and after serving here for fifteen years he joined Bankura Christian College in 1987. He taught at Bankura Christian College (P.G. College) for seventeen years and joined Vidyasagar University as Registrar on 30th April, 2004 and continued till 2007. As a Visiting Professor he taught Sociology at the University of Burdwan for six years. Finally, he served as Chairman, The West Bengal College Service Commission from 2007 to 2011. Moreover, Dr. Ghosh has published a number of books of P.G. and U.G. level. And specially to mention that he worked on Panchayat for which he was appointed Consultant of M.S. Swaminathan Research Foundation, Chennai.

Dr. Notan Bhusan Kar, M.A. (Sociology), M. A. (Pol. Sc. & Rural Administration), Ph.D., is an independent researcher, who has presented his research papers in numerous National & International Seminars. He is a teacher in IGNOU, Kolkata, His research interest are: Gloablization and its impact, Tribal communities and their problems, Rural Development, Gender Issues, Social problems, Backward & Marginalized people. At present he is an Assistant Editor of an inter-disciplinary journal of social sciences, "Society Today."

Social Problems in India

Edited by
Bhola Nath Ghosh
Himansu S. Ghosh
Assisted by
Notan Bhusan Kar

CONCEPT PUBLISHING COMPANY PVT. LTD.
NEW DELHI-110059

ISBN-13: 978-93-86682-02-4

First Published 2017

Published and Printed by

Concept
Since 1974

Concept Publishing Company Pvt. Ltd.
Regd. Office:
A/15-16, Commercial Block, Mohan Garden,
New Delhi-110059 (INDIA)
Phones : 25351460, 25351794, *Fax* : 091-11-25357109
Email : publishing@conceptpub.com
Website: www.conceptpub.com

Cataloging in Publication Data—DK Courtesy: D.K. Agencies (P) Ltd. <docinfo@dkagencies.com>

Social problems in India / edited by Bhola Nath Ghosh, Himansu S. Ghosh ; assisted by Notan Bhusan Kar.
pages cm
Contributed articles.
Includes index.
ISBN 9789386682024

1. Social problems—India. 2. Social problems—India—West Bengal. I. Ghosh, Bhola Nath, 1954- editor. II. Ghosh, Himansu S., editor. III. Kar, Notan Bhusan, editor.

HN687.S63 2017 DDC 361.10954 23

Preface and Acknowledgements

We have tried to bring together the scientists, researchers and policy-makers into one forum to explore and understand the issues concerning social problems in our society. This is also based on the realization that in order to understand these complex issues, we need a multidisciplinary and inter-disciplinary approach. There are five papers out of fifteen included in this volume that are presented in the lecture series of the Sociological Research Unit, Indian Statistical Institute, Kolkata.

We are thankful to the paper contributors for their enthusiastic cooperation. We also thank all the colleagues of Sociological Research Unit, Indian Statistical Institute, Kolkata and Giridih for their understanding and kindness. A word of special thanks goes to Concept Publishing Company (P) Ltd., New Delhi. We hope this book would help to the academicians, researchers and practitioners.

Contents

Preface and Acknowledgements v

List of Contributors ix

Introduction xi

1. Combating Corruption: The Issues and Challenges 1
Swapan Kumar Pramanik

2. State, Law and Domestic Violence Against Women in India: A Critical Review 13
Biswajit Ghosh

3. Student Radicalism in Contemporary Bengal 36
Anirban Banerjee

4. Problems of Healthcare Facilities among the Tribals A Case from Malda District in West Bengal 51
Arpita Ghosh

5. Corruption in India: Can the Hydra Headed Monster be Chopped! 64
Amal Mandal

6. Globalization, Development induced Displacement and the Livelihood Issues of Tribal: A Case of Mineral-based Industries in India 86
Notan Bhusan Kar

7. Maternal Mortality and Associated Risk Factors: A Study in Kolkata Metropolitan Area of West Bengal, India 100
Partha De

8. Status of Women in East India: Its Measurement and Determinants 123
Chaiti Sharma Biswas

9. Cancer Care and Social Support: Challenges and Key Issues 136
Sourav Madhur Dey

10. Education and Identity: A Case Study of A Santal Village of West Bengal 162
Sujata Chakraborty and Bhola Nath Ghosh

11. Development or Counter-development? Response of the Jharkhand Movement 177
Jyotiprasad Chatterjee

12. Bullying: A Social Issue 203
Rumki Gupta and Jayeta Dhara

13. Right to Equality: Indian Women 215
Himansu S. Ghosh

14. Woman on Trial in Mainstream Hindi Films: An Analysis with Special Reference to 'Aradhana' (1969), 'Andaz' (1971) and 'Daag' (1973) 228
Pallav Mukhopadhyay

15. Population Ageing and Demographic Transition: Indian Experience 239
Sidhartha Sankar Laha

Index 258

List of Contributors

Dr. Amal Mandal, Associate Professor, Department of Political Science, Tufanganj College, Cooch Behar, amalcob@rediffmail.com, 09434689831 (M)

Dr. Anirban Banerjee, Professor of Sociology, The University of Burdwan, Anirban_2banerjee1961@yahoo.co.in, 09153085106 (M)

Dr. Arpita Ghosh, Assistant Professor, Department of Human Rights and Human Development, Rabindra Bharati University, Aghosh.hr08@gmail.com, 09433938454 (M)

Dr. Bhola Nath Ghosh, Associate Professor and Head Sociological Research Unit, Indian Statistical Institute, Kolkata, bholanathghosh@hotmail.com, 09433018495(M)

Dr. Biswajit Ghosh, Professor and Head, Department of Sociology, University of Burdwan, bghoshbu@gmail.com, 900276 9014 (M)

Dr. Chaiti Sharma Biswas, Scientist, Economic Research Unit, Indian Statistical Institute, Kolkata, csharmabiswas@gmail.com, 094330069580 (M)

Dr. Himansu S. Ghosh, Professor of Political Science, Ex. Chairman, West Bengal College Service Commission, Kolkata himansughosh1947@gmail.com, 09433568449 (M)

Dr. Jayeta Dhara, Research Associate, Psychology Research Unit, Indian Statistical Institute, Kolkata.

Dr. Jyotiprasad Chatterjee, Associate Professor, Sociology, Rastraguru Surendranath College, Barrackpore, jyotichatto@rediffmail.com, 9143005702 (M)

Dr. Notan Bhusan Kar, Independent Researcher in Kolkata based and Academic Councellor in IGNOU, notanbhusankar@gmail.com, 09477560129 (M)

Dr. Pallav Mukhopadhyay, Assistant Professor, Department of Journalism and Mass Communication, West Bengal State University, pmy_m@rediffmail.com

Dr. Partha De, Scientist, Population Studies Unit, Indian Statistical Institute, Kolkata, parthade@hotmail.com, partha@isical.ac.in, 09831321179 (M)

Dr. Rumki Gupta, Scientist, Psychology Research Unit, Indian Statistical Institute, Kolkata, Gupta.rumki@gmail.com, 09433054024 (M)

Dr. Sidhartha Sankar Laha, Assistant Professor, Department of Economics, Tufanganj Mahavidyalaya, Cooch Behar, sidharthasankar09@ gmail.com, 09434689831 (M)

Dr. Sourav Madhur Dey, Professor, Department of Sociology, University of Burdwan, smdey@soc.buruniv.ac.in, 09433410542 (M)

Dr. Sujata Chakraborty, Independent Researcher in Navi Mumbai based, sujatachakraborty102@gmail.com, 09987799404 (M)

Dr. Swapan Kumar Pramanik, Professor of Sociology, Ex. Vice Chancellor, Vidyasagar University, Medinipur, 033–25771316

Introduction

Sociologist does not fully agree on how to define a "social problems." Jermoe Manis states in his *Social Problems* text book that "....any condition identified by the knowledge values of science as detrimental to human well-being" is a social problem. By this definition, it is sociologists, not the general public, who define social problems. Yet whatever formal definition is used, most books treat pretty much the same series of problems. Although most people know something about social problems, their knowledge is generally unorganized, frequently contradictory, often incorrect. In addition, their knowledge is also generally influenced by political ideologies.

We now turn our attention to the chapters included in the book and see how the social problems is addressed. This volume first introduces general issues of social problems.

In this volume, we consider social problems to be those conditions that concern and disturb people.

Fifteen following chapters deal with specific problems. Each presents a body of data bearing on the problem and interprets these data in terms of the basic approaches.

According to *Swapan Kumar Pramanik,* chapter-1, corruption is the use or abuse of official power for promoting personal interests. Decades back, Mahatma Gandhi, while reacting against rampant corruption in the Congress Ministries formed under the Government of India Act, 1935, said, "I would go to the length of giving the whole Congress a decent burial rather than put up with corruption that is rampant". Nehru, in one of his famous post-independence speeches promised to hang in the open street posts the black marketers and smugglers to fight the menace of corruption. All these promises have remained rhetoric, whereas corruption is thriving.

Guner Myrdal in his "The Asian Drama" has depicted the extent of corruption thus in India, from the gateman in the railway level crossing up to the topmost bureaucrat and politicians—everyone exploits his official position and in many cases, with a pecuniary benefit. One Central Minister along with some top bureaucrats, politicians and businessmen are in jail for the biggest ever telecommunication scam involving an amount of a staggering Rs. 1,80,000/- crore. In an India corruption study, 2010, made by the Centre for Media Studies, a Survey on 10,000 rural households was made to gather corruption data in four key sectors impacting the poorer public distribution, school education, water supply and health services. It was revealed that in these basic services the quality of service provided is very weak and corruption is very high. Despite great emphasis on Bharat Nirman, Right to Education, National Rural Health Mission and Food Security in recent years, the beneficiaries are very few and the extent of corruption is very high. Hundreds of billions of rupees are spent on these programmes, but the poor are not benefiting adequately. Media generally projects corruption at high levels. While this is true, the corruption faced by common person in their day to day lives, is equally important. It seems that our democracy has degenerated to kleptocracy, a consideration state, where everything, either basic necessities or things worthy to get, can be had for a consideration. But the silver line in this gloomy situation is the level of public awareness on the menace of corruption and the formation of a very strong public opinion to fight it out. This is also compelling the state to adopt various measures at least to check corruption, if not to eliminate it.

Chapter-2, *Biswajit Ghosh* concentrates on state, law and domestic violence against women. It is a normal practice for the modern states to rely on the legal and administrative structures to ensure gender equality and gender justice. This chapter critically reviews the performance of this legal structure to curb domestic violence against women in India. It is widely known that instances of officially claimed number of domestic violence against women have increased tremendously during the last few decades in the country. This is despite several amendments to the old laws and enactment of a new law. There are several arguments and counter-arguments explaining this trend. A review of the performance of these laws however proves that mere passing of law may not guarantee reduction in the number of violence as well as improvement in justice delivery system in India. Much remains to be done to ensure gender justice and equality in a patriarchal society.

Chapter-3, *Anirban Banerjee,* seeks to examine the present state of student radicalism in West Bengal. Since mid-May 2011, there has been a political change in West Bengal which has been hailed as **parivartan.** The ruling Left Front government was ousted from power and the Trinamul-Congress combine stormed into power. **Parivartan** has had a wide ranging impact on the social, political and cultural life of West Bengal. The education system has been also affected by political change. And this has also affected the student movement. The major research questions posed by the author are—(1) In what direction is the student movement going? (2) Do today's students have the same ideas about radical social change as their predecessors? These questions prompted the author to do a UGC sponsored Major Research Project entitled "Student Radicalism in Post-Left Bengal". The project is now in its early stages. On basis of some primary and secondary data, collected for the project, the author seeks to answer these questions.

Chapter-4, *Arpita Ghosh*, concentrates on health and well-being are the great concern of our contemporary era. While studying with the health situation of the tribal it has been observed that with regard to access to and benefits from the public health system the tribal have always remained at the receiving end of the system. The public health system has remained largely uneven and concentrated among the better endowed sections of the society. So, the socially disadvantaged sections of the society have always lagged in this respect and the tribal have remained excluded. Health rights have never been accredited from a rights approach and more so for the tribal. The developmental projects meant for tribal development have not been holistically treated to include health rights.

Even after so many decades of independence, access to health institutions and civic amenities have had very poor turnouts in the rural areas and especially the tribal dominated belts. The present chapter deals with the access of the tribal families in Malda district of West Bengal to healthcare facilities.

Chapter-5, *Amal Mandal*, taking corruption in its holistic embrace and describing the general causes of its proliferation, this chapter argues that corruption in India can only, for many reasons as elaborated, be cured or controlled and the fight against corruption heavily hinges on the commitment and determination of the political leadership which is, indeed, lacking in India.

Chapter-6, *Notan Bhusan Kar* says that in India, the economic liberalization, privatization and globalization (LPG) model of development and its consequences depriving the marginalized people especially the tribal people who are customarily dependent on forest resources for their sustainable livelihood. But at present both the Central and various State Governments are encouraging the neo-liberal trade of mineral based industries in the tribal regions and neglecting the PESA Act and other laws. In the name of globalization and the country's economic development, the Multi-National Companies (MNCs) including Indian big corporate are taking over the livelihood resources of the poor tribal and pushing them into a further marginalized condition and displacing them from their land and homes. Such development serves the interests of these privileged classes while on the other hand it is impoverishing the tribal people in these regions. The mining and other industries are taking over the resources from these tribal people forcefully with the help of State. So, the present development paradigm cannot be able to provide them better social and economic upliftment. Henceforth, when people protest against these so-called development model, the Government then termed it as "Maoist" movement against the State. As a result, conflicts between tribal people and State growing across the country. This chapter is an attempt to understand the present LPG development model that is creating acute problem of the tribal people, their resistance against displacement, consequences affects on tribal communities with specific reference to Odisha, Chhattisgarh and Jharkhand states where tribal people inhabit largely.

Chapter-7, *Partha De* says that in India women bear many children where obstetric care is poor and thus their lifetime risk of maternal death is much higher. The available studies related with maternal mortality in India are based mainly on hospital records. But, a significant portion of the delivery is still done by traditional birth attendants (TBAs) at home in both the urban slums and rural areas resulted in high maternal mortality in the country. However, findings from hospital-based studies are not representative of a particular area or community, but only the segment that sought care at the hospital. This study has collected information directly from the households where such death happened. The objective is to determine different socio-economic, demographic and health care characteristics associated with the causes of maternal mortality in the large metropolitan area of Kolkata. The relationship between the prevalence of each cause of maternal death and various background characteristics are evaluated using bivariate and multivariate statistical analysis. Findings show that the leading causes of maternal deaths are haemorrhage, eclampsia, infection, retained placenta, anaemia and viral hepatitis in pregnancy. Important background causes for maternal death are pregnancies in the youngest and oldest reproductive age groups, higher birth order, woman's illiteracy, inaccessibility in health care services and delivery by TBAs at home.

Chapter-8, *Chaiti Sharma Biswas* tries to measure the status of women in East India. She says that as a backward section, women are generally neglected in the development process. Mainstreaming of women is recommended to place them properly into this process. As a means of mainstreaming, various policy-makers suggested for "empowering women". Despite earnest efforts, it is observed that the achieved level of women empowerment remains well behind the third MDG goal (to empower women). Based on Third National Family Health Survey present study aims to assess the level of women empowerment in Jharkhand and tried to identify the reasons for this lag. As a measure, an Empowerment Index (EI) is developed, and to identify the determinants of EI, it is regressed on various socio-economic factors. It is found that majority of the women in Jharkhand has medium level empowerment and lag behind the average empowerment level of Indian women. Percentage of highly empowered women is found to be low here. Women's education, occupation, income higher than husband, economic status, household structure, media exposure etc. emerged as significant determinants of women empowerment.

Chapter-9, *Sourav Madhur Dey* concentrates on cancer care and social support. He says that there are more than 30 million people living with cancer in the world today, the majority of them live in the developing world. 14 million cancer cases occur annually throughout the world. Caring and supporting those affected by cancer is a challenging task for all. Cancer affects not just those who have the disease, but also their caregivers and families. Very few studies have examined the effects of long-term cancer survivorship on the family. Most studies that have addressed this topic have focused on breast cancer survivors and are limited to three years after diagnosis. This chapter raises issues about the role of family members in providing support for cancer patients. This article will examine the family dynamics in dealing with cancer, emotional interplays within family, extent of isolation among cancer patients as well as the significance of professional intervention in holistic care of the patient.

Chapter-10, *Sujata Chakraborty* and *Bhola Nath Ghosh* concentrate on education and identity of a Santal village in West Bengal. They seek to develop a clearer understanding of the role of education in the formation of ethnicity. The basic meaning of the term 'ethnicity' is that it gives a distinct identity to a community and distinguishes one community or an individual from another. It has been found that ethnic consciousness or ethnic identity has increased even in the most developed countries of the World. Ethnic strife and conflict are the topic of the day everywhere. Education being one of the most potent components of development, it can be considered that it does play a very distinguishing role in the formation of ethnic identity. Therefore, in this chpater an evaluative study has been made to know how and in what ways the education is helping in building up the ethnic awareness amongst the people. This study raises two questions: (1) how did the educational initiatives undertaken by the Governmental and non-governmental agencies helped in enhancing social integration and social mobility of the ethnic minority groups? (2) What impact did educational initiatives had on the ethnic minority groups (both negative and positive side of education)?

Chapter-11, *Jyotiprasad Chatterjee* concentrates on development or counter-development in the Jharkhand Movement. He says that traditionally, India is characterised by a vivid range of cultural and social diversities. The colonial administrators, in their attempt at political integration of the country, blatantly ignored this. Coupled with the severe economic exploitation of the people, the imperialist colonial state in India also acted as an instrument of cultural oppression. Ethnic discontent, as one of the emerging concerns for the society and body politique of contemporary India, hence, necessarily has its root in British colonialism. The same odyssey of socio-economic and cultural oppression has been continuing in independent India too. The state in India, in the post-colonial era, rather than adopting measures to resolve the various issues relating to ethnic deprivation has actually taken recourse to such a development model which marginalises the indigenous people further. The present exercise attempts to examine the impact of such development initiatives in the specific context of Jharkhand, a newly formed state of the Indian Republic famous for its rich mineral storage and inhabited by a large number of *adivasis* (tribes), the ethnic groups of India. Adopting a historical and comparative methodology, the present chapter shows how the feelings of socio-economic and cultural deprivation of the *adivasis* have been accentuated by the development programmes being pursued in India under the aegis of capital—national or multinational. It is no wonder then that such a development process has been appearing to be counter-development to the marginalized adivasis.

Chapter-12, *Rumki Gupta* and *Jayeta Dhara* try to find the bullying as a social issue. They say that during the last decade, bullying of and by children of all ages has become a prominent social, educational, legal and media issue. Many recent studies have sought to quantify students' experience of bullying in schools. A bully is defined as a person who uses superior strength to influence or intimidate another person or to force him or her to do what they want. Olweus described bullies as having an aggressive personality pattern that predisposes them to respond aggressively. By bullying, these children employ their aggression to assert power and dominance. Bullying is an issue of concern to educators because it has the potential to affect student's academic and social development. In this study, the sample comprises 1,147 students reading in classes VII and VIII of Government aided schools under West Bengal Board of Secondary Education (WBBSE). These students are categorized into bully and non-bully according to their scores in bully scale by Ken Rigby and Phillips Slee. Out of 1,147 students, 262 were (23%) bully and 885 (77%) were non-bully. Academic achievement of the students was measured by the Annual Examination marks on Bengali, English, Mathematics and Science subject individually as well as totals of all the subjects. While considering total group, bully and non-bully students differed significantly in bully scores and Mathematics scores. In case of bully and non-bully group, analysis was done from different angles.

Chapter-13, *Himansu S. Ghosh* tries to concentrate on right to equality on Indian women. He says since the dawn of civilization "Equality" is a matter of enquiry. Pericles, Plato, Aristotle and others threw light on this concept, but in eighteenth century it became a part of battlecry of French Revolution, 1789. Ultimately, it became universal phenomena through Universal Declaration of Human Rights, 1948.

India was under British Rule and became free in 1947 and adopted its own Constitution in 1950 where Indian people were guaranteed "Right to Equality" in Articles 14 and 18.

Therefore, the question raised in my mind, does the Indian women enjoy equal right with male counterpart? Obviously, the answer would be negative. This kind of inequality is not only exit in India but all over the countries to some extent. "Global Gender Gap Report 2013" indicates so.

In this chapter, we will try to verify the four indicators of inequality, i.e. economic participation and employment opportunities, political participation, educational attainment and health and survival, which are considered by World Economic Forum for measurement and we will find that the women are to go a long way to achieve equality with male counterpart.

Chapter-14, *Pallav Mukhopadhyay* concentrates on Woman on Trial in Mainstream Hindi Films. He says in the 1950s and 1960s, towards the end of the black and white era, the Indian heroine was a silent, suffering entity who believed she was to be seen and not heard; so deep was her feeling of unworthiness, what the men in India wanted their women to be. The 1970s, reflected the two sides of the Indian woman—one traditional and the other Western but still a part of a man's world fulfilling his needs for romance, sexual gratification and procreation. The films of those decades were so simple. It began and ended with whether the man would marry her or not. They had no link with real life, yet they were so thoroughly entertaining. The 1980s saw a change in the way the Indian woman was viewed, which was not reflected in the mainstream. The 1990s and the first decade of twenty-first century swung in another direction yet again. Although, it was still about sex and romance, this time the woman was an equal partner and not a human being who could not even think about her self-dignity.

Chapter-15, *Sidhartha Sankar Laha* concentrates on population ageing and demographic transition and he says that the ageing of a population is consequence of the process known as demographic transition. The population of India is currently moving toward an old age structure and it is certain that there will be rapid growth in the elderly population in the near future. The chapter explores the demographic profile of older persons in India and population projections "A Long-range Demographic View" on the basis of various demographic parameters to better understand the implications of changing population age structure. Results of the present analysis further indicate that some states, particularly in the southern region are at the forefront of this transition. The shift to an older age structure has important implications for the country as well as elders and their families. There is therefore a need to promote harmony between development and demographic change by increasing the economic and social supports for the elderly.

Nothing less than the word "gratitude" to be appropriate to express our emotion for the confidence Viva reposed on the sincere and honest work of our contributors.

REFERENCE

Jerome Manis (1984), *Analyzing Social Problems*, New York: Praeger, p. 12.

Bhola Nath Ghosh
Himansu S. Ghosh
(*Editors*)

1

Combating Corruption: The Issues and Challenges

Swapan Kumar Pramanik

INTRODUCTION

Decades back, Mahatma Gandhi, while reacting against rampant corruption in the Congress Ministries formed under the Government of India Act, 1935, said, "I would go to the length of giving the whole Congress a decent burial rather than put up with corruption that is rampant". Nehru, in one of his famous post-Independence speeches promised to hang in the open street posts the black marketers and smugglers to fight the menace of corruption. All these promises have remained rhetoric, whereas corruption is thriving.

Guner Myrdal in his "The Asian Drama" has depicted the extent of corruption thus in India, from the gateman in the railway level crossing up to the topmost bureaucrat and politician—everyone exploits his official position and in many cases, with a pecuniary benefit. One Central Minister along with some top bureaucrats, politicians and businessmen are in jail for the biggest ever telecommunication scam involving an amount of a staggering Rs. 1,80,000/- crore. In an India corruption study, 2010, made by the Centre for Media Studies, a Survey on 10,000 rural households was made to gather corruption data in four key sectors impacting the poorer public distribution, school education, water supply and health services. It was revealed that in these basic services the quality of service provided is very weak and corruption is very high. Despite great emphasis on Bharat Nirman, Right to Education, National Rural Health Mission and food security in recent years, the beneficiaries are very few and the extent of corruption is very high. Hundreds of billions of rupees are spent on these programmes, but the poor are not benefited adequately. Media generally projects corruption at high levels. While this is true, the corruption faced by common person in their day to day lives, is equally important. It seems that our democracy has degenerated to kleptocracy, a consideration state, where everything, either basic necessities or things worthy to get, can be had for a consideration. But the silver line in this gloomy situation is the level of public awareness on the menace of corruption and the formation of a very strong public opinion to fight it out. This is also compelling the state to adopt various measures at least to check corruption, if not to eliminate it.

WHAT IS CORRUPTION?

In the formal sense, corruption is the use or abuse of official power for promoting personal interests. Elliott and Merrill view corruption thus: "Political corruption in a technical sense is the wilful exploitation of political office or opportunity for personal gain. Corruption involves an unlawful act (or failure to act) and a tangible or intangible benefit. The corrupt individual defines the situation in terms of personal aggrandizement, rather than community service. The machinery of Government is manipulated in the interests of predatory groups. Politicians, criminals, businessman employ the resources of community for their own ends, rather than for those of the general welfare (Elliott and Merrill, 1961:520)". According to Andriski, corruption is the use of public power for private advantage in ways which Nanogress some formal rules of law (Machael, 1983). The Santanam Committee (1964) defined corruption thus: "In its widest connotation, corruption includes improper or selfish exercise of power and influence attached to a public office or to a special position one occupies in public life" (*Report on the Committee on Prevention of Corruption*, p. 6). According to World Bank Report 1997, abuse of public power for private gain is described as corruption.

But all the above definitions appear to be too simple to comprehend a complex phenomenon such as corruption. Corruption is a multifaceted phenomenon. It erodes the whole system and gradually kills it. Corruption directly works against such principles as transparency, responsiveness, accountability, probity in public life and good governance. The criminal—mafia, politician linkage operates in much more subtle ways than can be comprehended by the formal structure of law, and corruption is not only abuse of public office. Private players, corporate and farm houses play equally important role in abetting corrupting and resulting in loss of efficiency and loss of national income. The World Bank has identified corruption as among the greatest obstacles to economic and social development. Corruption results in absence of transparency and the incompetent get selected for projects resulting in increase in overhead cost and low level output. Economists have said that a country with a higher perception of corruption not only deters financial institutions from long term investment, but also can result in withdrawal from that country with consequent capital outflows and creating a volatile economic environment. The World Economic Forum's global competitiveness Index 2010 indicated that for a country's economy to become competitive internationally, apart from such factors like business freedom, trade freedom, fiscal freedom etc., freedom from corruption is the factor that enhances an economy's competitiveness. In a survey on Bribery and Corruption and its Impact on Economy and Business Environment conducted by the KPMG in 2011, over 2/3 of the respondents (mostly CEOs) perceive that India can achieve more than the projected 9 per cent GDP growth if corruption is controlled, while the rest feel that corruption is definitely a key risk to the projected growth rate. 93 per cent of the respondents said that corruption negatively impacts the capital market.

POLITICAL CORRUPTION

Among all the forms of corruption, political corruption is most important and its capability to penetrate and disorganize the society is most pervasive. Corrupt politicians not only rot the system, but also help develop a cynical attitude among the common people about politics and have a chain effect on others in spreading the tentacles of corruption. In the last few decades in our country severe scandals and financial irregularities including paying of massive commissions, pay-offs and kickbacks have come to light. The Bofors Scandal in 1986, the Securities Scandal in 1992, The Treasury Fraud Scandal in Assam in 1995, the Animal Husbandry Scam in Bihar in the nineties, the Telecommunications Department Scam of 1996 and the same repeated in 2010, bribery of MPs on several occasions, paid news system and paid Question System in the parliament—are several such examples which have rocked our body politics and in fact the whole society. But they constitute only the tip of the iceberg—the extent of political corruption is far more pervasive than what has been unearthed.

Of course, political corruption is a worldwide phenomenon. And it emanates from the very basis of a capitalist society where success is assessed in monetary terms and where end justifies the means. As P.H. Odegard says, "Political corruption is in a sense a product of the mores of an acquisitive society, where financial values are predominant and the pragmatic sanction of behaviour lies in its pecuniary success" (Odegard, 1934).

The intimate connection between political corruption and the social structure has been exhaustively discussed by R.K. Merton, the famous sociologist, with reference to the United States. He uses the term "political machine" in the United States to denote these extra legal and mostly corrupt procedures. But being a functionalist, he attempted to show how in a rapidly changing metropolitan milieu in the United States, the needs of various groups, which cannot be accommodated within the formal constitutional procedure, the political machine provides extra legal satisfaction of the variety of needs. As Merton says "....... the functional deficiencies of the official structure generates an alternative (unofficial) structure to fulfil existing needs somewhat more effectively" (Merton, 1949:73). Some such "needs" in the United States, as stated by him, are the needs of underprivileged groups, the needs of over-privileged groups, the needs of 'illegitimate' groups and the needs of minority groups.

In a capitalist country like the United States, the close connection between big business and politics becomes evident at every stage. The corporate groups functioning within its city like the banks, the railways, the big manufacturing concerns, the contractors and the service providers frequently collaborate with the corrupt political interests. Elliott and Merrill say, "these business groups were seeking favours from the local government, in the form of franchisees, tax reductions and other privileges, and its behooved them to influence the government in their favour. In return for special privilege, the corporate interests furnished financial backing for machine both during and between elections" (Elliott and Merrill, 1961:525). William Whyte, in his book "*Street Corner Society*" has shown how this corporate house-political nexus has turned into a political criminal symbiosis. Whyte says, the success of certain political organizations and politicians is a matter of vital interest to the racketeer. In the slum areas of the large cities, elections often assume the characteristics of a war between rival political factions. Each group mobilizes its underworld supporters and there is often bitter feeling between them. Each side is convinced that if they do not steal the election, the other side will. The end justifies the means (W. Whyte, 1955:240). The net result of all these is that in the United States, political corruption has been institutionalized. It is true that this criminalization of politics is on the decline in the United States today, but the nexus continues in essence.

Regarding the nature of political corruption in India, we can mention here the report of the Vohra Committee which was constituted in 1993 to take stock of all available information about the activities of crime syndicates/mafia organizations which had developed links with and were being protected by Government functionaries and political personalities. Some of the points contained in the proceedings and report of the Vohra Committee are mentioned below:

1. CBI has reported that all-over India, crime syndicates have become a law unto themselves. Even in the smaller towns and rural areas, muscle men have become the order of the day. Hired assassins have become a part of these organizations. The nexus between the criminal gangs, police, bureaucracy and politicians has come out clearly in various parts of the country. The existing criminal justice system is unable to deal with the activities of the mafia; the provisions of law in regard to economic offences are weak; these are insurmountable legal difficulties in attaching/confiscation of the property acquired through mafia activities.
2. There has been a rapid spread and growth of criminal gangs, armed senas, drug mafias, smuggling gangs, drug paddlers and economic lobbies in the country which have, over the years, developed an extensive network of contacts with the bureaucrats/government functionaries at the local levels, politicians, media persons and strategically located individuals in the non-state sector. Some of these syndicates also have international linkages, including the foreign intelligence agencies.
3. These syndicates have acquired substantial financial and muscle power and social respectability and have successfully corrupted the government machinery at all levels and weild

enough influence to make the task of the investigating and prosecuting agencies extremely difficult; even the members of the judicial system have not escaped the embrace of the mafia. The costs of contesting elections have thrown the politicians into the lap of these elements.

4. The mafia is virtually running a parallel government, pushing the state apparatus into irrelevance.
5. The linkages developed by crime syndicates get generally confirmed when pressure is mounted on the concerned agencies not to take action against the offenders or to go slow in the cases against them. Such pressures are mounted either immediately after a raid or at the time when prosecution is about to be initiated.
6. Narcotics trade has a worldwide network of smugglers who also have close links with terrorists. Terrorists indulge in narcotics trade to amass huge funds, in various foreign currencies, from which they source their procurement of weapons etc.
7. In view of the above dangerous trends, the Vohra Committee had suggested setting up a Nodal Centre to which all existing intelligence and enforcement agencies shall promptly pass on any relevant information and the Centre will function under the direct control of the Home Secretary. But nothing worth mentioning has been done as yet to implement the Vohra Committee report.

CORRUPTION: THE SPREAD OF THE MENACE

Such cases of grand corruption network, dangerous as they are from the development and national security point of view, do not exhaust the list of corruption. Petty corruption, which affects the basic rights and services of the common man, have become quite rampant and affect the day to day lives of the citizens and quality of services provided to them. In the above mentioned corruption study (2010), in the four basic services provided for the people, viz., public distribution system, school education, water supply services and hospital services which was conducted by the Centre of Media Studies by seeking the perception and experience of about 10,000 households spread over 12 states, it was found that a significant part of the respondents feel that corruption has increased (45%) or remained at the same level (19%) compared to the 2005 situation, when the previous CMS Survey was conducted. What is a matter of more concern is that, as per the report, "Amongst the most affected by corrupt practices are socio-economically weaker sections of the society, particularly in the rural areas. Review of the findings of India Corruption Study 2010 (show that) more than 40 per cent of the rural households belonging to OBC and SC Social group felt that the level of corruption has increased in Public services during the previous one year, while 28 per cent each from OBC, SC and ST categories opined that the level of corruption has remained same as in previous year". These figures are really alarming as the above services constitute the core of good governance.

Another alarming figure regarding the involvement of public servants in abetting Corruption in India was published by Trace International in January 2009 which, while studying cases of bribery in India, state that—

- 91 per cent of the bribes were demanded by government officials;
- 77 per cent of the bribes demanded were for avoiding harm rather than to gain any advantage; and
- Of these, 51 per cent were for timely delivery of service to which the individual was already entitled, examples being clearing customs or getting telephone connection.

That really places India in a very paradoxical position. While our economy is the sixth largest in the world and while our economy is much sophisticated and use cutting edge technology in many spheres, we rank eighty-fifth in the Corruption Perception Index of Transparency International. That means that half of the countries of the world are less corrupt than India. The Transparency International's Bribe Payer Index of 2008 also ranks India very poor—19th among 22 countries. This indicates that Indian farms are perceived by International business as highly likely to engage in bribery when doing business abroad. This affects India's international business both in terms of capital inflows and outflows (CVC, 2009).

Some attempts have been made to delineate the impact of corruption on Indian Economy. Some estimates show that the loss due to tax evasion alone is to tune of Rs. 2 lakh crore annually while about Rs. 40,000/- crore is lost due to delay in Project implementation. As per one World Bank estimate, the average bribe to obtain a Public contract is estimated at 15 per cent of the contract value. According to another estimate, public sector enterprises would have improved their profit margin by about 20 per cent, if corruption was not there. According to a release by Washington based Global Financial Integrity on the Drivers and Dynamics of Illicit Financial Flows from India 1948-2008, India lost about 462 billion US$ in illicit financial flows due to tax evasion, crime and corruption. What is a matter of more concern is that 68 per cent of this loss occurred in the Post-1991 period which indicates that deregulation and trade liberalization have actually accelerated the process of illicit money flow abroad.

Post-liberalization period has also ushered in an era of big scams. During the days of regulative government policies, petty payments or baksish to babus was there but it was at a tolerable level. But after the introduction of new technology or IT in various spheres, the role of middle men in many cases has been eliminated, e.g. in tax filing return, telephone connection or railway reservation. As per KPMG's Bribery and Corruption Survey 2011, "India today is faced with a different kind of challange. It is not about petty bribes (*baksish*) any more but scams to the tune of thousands of crores that highlight a political/industry nexus which, if not checked, could have a far reaching impact". In the above mentioned CMS study 2010 of the extent of corruption in public services, it is true that corruption was found to affect 40 per cent of the respondents, but the same study mode in 2005 had shown that about 60 per cent had been adversely affected due to corruption. This was due to the fact that in many cases machines/technology minimized human manoeuvrability. It is not our position that small corruption has been eliminated. While they have remained more or less at same place, big corruption has far outpaced small corruption.

COMBATING CORRUPTION

R.K. Merton, a great sociologist, defined deviance (corruption included) as the result of a gap between the desires of an individual and socially accepted means of fulfilling that desire. In an acquisitive society, where wealth is the indicator of social status, one has to acquire that wealth, whatever may be the method or the means. This gives rise to corruption. So, in the ultimate sense, corruption originates from the very basis of our class divided society and unless this social order is changed drastically, corruption cannot be eliminated. That explains why corruption exists in every capitalist society. Our earlier example of corruption in the US proves the point. The difference is only a difference of degree, not of kind.

But this overall position does not minimize the importance of combating corruption within the present set-up. Our own record of combating corruption shows that along with increase in corruption, more and more stringent laws have been made. Or from a cynical point of view, in spite of the passing of more and more stringent laws, the incidence of corruption has increased as corruption has acquired new dimensions.

As early as in 1960, a committee on Prevention of corruption was appointed by the Government of India, known as the Santhanam Committee which submitted its report in 1962. On the basis of the recommendations of this committee, the Central Vigilance Commission was appointed in 1964 for looking into the cases of corruption against the Central Government and other employees. But the CVC, though created in 1964, became an independent Statuary body only in 2003.

The Prevention of Corruption Act was passed in 1988 by which it consolidated the provisions of the Prevention of Corruption Act, 1947, some Sections of the IPC, the CPC and the Criminal Law Act, 1952. The 1988 Act brought all the previous Acts within a single umbrella while at the same time modifying it and enlarging its scope. It covers all the corrupt acts like bribery, misappropriation, obtaining pecuniary advantage, possessing assets disproportionate to income etc.

But as stated by one Central Vigilance Commissioner, significant levels of corruption exist in India despite the existence of a strong governance structure, institutions, legal framework and policies. The anticorruption laws and institutions coupled with a strong oversight system consisting of the CVC, CAG and the CIC have been well acknowledged. The problem lies in implementation and there is a huge gap between policies and implementation (CVC, 2010).

But the question is whether the CVC is empowered enough or independent enough to initiate action against corruption. The CVC does not have any administrative power. It is an advisory/ recommending body, whose views are not binding on anyone. It is not an investigating agency. It works through the CBI and departmental vigilance officials, but has no direct or effective control over them. It cannot initiate enquiry against senior bureaucrats without prior permission. If, with regard to corruption, the CVC is a watchdog, it is a toothless body, a slumbering watchdog. The CBI another investigating authority also is under the Home ministry. And there are umpteen evidences which show that the CBI has been used as a political weapon against political adversaries.

The Government has introduced another Bill, popularly known as the Whistleblower's Bill or the Public Interest Disclosure and Protection to Person Making the Disclosures Bill, 2010, in order to protect the persons who provide information about corruption. But here also, the CVC has been given the authority to take up the matter. So, taking all these into consideration and taking into consideration the existence of corruption in high places, it is obligatory that an independent authority of Lokpal be created to deal with cases of corruption. In a deliberation on the subject "Deficiencies in the Present Anti-Corruption System" held in August, 2010, the recommendation was "the government should immediately institute a "Lokpal" at the Centre and "Lokayukta" in the States (which do not have them) with adequate powers to act as "apex", independent and effective" anti-corruption agency. But the performance sheet of the government on this matter over the last several years is not at all encouraging. The turbulent scenes in the Parliament on the Lokpal Bill only proved the governmental indifference on the point of creating an independent institution of Lokpal. It is gratifying to note that after much hesitation and didly-dalezing, the Parliament has passed the Lokpal Bill, though the highest political dignitaries have been excluded from its purview.

In the above mentioned Survey [KPMG's Bribery and Corruption Survey (2011)], the respondents were asked why, in spite of so many enforcement agencies and the laws, these are not proving effective enough. Their answer was the following:

(a) Belief that there is political interference (20%).
(b) That there is delayed justice (17%).
(c) That there is the involvement of multiple agencies in investigating claims and in filing charges—thereby further delaying the process (14%).
(d) That the penalties are not harsh enough to deter repetition of the same crime (15%).
(e) That there is the fear of retribution or victimisation by the affected parties (13%).

So unless all these issues are properly addressed, there cannot be any decisive step against Corruption. There is another important point to note. The entire effort so far has been to prevent Corruption in public offices by public servants. The regulations in India focus on the bribe taker rather than on the bribe giver. Corporates escape the provisions of law although they are very much involved in the process and are the beneficiaries of the System. In most of the cases, corruption is induced by the private sector. Taking this into consideration, regulations in developed countries are bringing the private sector also within the ambit of anti-corruption law. The United States Foreign Corrupt Practices Act and the UK Bribery Act, 2010 are two examples of this type of law wherein the government has attempted to grab the private sector also. Government of India is also contemplating a similar type of law. It is already the signatory to the UN Convention Against Corruption (UNCAC). At the G 20 Summit in 2010, India signed the group's anti-corruption action plan, which requires it to ratify and fully implement the anti-corruption convention intended to check corruption in the private sector.

One last point regarding combating corruption: This is about the crucial importance of the role of civil society. A congenial social environment has to be built-up regarding zero tolerance of corruption, sustenance and success of efforts to combat corruption in India is directly related to the extent of participation of the civil society in these efforts. As it has been rightly said, "Combating corruption is, therefore, not just a matter of making laws, but rather it is deeply rooted in the activities of the civil society itself" (Sondhi, 2000:4). The movement initiated by Anna Hazare, the participation of the civil society in that movement and the public outburst against corruption—are all indicative of the society's growing consciousness against corruption. That is the silver line in India's fight against corruption.

REFERENCES

Central Vigilance Commissioner's address to the India, *Battling India's Malaise of Corruption,* New Delhi.

Elliott and Merrill (1961), *Social Disorganization*, Harper and Row Publishers, New York.

Elliott and Merrill, *op.cit.*, p. 525.

KPMG, *Survey on Bribery and Corruption*, (2011), (www.worldbank.org).

Machael, Clarkel (ed.) (1983), *Corruption: Causes and Consequences*, Francecis Publishers, London.

Peter H. Odegard (1934), "Corruption: Political: United States" in *Encyclopaedia of the Social Sciences*, New York.

Prsanna Mohanty (2010), "CVC: A Slambering Watchdog" in *Governance Now*, October 15.

Report of the Committee on Prevention of Corruption, Government of India (1964), Ministry of Home Affairs, New Delhi.

R.K. Merton (1949), "Manifest and Latest Functions" in *Social Theory and Social Structure* (The Free Press).

Sondhi, Sunil (2010), "*Combating Corruption in India—The Role of Civil Society*", July, (sunilson@bol.net.in)

William F. Whyte (1955), *Streets Corner Society*, University of Chicago Press, Chicago.

2

State, Law and Domestic Violence Against Women in India: A Critical Review

Biswajit Ghosh

INTRODUCTION

Increasing instances of violence against women in India is a matter of deep scrutiny in these days. A country, which has had the tradition of worshipping goddesses symbolising *shakti* (power), is today faced with the ugly reality of regular humiliation, insult, sexual abuse, molestation, rape, physical torture, and even death of women in the hands of their 'close relatives'. This issue of domestic violence against women is, however, not new and it is found in all societies across all economic and age groups. One major reason for the colossal prevalence of domestic violence against women in a society like India is the subordination of women in traditional custom or practice. Domestic violence is a 'silent crime' and wife beating is a complex problem that involves much more than the act itself. The myth that wife battering is a 'private matter' has silenced many victim's for centuries (Bhattacharya, 2004: 18). Moreover, there is a strengthening of male-biased norms and values across all castes and classes in India along with increasing economic development (Kapadia, 2002: 4). As a corollary, the findings of the National Family Health Survey-3 show that that 34 per cent of all women age 15-49 have experienced violence at any time since the age of 15 (International Institute of Population Sciences, 2007: 499). Official data supplied by the *National Crime Record Bureau* of Government of India also show that, a total of 3,09,546 cases of crime against women were reported in the country during the year 2013 as compared to 2,44,270 in the year 2012, thus showing an increase of 26.7 per cent during just one year. Out of these crimes committed against women, 1,37,658 or 44.47 per cent of crimes may be classified as 'domestic violence' (Dowry Death, Cruelty or Torture by Husband and other Relatives, and Dowry Prohibition Act) caused mainly at matrimonial home (GoI, 2013: 79). Even though we very often doubt the efficacy of official method of counting of crimes for social, cultural and economic reasons, even such data acknowledged rising reportage of domestic violence against women during the last few decades. Thus, a decade ago, in 2004, the total number of officially recorded 'domestic violence' against women was 68,739. In other words, there has been 50 per cent rise in the incidences of such crime during the last one decade. It is worth arguing here that "what is captured in official data is crime and not the more widespread, generalized and indeed at times latent forms of violence and oppression" (Karlekar, 2005a: 296). We need to explain this rising trend from sociological point of view as there are several arguments and counter-arguments explaining this trend. It is in such a context that this chapter seeks to review the performance of the laws framed by the Indian state so far to prevent domestic violence. Thus, to begin with, it must be acknowledged that the Indian state has attempted to prevent all types of violence against women including domestic violence through legal reforms, and the tendency to depend on legal measures to cure social evils still follows. Perhaps, the most notable and talked about Act in this respect is the Dowry Prohibition Act, 1961. The Act not only declares the transaction of cash and valuable items at the time of marriage as illegal but also prescribes punishments for the offenders. Along with this, there are other related laws to deal with 'Torture' or Cruelty by Husbands and Other Relatives (Sec. 498-A IPC) and also to book and convict the guilty persons responsible for Homicide for Dowry, Dowry Deaths or their attempts (Sec. 302/304-B IPC). The Protection of Women from Domestic Violence Act, 2005 (PWDVA) has been a new addition to the existing laws. This law has emerged from the criticisms directed against "The Protection From Domestic Violence Bill 2001", which was drafted by the Lawyers Collective and introduced in the parliament by the National Democratic Alliance Government on 18th February, 2002. In the wake of the communal riots in Gujarat, the Bill could not be introduced for voting in parliament and it got annulled. Later, the United Progressive Alliance Government introduced a new Bill—The Protection of Women from

Domestic Violence. The Act has come into force with effect from the 26th October, 2006. The Government including many others have hoped that this effort would go a long way in providing relief for women from violence (Agnes 2005; Jaising 2005). Discussion here is basically based on official reports and field experience from West Bengal.

PREVALENCE OF DOWRY, DOWRY DEATH AND DOMESTIC VIOLENCE

Ranjana Kumari (1989) has argued that *while* all dowry practises *universally*, desertion and harassment cases are more among higher income groups, but upper and middle-income groups show higher dowry deaths. Women belonging to these income groups are unprepared for the trauma as compared to working and lower classes of women who are not intimidated by loss of self-esteem (Bhattacharya, 2004: 22). Among certain dominant (socially, economically and politically powerful) castes, dowry is viewed almost like a norm, which is hard to be broken. Within those social groups, illegal transaction is considered to be a matter of pride by all. It is obvious that there are exceptions, but the supporters and the practitioners of dowry overwhelmingly outnumber such sections (Ghosh, 2010).

One of the major reasons for the existence of dowry in India is the fact that women largely link the idea of dowry to the notion of inheritance of parental property (Caplan, 2000: 357). Some Anthropologists like Goody and Tambiah (1973) have represented dowry as a form of inheritance. It is not at all difficult to find a large number of women, both in rural and urban settlements, who view dowry as their legitimate right. Girls, therefore, often expect dowry from their parents at the time of marriage.

Furthermore, females in considerable number support dowry due to the strong influence of imitational patriarchal values in the society. Women's domestic productivity is perceived to be less valuable than her sustenance cost. This is due to undervalue of women's work in patriarchal society. Ursula Sharma (2000: 354) rightly points out that dowry divides women into two categories: 'mother' (who pays dowry at the time of marriage of her daughter) and 'mother-in law' (who receives dowry at the time of marriage of her son). This is probably one of the reasons for which anti-dowry movement launched by many women's organizations have remained either restricted to a limited space or on paper.

In the present Indian social context, rise in dowry demands is closely linked to the wide expansion of consumerism (Menski, 1998). The practice of dowry continues because firstly, there is little respect for law, secondly, for many, it represents the social tradition, and thirdly, punishment in these cases is rare. It appears that legal sanctions can hardly do away with a cultural practice if implemented from top by legal and administrative machinery without any socio-cultural reform at the grassroot level.

In the Indian society, the reasons for domestic violence against women are very similar to that of dowry related crimes. The patriarchal culture views women only as 'mothers' and therefore, it is believed that marriage is essential for women, and after marriage, their primary task is to give birth to children and look after the household. Feminists, therefore, often argue that marriage leads to 'control' of sexuality of women and its safe transference into the hands of the husband. The dominant family ideology considers a girl as '*paraya dhana*' or another's property. This point of view neglects the productive role of women, their capacity in nation building and the need for their education. Violence against women is a function of the belief that men are superior to women. Hence, incidences of domestic violence should be situated in the wider socio-economic and political context of power imbalance. Patriarchy prescribes that in every stage of her life, a woman should remain dependent on the male relatives for existence. Problem starts when someone tries to break the barrier and wishes to enter into the 'men's spheres', such as workplace, educational institutions, etc. Those who remain unmarried or fail to become mother after marriage meet similar consequences.

Surprisingly, certain myths are also prevalent as part of the patriarchal ethos which show that (a) wife beating is an act of love; (b) it takes place among uneducated lower class people; (c) only unsuccessful men beat their wives; and (d) some women deserve beating at the hands of their husbands (Ahlawat, 2005: 389). It has also been argued that the structure of capitalism keeps women at home, not men; and frustration at the class system is regarded as the determining factor in men's abuse of women (Saunders, 2004: 8). Often the abusive men is stereotyped as 'alcoholic', 'mentally ill', or 'very angry in nature', who would normally not commit any violence! These myths are dangerously misleading and research has proved that domestic violence cannot be controlled unless the rhetoric of male domination is challenged seriously. It would be interesting in this context to review the performance of laws related to dowry, dowry death and domestic violence in India.

PERFORMANCE OF LAWS RELATED TO DOWRY, DOWRY DEATH AND DOMESTIC VIOLENCE

Let me begin by analysing the performance of laws related to dowry, one of the prominent oppressive practices of South Asia (Menski, 1998). Dowry demands and conflicts related to such claims constitute a major reason of violence committed against women at matrimonial home. Steady rise in dowry deaths in India since Independence compelled the Government to enact the Dowry Prohibition Act in 1961. Under the provisions of this Act, dowry practice is officially outlawed. According to the Act, "giving dowry is an offence, taking dowry is an offence, to help in giving and taking dowry is an offence, asking for dowry is an offence, and advertising for dowry is an offence". In 1983, the then Congress Government had to introduce Section 498A in to the IPC being alarmed by rising instances of "stove bursts" (Jaising, 2014). It was a bold step to prevent Cruelty by Husbands and Other Relatives, many of which are connected to disputes originating from dowry transactions. In 1986, the IPC was once again amended to introduce Section 304B to define 'dowry death'. It provided that if the death of a married woman occurs in unnatural circumstances within seven years of the marriage, and it is shown that just before her death she was treated with cruelty in relation to a demand for dowry, it shall be presumed that her husband or his relatives caused the death. This Section states that whoever commits 'dowry death' shall be punished, with imprisonment for a term, which shall not be less than seven years, but which may extend to imprisonment for life.

Despite these legal provisions, which were amended from time to time to strengthen the laws and make punishment more rigorous, more than eight thousand cases of dowry deaths and over one lakh eighteen thousand cases of tortures/cruelty by husband/relatives were recorded in 2013 in India (see Table 2.1). Along with this, reportage of cases under the Dowry Prohibition Act has also increased steadily. Yet, the dowry law "had either been ignored or criticised and dismissed as inadequate" (Menski, 1998: 104). One of the major defects of the dowry law was to exempt "voluntary and customary gifts of love and

Table 2.1: Incidence of cases under Dowry Death, Torture and DPA in India, 2000-2013

Year	*Dowry Deaths*	*Torture*	*DPA*
2000	6995	45778	2876
2001	6851	49170	3222
2002	6822	49237	2816
2003	6208	50703	2684
2004	7026	58121	3592
2005	6787	58319	3204
2006	7618	63128	4504
2007	8093	75930	5623
2008	8172	81344	5555
2009	8383	89546	5650
2010	8391	94041	5182
2011	8618	99135	6619
2012	8233	106527	9038
2013	8083	118866	10709

Source: *Crime in India 2000-2013*, National Crime Record Bureau, New Delhi.

affection" given by the bride's family to her or her husband from the definition of 'dowry'. Obviously, legal remedies did not take into account feminist critique, such as gendered differences in power of the parties to the marriage, and the problem of looking to dowry as women's optimal, if indirect, access to property resources (Basu, 2009: 197). The second major loophole is that both giver and taker of dowry are treated equally as offender under the Act (Chowdhary, 1998: 153). Along with these legal loopholes, the implementation of anti-dowry laws in India remained grossly inadequate due to their weak enforcement by the concerned agencies.

It is worth noting here that officially recorded crime statistics against women clearly tell that cruelty within matrimonial home (torture) accounts for most of the recorded crimes of domestic violence against women in any year. In 2013, it is 88.47 per cent. In this sense, matrimonial family is the major arena for legitimate physical and mental oppression of women and girls (Karlekar, 2005a: 297). Obviously, marriage does not guarantee any social security of married women at in-laws home. The Feminist critique of family and marriage, therefore, holds some strong ground in the Indian context.

It is revealing to further interpret that data cited in Table 2.2 They show that dowry death rate is high in states like Bihar, Uttar Pradesh, Madhya Pradesh, Haryana, Jharkhand, Odisha and Delhi in 2013. But, so far as Cruelty/Torture crimes are concerned,

Table 2.2: Incidence (I), Rate (R) and Rank by Rate (RR) of Dowry related Crimes and Torture in Major States in India, 2013

Major States	*Dowry Death*			*Dowry Prohibition Act*			*Torture/Cruelty*		
	I	R	RR	I	R	RR	I	R	RR
Andhra Pradesh	492	1.14	6.09	1632	3.79	15.23	15084	35.06	12.69
Assam	170	1.11	2.10	40	0.26	0.37	8636	56.39	7.27
Bihar	1182	2.43	14.62	1893	3.90	17.68	4533	9.33	3.81
Delhi	144	1.64	1.78	15	0.17	0.14	3033	34.54	2.55
Gujarat	29	0.10	0.36	84	0.29	0.78	7812	27.11	6.57
Haryana	263	2.17	3.25	13	0.11	0.12	3617	29.86	3.04
Jharkhand	307	1.95	3.80	1428	9.06	13.33	2084	13..22	1.75
Karnataka	277	0.92	3.43	1693	5.65	15.81	3276	10.93	2.76
Kerala	21	0.12	0.26	03	0.02	0.03	4820	26.83	4.05
M. Pradesh	776	2.17	9.60	72	0.20	0.67	4988	13.94	4.20
Maharashtra	320	0.58	3.96	43	0.08	0.40	8542	15.41	7.19
Odisha	395	1.92	4.89	2014	9.79	18.81	2792	13.57	2.35
Punjab	126	0.96	1.56	03	0.02	0.03	1741	13.30	1.46
Rajasthan	453	1.35	5.60	57	0.17	0.53	15094	44.92	12.70
Tamil Nadu	118	0.35	1.46	305	0.89	2.85	2471	7.25	2.08
Uttar Pradesh	2335	2.36	28.89	1277	1.29	1.92	8781	8.88	7.39
West Bengal	481	1.08	5.95	107	0.24	1.00	18116	40:78	15.24
All India	**8083**	**1.36**	**100**	**10709**	**1.81**	**100**	**118866**	**20.06**	**100**

Source: *Crime in India 2013*, National Crime Record Bureau, Government of India, New Delhi.

states like Assam, Rajasthan, West Bengal, Andhra Pradesh, and Delhi have recorded higher rates. The states like Bihar, Uttar Pradesh and Madhya Pradesh have recorded least number of Cruelty/Torture crimes. One may raise some serious questions about the methodology of recording crimes by police in different states. How are we to accept that in Bihar, Uttar Pradesh or Madhya Pradesh violent crime (dowry death) over dowry takes place without disturbing the domestic sphere (Torture)? The reverse instance of torture cases outnumbering dowry death seen in states like Kerala, Karnataka, Tamil Nadu, Punjab or Gujarat may be normal as death may precede conflict. There is, therefore, diversity in police approach to record a crime under different sections of Indian Penal Code (IPC) and Special and Local Laws (SLL). It may also be argued that incidences of domestic violence are kept 'under the carpet' and not reported to the police until they reach an intolerable level or become fatal.

Explanations regarding rising reportage of crimes against women in general and domestic violence in particular have many shades and colours. To some, what has been captured in the legal framework now only reflects growing awareness among the people and particularly women to report these crimes to the authority. This must have resulted due to rising literacy, mass media exposure as well as expanding activities as well as campaign by various women's organizations and NGOs. This line of argument seeks to explicate that the incidences of gender violence are common in Indian society and there has not been any spurt of such violence in recent times. Hence, rising reportage of crimes against women is a positive sign.

It is true that reportage of gender crimes has gone up with increasing literacy and awareness campaign during the last few decades. But, it is a difficult proposition to argue that just within a year or so, such reportage has increased stupendously. A comparison between figures of two decades may hold good logically. But, how would one justify the fact that literacy and awareness level was exceptionally low in 2012 or so in the country. Hence, we need to look for alternative arguments to explain this rise. Here, I aver that in a patriarchal society like ours, assertion of rights by women as well as increasing participation of women in public life including employment may also engender hostile responses from their male counterparts in both public and private spheres. In other words, the more women speak out, try to exercise their rights, change their options and choices in a 'global village', join late night occupation, go out in public to participate equally with the male folk, the more they become victim's of violence, torture, rape and molestation.

From such a viewpoint, 'development' alone is not a solution to the problems of women. Rather in a certain stage of 'development' women are exposed to new forms of violence. Rising instances of vulnerability, forced migration and labour trafficking in India since economic globalization is a case in point (Ghosh, 2014). Also the example of rise in the instances of female infanticide and foeticide and consequent 'missing girl child' in the so-called 'developed' states of India speaks about this trend. It is equally true that Sex-Ratio and Child Sex-Ratio is low particularly in urban India and among general category of population as compared to Scheduled Castes and Scheduled Tribes. From this point of view, the rising trend of violence against women in India is an expression of patriarchal domination in general and hidden male 'frustration' to control the so-called 'docile and subjugated subject' in particular. The ever-increasing volume of violence against women in contemporary India is, therefore, a matter of serious concern for all of us.

A cursory look into the official crime statistics would also confirm our apprehension that we are far from realizing a better reportage of crimes committed against women. Thus, very few cases are booked under the Dowry Prohibition Act, 1961 over the last one-decade or so. This low registration points out that normally, in the Indian society, dowry disputes are not reported outside the domestic sphere. Research has revealed that women perceive an incidence as abuse only if the beatings are very serious; the odd slap or blow is regarded as routine affair (Karlekar, 2005b: 311). The logic of 'increasing reportage' also fails to explain the fact that incidences of child marriage is hardly reported to the police. Thus, only 222 cases are reported to the police in 2013. But there is a silent complicity to this practice in many parts of the country with rural and backward communities (Ghosh, 2011).

There is, therefore, every reason to doubt the official figures on most of the crimes committed against women (and children) in the country. It is a matter of serious concern that despite problems with our case registration system and the general tendency to hide or suppress women related issues, the incidences of violence against women in the last one decade have gone up from 1,54,553 cases in 2004 to 3,09,546 cases in 2013 in the country. The increase is more than 100 per cent and it appears simplistic to argue that 'only reportage' of violence has increased and not its intensity. Apart from the explanations discussed earlier, another strong reason for such a rising trend is the general failure of the police and judiciary to put up adequate resistance through timely and proper conviction of the offender. This is in spite of the fact that police have filed chargesheet in more than 90 per cent of dowry death cases (see Table 2.3). The same is equally true regarding cases related to Cruelty by Husbands and Other Relatives, or cases under the Dowry Prohibition Act. But, ironically, most of the cases could not be sustained and justified in the court of law leading to a very low rate of conviction in dowry related crimes (see Table 2.4).

Organizations like *Save Indian Family* however claim that provisions of 498A are being misused by the women to frame false charges on their husbands. This organization claims that it is approached for help by a large number of husbands complaining of harassment by their wives, committing even physical violence. On

Table 2.3: Charge sheeting Rate of Selected Dowry Related Crimes in India, 2001-2013

Year	Charge Sheeting Rate		
	Dowry Death	Cruelty by Husband/ Relatives	Dowry Prohibition Act
2001	92.70	91.60	89.70
2002	93.70	93.00	88.70
2003	94.30	95.10	91.70
2004	94.30	94.20	91.90
2005	95.20	94.60	92.10
2006	94.00	94.10	87.10
2007	92.80	93.90	90.70
2008	92.80	93.70	91.00
2009	91.70	93.90	89.70
2010	93.20	94.20	91.70
2011	92.00	94.40	93.60
2012	94.00	93.60	93.80
2013	94.00	92.30	81.20

Source: Compiled from *Crime in India 2001-2013*, NCRB, Government of India, New Delhi.

Table 2.4: Conviction Rate of Selected Dowry Related Crimes (I.P.C. & SLL) in India, 2001-13

Year	Conviction Rate		
	Dowry Death	Cruelty by Husband/ Relatives	Dowry Prohibition Act
2001	32.30	22.20	29.90
2002	34.00	21.40	28.80
2003	32.40	18.20	21.10
2004	32.01	21.50	25.00
2005	33.40	19.20	25.50
2006	33.70	21.90	27.30
2007	33.00	20.90	23.10
2008	33.40	22.40	23.90
2009	33.40	19.80	21.50
2010	33.60	19.10	20.00
2011	35.80	20.20	20.80
2012	29.50	15.00	19.30
2013	32.20	15.90	14.70

Source: Compiled from *Crime in India 2001-2013*, NCRB, Government of India, New Delhi.

July 2nd, 2014, the Supreme Court of India in Arnesh Kumar *vs.* State of Bihar & Ors case has also opined that disgruntled wives are misusing the provision of 498A to put "bed-ridden grandfathers and grandmothers" behind bars. The judgement offers statistics of the high rate of acquittals as evidence of the fact that these wives have misused the law. This argument has its opposite version too. It has been observed that that low conviction rate are mainly due to lack of evidence, delay in taking action, want of community support and in many instances, the poor financial condition of the victim's family to pursue the case for punishing the offender (Ghosh, 2013). Indira Jaising (2014: 35) has equally argued that—

> "While rendering the judgement, the Supreme Court ought to have been more conscious of the prevalence of domestic violence, and the difficulties women face in approaching the police. Filing a first information report (FIR) is indeed an ordeal as the police invariably try numerous techniques to avoid registering one, ranging from sermons to reconcile, to threatening the abuser—everything but filing a FIR! Hence, it is hard to imagine that the police are registering frivolous FIRs leading to acquittals".

There might be certain instances to book each and every matrimonial conflict under a stringent law. But, as opposed to such a negative view, field experience including those of activists reveal that such 'false case filing' are not many and conversely many instances of domestic violence are not just reported to the police (Ghosh and Choudhuri, 2011, Jaising, 2014). The opinion of the police and judiciary also support certain stereotypes. Indira Jaising (*Ibid.*: 36), thus writes,

> Courts are quick to convict for dowry death. Our law reports are replete with cases of husbands and their family members convicted for dowry death under Section 304B. No court has ever suggested that the dead woman lied, or misused the law, as indeed the dead body is proof of the cruelty she faced when alive and dead women tell no lies. Judges, when convicting under Section 304B, are quick to condemn the institution of dowry and bemoan the fact that it exists till today. Yet when it comes to the invocation of Section 498A, the first suggestion is that "disgruntled wives" are misusing the law.... How does one explain this concern of the courts

for the dead and condemnation for the living? Could it be that dead women exercise no rights nor claim a right to reside in the shared household? And what does one understand by the expression "disgruntled wife", a wife claiming her right to reside in the shared household?

PROVISIONS UNDER THE NEW DOMESTIC VIOLENCE LAW

Before the enactment of the Protection of Women from Domestic Violence Act, 2005 (PWDVA), the term 'domestic violence' was defined narrowly to refer to only cruelty and harassment of wife, and wife's murder under section 498A and 304B of the IPC (Ray, 2006: 428-29). Continuous struggle by women's groups has changed the situation and ultimately the law-makers of India have realized that domestic violence mean not only violence related to dowry, but several other forms of crimes. PWDVA is a comprehensive law and it addresses all issues related to women in the domestic sphere. It is for the first time that an Act has been made to address women's issues in such detail. The Act has categorized 'domestic violence' into four categories, namely (a) physical, (b) sexual, (c) verbal and emotional, and (d) economic violence, and attempted to define such violence comprehensively.

Thus, *Physical Violence* covers slapping, hitting, beating, kicking, pushing or any kind of bodily harm or injury in any other manner, and even a threat of such harm. *Sexual Violence* includes offences such as forced sex, forced exposure to porn, any act of sexual nature to abuse, humiliate or degrade a women and child sexual abuse. *Verbal and Emotional Violence,* recognized for the first time in India over and above physical violence, covers a lot of issues like any kind of accusation on a woman's character or conduct, insults for not bringing dowry, forced marriage or preventing a women from marrying a person of her choice, any form of threat or insult for not producing a male child, not allowing a women to pursue her study, preventing a women from taking a job, preventing woman from meeting someone, preventing a woman or her child from leaving the house, demeaning, name calling, ridicule, threat to commit suicide, etc.

Economic Violence includes denial of food, cloth, medicine and money at the time of necessity to a woman or her children, forcing a woman to quit her job, not allowing a woman to take up employment, preventing her to use or access any part of the house, refusing to pay house rent in case of a rented accommodation or other bills like electricity, forcing her out of the house, selling or disposing her *stridhana* (property gifted to the bride at the time of marriage) forcefully, taking away her salary forcefully and any other economic violence. As is apparent, the inclusion of such actions as 'domestic violence' would be very helpful to those married women who face deprivations and threats at their matrimonial home.

The Act has laid down stringent rules to prosecute a man for any type of violence committed against woman at home. All crimes in the PWDVA are non-bailable and no complaint can be lodged against any women under this Act. A victim also has the right to simultaneously file her own complaint under section 498A of the Indian Penal Code (IPC). For committing a crime under the Domestic Violence Act, a man can be jailed for one year, or fined up to Rs. 20,000. He also faces the risk of being booked under sundry sections of the IPC. The new Act goes beyond the 498 (A) of the IPC and extends protection to wives, sisters, mothers, daughters, single women and even to female live-in partners. The law has made strong provisions for protection of women from domestic violence under sections 18 and 19 of the Act. Thus, under section 18, the law empowers the court to stop any further acts of domestic violence on the woman or her children. It also prescribes for giving possession of *stridhana*, jewellery, clothes etc., to woman and stops all transactions of any joint bank accounts/lockers. Further, under section 19, the Act provides for the right of woman to live in her matrimonial or shared household peacefully, her right to property in which she is residing, and stops any disposing of the house without the permission of the court. In other words, an aggrieved wife cannot be harassed for lodging a case against her husband or other male members of the house.

The law also makes a provision for positive entitlements under sections 20 and 22 through an interim monetary relief order related to (a) maintenance for the victim or her children; (b) compensation for physical injury including medical expenses; (c) compensation for mental torture and emotional distress; (d) compensation for loss of earning; and (e) compensation for loss caused by destruction, damage, removal of any property from her possession or control. The court has also been empowered to pass general orders to stop domestic violence and special orders to prevent the tormentor from entering into a woman's place of residence or workplace or places used by her children, communicating with her, or isolating any assets that are shared by both.

Thus, the Act for the first time extends beyond the framework of mere 'punishment' to the offender of crime and tries to help and protect women from violence at home. One important characteristic of this new legal measure is its emphasis on the provision of positive entitlements—maintenance order, protection from future violence, and the right to custody of children—as opposed to mere penalization of the husband (Suneetha and Nagaraj, 2005: 4101-03).

The creation of an official cadre called Protection Officers (POs) and recognition of NGOs as Service Providers (SPs) are two other salient features of the new law. The State Governments have been given the responsibility to appoint a PO, preferably woman, at every district across the country to help the victim's file cases before the magistrates. They will also provide free legal, medical, shelter and other services to the aggrieved woman. The POs can be penalized for failing to discharge his/her duty with the permission of the State Government.

Besides, the law takes into consideration the issues like speedy justice and easy accessibility to justice. First, the cases under this new Act will be adjudicated under the magistrate's court, which is located at the sub-district level. The measure will enable a large number of women to access it. Second, there is emphasis on speedy disposal of cases. The first court hearing has to be fixed within three days of the date of receipt of application. The section 12 of the Act directs the courts to dispose of the application within sixty days of first hearing. In addition to these steps, the Act makes provision that the sole testimony of the aggrieved person may be sufficient for the court to reach a conclusion.

This Act has been criticised for favouring the women, targeting the male offenders including its potential for misuse to harass the male relatives. Though one cannot deny such possibilities, in a context of rising instances of domestic violence in the country, one can neither undermine its necessity. The Act has for the first time provided some legal options to those young women who are not allowed by the conservative family members to go out for study or for jobs. The provisions of positive entitlements for the victim are also unique. The Act also attempts to tackle many other types of violence against women within the family circle, which normally remain unreported.

It has been noted earlier that domestic violence constitutes the major type of crimes committed against women in the country. Most strikingly, such crimes have perilously increased stupendously during the last two decades despite educational improvement and socio-economic development. This is a pointer to the fact that women in India, irrespective of socio-cultural differences, continue to be exploited, harassed and tortured in domestic sphere. Their capabilities and choices are commonly thwarted by so-called traditions, customs and culture that are legitimised by a patriarchal social order. The persistence of different types of social evils and crimes like rape, molestation, dowry, domestic violence, child marriage and trafficking in women and children have plagued and hindered the development of Indian society (Ghosh, 2007). Hence, the 'female bias' of the recent Act or its potential for being misused should not be exaggerated, even though it is necessary to be careful about such deviations.

IMPLEMENTATION OF THE ACT

Looking into the awful experience of the laws related to dowry and domestic violence, one would rather like to know the way the well drafted new Act is being implemented. There is, however, no official data or report to analyse the functioning of the new law throughout the country. The only agency that persistently kept on reporting the functioning of the Act is Lawyers Collective, a Delhi based NGO, which earlier took a leading part in framing the law. Since 2007, this NGO has published six Monitoring and Evaluation Reports and all of them have stated the impediments faced by law implementing agencies in providing justice to the victim's. The Third Monitoring and Evaluation Report (2009) particularly mentioned the need for effective and adequate infrastructure apart from maintaining the "need to review certain aspects of the substantive and procedural law" (Lawyers Collective, 2009a). The Fourth Monitoring and Evaluation Report (2010) had noted some positive changes, despite several challenges in the implementation of the law. Among the positive changes, multiplication of number of cases from 10,000 in 2007 to 33,000 in 2009 is noted. Similarly, the report praises the efforts of the Magistrates to understand the 'Spirit of the Act' and pass appropriate orders.

The Fifth Report (2012: iii) equally speaks about continuity in positive framework and it particularly mentions three changes: (a) judges have understood the law better; (b) POs have been used by courts in fact finding to give orders; and (c) most importantly women in large numbers have used the law to their benefit. Yet, this report acknowledges that there are several challenges ahead—structural and attitudinal. It is a matter of serious concern that only a few states have so far appointed full time POs with independent change along with listing of SPs. Similarly, medical and shelter facilities have still not become visible in many states. Insufficient funds, lack of transparency in allocating resources, and under-spending of the money allocated are common complaints. For instance, only 13 of the 33 states and Union Territories have a "Plan Scheme" for implementing the PWDVA. Madhya Pradesh is the only state that has budgeted funds for Shelter Homes run by private organizations (*Ibid.*: 203). Surprisingly, only a few states have so far appointed full-time Protection Officers (POs). Attitudes of the implementing authority also require qualitative change. Due to a combination of these factors, there are delays in court judgements, victim's are asked to go for mutual settlement or compromise even before filing a case and the beneficiary of the new law has remained confined to a section of urban married women only. The Fifth Report has accordingly suggested steps like judicial reform, proper allocation of funds, and promotion of an attitude of zero tolerance to domestic violence by all stakeholders. The Report therefore concludes that "there has been some progress and some digression in the implementation of the Act" (*Ibid.*: xviii).

The Sixth Report (2013: 142-43) refers to both setback and good news in implementation of the law. Thus, it writes,

> As in previous years, the single largest users of the Act are still married women followed by widows, divorced women, daughters and sisters (women filing against members of their natal family) and women in relationships in the nature of marriage, in that order. The sheer numbers of Orders received by the Lawyers Collective Women's Rights Initiative indicates a significant growth in the use of the Act by women across the country. What has emerged is that most applications are filed after the woman leaves the Shared Household and is residing either with the natal family or on her own.
>
> The decisions on domestic violence analyzed this year highlight some path breaking judicial pronouncements that firmly support and enhance the objective of the Act. Still, as can be expected, the Courts have not been entirely successful in escaping entrenched patriarchal beliefs and biases. Ironically, in some cases, these beliefs have resulted in

positive Orders for women especially where they are couched in terms of moral duties of husbands or fathers to provide protection. In the vast majority of cases, bias is evident in the Orders. The area of greatest concern arising out of the analysis is the danger that judicial decisions may reduce the PWDVA to a mere shadow of the personal laws that govern women's status in the family, failing to understand that the dominant purpose of the law is to address the consequences of violence and provide relief.

The Sixth Report also laments about administrative failure to sanction adequate budget for the appointment of Protection Officers and for their training. Failure on the part of the activists to impress upon the government to create necessary infrastructure to implement the new law have led them to conclude that "women do not matter and least of all, violence against women does not matter" (Lawyer's Collective, 2014: V). An evaluation of more than 10,000 judicial decisions during 2011 and 2012 has led the Lawyer's Collective to lament on the approach of the judiciary to search for a "perfect victim", one worthy of relief. Let us look into the varieties of fastidious reasons used to deny protection/maintenance orders to the victim's:

(a) Women who leave the Shared Household for having faced violence are not in "imminent danger" of facing violence and hence not in need of Protection Orders.
(b) Women who live in the Shared Household must not be facing violence as otherwise they would have left, and hence are not in need of Protection Orders.
(c) Women who left matrimonial home of "their own volition" are not worthy of relief under the law.
(d) Women who refuse to restore conjugal rights are also not worthy of relief.
(e) Women who are earning do not need maintenance, those who do not also do not deserve relief under the law, as they ought to be earning.

FIELD EXPERIENCE FROM WEST BENGAL

In view of the above, I would like to use the findings of a research conducted in the district of Burdwan in 2008-10 to take a field view of the issue of implementation of the new Act (Ghosh and Choudhuri, 2011). Our field experience, based on a survey of 320 victim's of domestic violence, proves that the volume of cases filed under the PWDVA is close to only one-third of those of the old 'Torture/Cruelty' law. This proves that even after eight years of its existence, the PWDVA is yet to become an alternative to even those who are currently filing domestic violence cases under Section 498-A of IPC, although the scope of the new Act to provide immediate relief to the victim is much wider and the procedure for filing a case is also 'victim friendly'. Moreover, it appears from the meagre number of PWDVA cases in West Bengal that the law is not implemented equally in all the state districts. In particular, victim's from rural Bengal have not been able to take benefit from it. There is hardly any move by any organization, including the government, to popularize the provisions of the law across different sections of our population and particularly among the ruralites. We have noted following problems with several other aspects of the law:

(a) The promise of disposing a case within 60 days from the first date of hearing is hardly fulfilled even though most of the judgements in the lower courts in Burdwan have gone in favour of the victim's. It is true that compared to others, domestic violence cases are resolved more quickly at lower courts. One cannot at the same time seriously put the blame on overburdened judiciary lacking infrastructure. There is equally no guideline and training of judicial magistrates on different aspects of the law, in the absence of which subjective interpretations of the law by the judges in different courts are taking place. It may be noted here that Lawyer's Collective's (2012) also did not find a single court to keep the time line of 60 days for passing orders. The judges are often confused about the amount of punishment to be given to a person who has not complied with the previous order. Again, the legal option to punish an offender for repeating domestic violence following a 'protection order' is limited because victim's mostly abandon their matrimonial home before filing a case. Given these complicacies, victim's are often persuaded to reach a compromise with the accused. This supports the contention that the law attempts to settle domestic violence within the existing familial structure, and may not help those who lost all hope of reunion.

The judicial process of handling a PWDVA case is also not bereft of additional trouble. Dependency on the lawyers to file a case is also evident. Moreover, a victim is supposed to hire a 'good' lawyer to defend her case well, particularly in higher courts. As domestic battles are dragged to higher and higher courts, there is little reason for optimism. Besides, implementation of interim orders of the Magistrates appears to be a very complicated process, and here the victim's face tough legal hurdles. Delay in implementing protection/ maintenance orders has added to the misery of the victim's and exposed them to more violence.

(b) The apathetic and often negative roles of the police to stand by the sufferings of the victim's and implement judicial orders have been a major hurdle in providing timely and needed justice to women. The experiences of some of our respondents demonstrate this. Ironically, there are charges of corruption against the police. In certain instances, police seem to be reluctant to act against any influential person. Hence, women filing cases under the Act have to fend for their own safety. Moreover, the police often seem to be confused about their duty and obligation in 'protecting' a victim, and seek suggestions from the POs for intervening in the complex and critical domestic sphere.

(c) The apathy of the society at large to stand by the sufferings of a victim of domestic violence is a major hurdle in resolving any dispute. As we did not find any NGO providing the much needed service to the victim's in the district of Burdwan, the role of neighbours and other secondary groups become pertinent. Yet, none of the victim's whom we interviewed received timely help from their relatives, neighbours, and even political leaders. Because of the apathy of the civil society, there is little socio-political action in Burdwan to prevent such violence. This forces the victim's, as in the case of many of our respondents, to leave the matrimonial home and take shelter in the parental home. In the Indian condition, if a victim fails to garner such support in view of the poor economic conditions of the parents or other relatives, she is at the mercy of the abusive husband to continue a painful life. It is in this context that PWDVA has failed to rescue the victim's by implementing court orders or providing expedient justice to the victim.

(d) Besides such limitations, the Act is also not very clear about certain other modalities for its effective implementation. As such, the PO, who assists the aggrieved person to file a case, is not informed about the outcome of any case unless a 'protection order' is issued. Again, it is not mandatory on the part of the State Governments to employ a sufficient number of POs at the local levels, pay them adequately, or train them. Quite necessarily, lack of infrastructural facilities impinges on the process of investigation/implementation of a case.

Absence of NGOs as Service Providers (SPs) in Burdwan has aggravated the problem. Although there are 69 Service Providers in West Bengal till the time of the research, there are none in Burdwan. The major reason for this is SPs do not receive any financial help from the Government. As a consequence, court orders related to protection/maintenance are hardly pursued. Additionally, the safety of a victim in an abusive matrimonial home cannot be guaranteed if SPs do not stand by them at the local level.

(e) It also appears that the provision of the PWDVA, regarding right to residence of wives in 'shared household', has some limitations. The Act defines 'shared household' as a household where the aggrieved person "lives or at any stage has lived in a domestic relationship either singly or along with the respondent". Thus, if an accused sells a matrimonial home or lives in a rented house/official accommodation after separation, it is difficult for a victim to get 'residential right'.

It may be noted that as per the judgement of Indian Supreme Court (S.R. Batra *vs.* Taruna Batra, 2007), an aggrieved wife may only claim her share in the property owned or possessed by her husband. Consequently, a wife has no right on property owned by her in-laws or owned by a third party (company/office) (Lawyer's Collective, 2009b). The apex court has observed that unlike in England, where the rights of spouses to the matrimonial home was governed by the Matrimonial Homes Act, 1967, no such right exists in India. This judgement has been a major impediment to the effective implementation of PWDVA. Very recently, the Delhi High Court has ruled that "a self-acquired property do not fall under the definition of a "shared household" enunciated in the Domestic Violence Act. Hence, daughter-in-law cannot assert her right, if any, in the property of her parents-in-law wherein her husband has no right, title or interest. She cannot continue to live in such a house of her parents-in-law against their consent and wish" (*The Times of India,* 2014). These verdicts have complicated the initial claim of the law makers to ensure a victim "the right to residence in shared-household".

(f) The experience of Burdwan district also demonstrates that not a single of the 320 women seeking 'protection' under the new law sought any counselling service to settle matters. The denial is due to the fact that the victim's have lost all hope to return to their matrimonial family. Neither do they expect the POs or the police to change the situation in their favour. The issue of 'protection' of the victim, therefore, defaults to mainly seeking 'economic compensation' from the separated husband or son. This partially unwraps the spirit of the new law to settle many types of domestic subjugation or exploitation of women/girls through counselling and persuasion. Again the option of 'free legal aid' to victim's remained almost on paper as women filing such cases had approached the PO through their respective lawyers. Similarly, victim's hardly sought shelter or medical facilities from the government. It appears that the victim's have less faith in the quality of services provided by the state agencies.

(g) In some instances, however, PWDVA is found to target male relatives even though the offender is female. Filings of a few of such false cases, however, do not represent a trend. Yet, they are a testimony to the fact that provisions of PWDVA may encourage false case filing against male relatives also.

CONCLUSION

It is quite clear from the foregoing discussion that mere presence of Acts in the law books is not enough to curb the crime, unless affirmative actions are seriously initiated. Enactment of a law for dowry prohibition or restricting cruelty at matrimonial home could not change the attitude of a large number of men and women, socialized in a patriarchal culture. Similarly, success of the new Domestic Violence Act is also dependent on the attitudinal change in society. In this context, civil society has a critical role to play. In a country, where women are socialized to consider marriage as 'essential' and domestic violence as 'normal' for the sake of her own and children's interest, the recent Act may not particularly help those majority who often fail to recognize even their basic human rights. Furthermore, the dwindling rate of conviction ranging between 15 per cent and 32 per cent in the domestic violence and dowry related cases is discouraging to those who hope for justice. It is a fact that even educated and resourceful women have to run from pillar to post to get justice. Hence, there remains serious concern about how the new law may be made effective to provide much needed justice to women coming from weaker sections. The stakeholders should generate motivation in public mind to abide by the laws, seek legal redress whenever required and stand by the suffering of women, apart from improving the infrastructure for the justice-delivery system. It is high time for the law-makers, seeking to protect the rights of women in the domestic sphere, to create appropriate institutions and mechanisms to realize the cherished goal. Since Independence, we have witnessed a lot of official commitment to the cause of women in the form of a law drafted with all good intentions. But our experience tells us that all these are mere palliatives rather than curing the malady. The problem of dowry and domestic violence cannot be tackled without addressing the basic question of power inequality under patriarchy.

REFERENCES

Agnes, Flavia (2005) "Reflections on Domestic Violence Act", *The Deccan Chronicle*, September 6, Hyderabad Edition.

Ahlawat, Neerja (2005), "Domestic Violence against Women: Emerging concerns in Rural Haryana", *Social Action*, 55, October-December: 387-94.

Basu, Srimati (2009), "Legacies of the Dowry Prohibition Act in India: Marriage practices and feminist discourses", in T. Bradley *et al.* (Ed.). *Dowry—Bridging the Gap between Theory and Practice* (177-196). New Delhi: Women Unlimited.

Bhattacharya, Rinki (ed.) (2004), *Behind Closed Doors—Domestic Violence in India*. New Delhi: Sage Publication.

Caplan, Lionel (2000), "Bridegroom Price in Urban India: Class, Caste and 'Dowry Evil' Among Christians in Madras", in Patricia Uberoi (ed.), *Family, Kinship and Marriage in India* (357-79). New Delhi: Oxford University Press.

Chowdhary, Manjaree (1998), "Miles to Go: An assessment of the enforcement hurdles in the implementation of the anti-dowry law in India", in Werner Menski (Ed.), *South Asians and the Dowry Problem* (151-162): New Delhi Vistaar Publications.

Ghosh, Biswajit (ed.) (2007), *Trafficking in Women and Children, Child Marriage and Dowry: A Study for Action Plan in West Bengal*. Kolkata: UNICEF and Government of West Bengal.

——(2010), "Persistence of the Practice of Dowry in Rural Bengal", *Journal of Social Work and Social Development*, 1 (1): 01-17.

——(2011), "Child Marriage, Society and the Law: A Study in a Rural Context in West Bengal, India", *International Journal of Law, Policy and the Family*, 25 (2): 199-219.

——(2013), "How Does the Legal Framework Protect Victims of Dowry and Domestic Violence in India? Critical Review", *Aggression and Violent Behaviour—A Review Journal*, 18 (4): 409-416.

——(2014), "Vulnerability, Forced Migration and Trafficking in Children and Women: A Field View from the Plantation Industry in West Bengal, India", *Economic and Political Weekly*, Review of Rural Affair, 28th June, 49 (26 and 27): 58-65.

Ghosh, Biswajit and Tanima Choudhuri (2011), "Legal Protection against Domestic Violence in India: Scope and Limitations", *Journal of Family Violence*, 26 (4): 319-330.

Goody, Jack and S.J. Tambiah (1973), *Bride Wealth and Dowry*. Cambridge: Cambridge University Press.

Government of India (2001-2013), *Crime in India (2001-2013)*, New Delhi: National Crime Record Bureau.

International Institute of Population Sciences (IIPS) (2007), *National Family Health Survey (NFHS-3), 2005-6*. Mumbai: International Institute of Population Sciences.

Jaising, Indira (2005), "Home is where the law is", *Indian Express*, September 8, Delhi Edition.

——(2014), "Concern for the Dead, Condemnation for the Living", *Economic and Political Weekly*, 49 (30): 34-37.

Kapadia, Karin (2002), *The Violence of Development: The Politics of Identity, Gender and Social Inequalities in India*. New Delhi: Zubaan.

Karlekar, Malavika (2005 a), "Encountering Violence", in Mala Khullar (Ed.), *Writing the Women's Movement—a Reader* (296-99). New Delhi: Zubaan.

——(2005 b), "Breaking the Silence", in Mala Khullar (Ed.), *Writing the Women's Movement—a Reader* (300-24). New Delhi: Zubaan.

Kumari, Ranjana (1989), *Brides are not for Burning: Dowry Victims in India*. New Delhi: Radiant Publishers.

Lawyers Collective (2009 a), 2010, 2012 and 2013. *Staying Alive: Second, Third, Fourth, Fifth and Sixth Monitoring* and *Evaluation Report*. www.unifem.org.in/violenceagainstwomen.html, accessed on 18-12-2012 and 15-8-2014.

——(2009 b), Landmark Judgements and Orders. http://www.lawyerscollective.org/wri/projects-activities/domestic-violence-landmarks, accessed on 31-3-2010.

Menski, Werner (ed.) (1998), *South Asians and the Dowry Problem*. New Delhi: Vistaar Publications.

Ray, Sawmya (2006), "Legal Constructions of Domestic Violence", *Sociological Bulletin*, 55 (3), September-December: 428-29.

Saunders, Kriemild (2004), *Feminist Post-Development Thought*. London: Zed Books.

Sharma, Ursula (2000),"Dowry in North India: Its Consequences for Women", in Patricia Uberoi (ed.), *Family, Kinship and Marriage in India* (341-56). New Delhi: Oxford University Press.

Suneetha, A. and Vasudha Nagaraj (2005), "Adjudicating (un)domestic battles", *Economic and Political Weekly*, 40 (38): 4101-03.

The Times of India (2014), "Bahu Can not Claim in-laws' property: HC", August 11, p. 9, Kolkata edition.

3

Student Radicalism in Contemporary Bengal

Anirban Banerjee

INTRODUCTION

I have been studying student radicalism since 1986 when I started my Ph.D. research as an ICSSR Doctoral Fellow at the Centre for Studies in Social Sciences in Kolkata, under the supervision of Prof. Surajit C. Sinha. The present chapter is based on an ongoing UGC Major Research Project which was awarded in 2013 [Vide F. No. 5-449/2013(HRP) dated 25.03.2013]. The main objective of my study is to examine the impact of règime change on political attitudes of university students. On May 13, 2011, the Congress-Trinamul combine stormed into power in West Bengal, thereby ending the 34 years old rule of the Left Front. This change of guard has been hailed as *parivartan* (change). Since, then much water has flown down the Ganga. The right-wing turn in government had its impact on society and politics in contemporary West Bengal. It has also had an impact on education, especially higher education.

Our major research questions are as follows:

1. In what direction is the student movement moving?
2. Are students in favour of radical social change?
3. Are males more radical than females?
4. Do students of contemporary rural Bengal differ in their attitudes from their urban counterparts?
5. Do students of different income groups differ in their attitudes?
6. Are there any differences among students holding different ideologies with regard to joining politics?

7. Finally do students of today differ in their social and political attitudes from their predecessors? More specifically, what impact did règime change in West Bengal in 2011 have on the political attitudes of university students?

The present chapter is based on some early findings of my research. The author has tried to gauge the present direction of the student movement through an analysis of news reports. The primary data are from a Pilot Survey done by the author for a UGC Major Research Project "Student Radicalism in Post-Left Bengal" [Vide F No. 5-449/2013(HRP) dated 25.03.2013]. I am the Principal Investigator of this Project.

STUDENT RADICALISM IN THE TWENTY FIRST CENTURY: A BRIEF REVIEW OF LITERATURE

The literature on student radicalism is very scanty. The majority of works are either journalistic accounts or news reports. Very few researches have been reported. Our main focus will be on the researches done by social scientists during first and second decade of the twenty-first century. In her doctoral dissertation Rez (2008) studied the activities of the Student Federation of India (SFI) in Burdwan district. Her key finding is that although most of the students are members of the SFI, they are not willing to participate in politics. Research projects on student radicalism in Bengal have also been done. In his UGC Major Research Project, Banerjee (2009) distinguished between two levels of radicalism—systemic and interactional. Systemic radicalism means an attitude favouring change in the total social system in a socialist direction. The author found that compared to the session (1986-88) previously studied by him (Banerjee, 1991 & 2003), the majority of students of Calcutta University have become conservative, i.e., totally opposed to socialism. And this had negative implications for the Left Front which was then in power. Banerjee (2011) studied radicalism in Hungary, a former socialist state, while participating in the Indo-Hungarian Educational Exchange Programme (2011). He found that none of the students was a radical. The majority of the students were liberal. The students were totally dissatisfied with their government and saw no merit in its politics. From this brief discussion, we have uncovered a major research gap. There is no systematic study of student radicalism in contemporary Bengal. The author intends to fill this gap.

THE STUDENT MOVEMENT IN THE AGE OF *PARIVARTAN*

We will now try to answer our first research question, "In what direction is the student movement moving?" On May 13, 2011, the Trinamul-Congress combine stormed into power in West Bengal, thereby ending the 34 year old rule of the Left Front. This political change was hailed as *parivartan*. Bengal thus shifted to the right after 34 years. This had important implications for the society, polity and educational system of Bengal.

The first major election which the new government attempted to organize was the student union elections in colleges and universities of West Bengal. The function of a students union is to train college and university students for future citizenship responsibilities. Student union elections enable students to have a taste of democratic political participation. And those student leaders who are elected to positions of responsibility, like Class Representative, Secretary of the students union, etc., have hands on experience of running a democratic institution. Many Bengali student-leaders of yesteryears, like Biman Bose, Mamata Banerjee, Gautam Deb, Ashim Chattopadhyay etc. became well known political leaders today.

But were the student union elections in contemporary West Bengal held in the true spirit of democracy? Our answer is in the negative. We find that unprecedented violence started in all institutions of higher education from the moment students union elections were declared in 2011. This was mainly due to outside political interference. The new government had declared that its intention was to rid the education system of *dalatantra* (party control). But we find that during the student union elections, anti-social elements served as storm troopers for the ruling party and intimidated students, teachers and college principals. Anyone connected with higher education was a fair target for the stormtroopers. According to one estimate, there were 11 incidents of campus violence between 10th December, 2011 and 11th January, 2012. Fighting between right and left wing students also contributed to this situation. Meanwhile both left and right-wing students won elections. For example, the Students Federation of India won in Majhdia College while the Trinamul Chattra Parishad won in Purbasthali College.[1]

After a gap of one year, the government decided to hold elections to the student unions. The process had to be completed within January 2014. During this period (2013-14) we find growing criminalization of student politics. In Chapra Banganajhi College, bomb warfare between feuding student groups during filing of nominations, injured a passer-by.[2] Baliachak College in Malda witnessed a gang war between politicalised students. The recently concluded student union elections were replete with complaints of attacks on opposition student groups by the students owing allegiance to the ruling party. For example, in Bankura district, the SFI allegedly could not file nominations in any of the 27 colleges.[3] In Malda Women's College, it was alleged that the TMCP forcibly occupied all 18 seats.[4] There was also evidence of growing infighting within the TMCP itself. In Kalna College, for example, two TMCP leaders were allegedly assaulted by their co-workers.[5]

All these incidents show that democratic norms were randomly flouted by student activists in the student union elections. Goal displacement occurred. Far from being educational tools to teach students the ABC of political participation and responsible citizenship, the student union elections had actually fallen prey to the machinations of adult political leaders who saw in the student unions nothing more than another political powerbase like trade unions, *panchayats* and municipalities. And they encouraged the hotheaded politicalised students to fight it out, not through democratic processes, but through violence and intimidation of political opponents and ordinary students. Whoever won in this surcharged political atmosphere won a pyrrhic victory at best, because, as these examples show, the student leaders did not care for popular support. They rather willy-nilly followed Mao's maxim—"Power comes out of the barrel of a gun".

THE CONCEPT OF RADICALISM

Before we proceed further, let us examine the concept of 'radicalism'. The concept of 'radicalism' has had wide use in sociological and political literature. Menefee observes that radicals believe in drastic measures for improvement of social conditions. They advocate sweeping changes in the political and economic structure of society.[6] I have operationally defined *radicalism* as *advocacy of drastic social change along socialistic lines*. Radicalism differs from liberalism and conservatism. Liberalism advocates slow, orderly change.

Conservatives, on the other hand, are distinguished from radicals in that they oppose any substantive social change.

METHOD OF STUDY

Here, I have adopted three strategies. Firstly, to answer question 1, I have done content analysis of news reports on the student movement. Secondly, I will be doing a sample survey of university students. At present, Empirical data for the present chapter is based on a pilot survey. The *Pilot Survey* is any small-scale test of a research instrument run in advance of the main fieldwork, and used to test the utility of the research design.[7] The objective of this study is not to test any hypothesis, but to gain insights which will be used in the main survey. Thirdly, as part of this study, I have decided to construct an index of radicalism to determine whether the purpose of the study is being achieved.

The pilot survey was carried out in social science departments of Jadavpur University, Presidency University and Burdwan University. 72 students, who were selected through accidental sampling, were administered a questionnaire. Apart from seeking the respondents' opinion on a host of social and political issues, their advice was also sought on what to include and what to exclude in the main survey.

Determining Radicalism: To determine whether students are in favour of radical social change, we constructed an *index* of attitudes. Index construction is an accepted method of measuring attitudes (Henerson, Marlene, & Fitz-Gibbon, 1987: 72-73). Four items in the questionnaire were scored.

Item No. 51: The Ideal society is the socialist society.

Item No. 52: In a socialist society there are friendly classes.

Item No. 53: Socialist society abolishes private property through which people are exploited.

Item No. 54: A socialist society provides people with equal opportunities to develop.

Each question has three options: Agree/Neutral/Disagree

Scoring and Indexing

Item	*Score*
Agree	2
Neutral	0
Disagree	1

An *index* of attitudes was created on the basis of summated scores. The following is the index.

Scores	*Attitude*
1—3	Conservative
4—5	Liberal
6—8	Radical

Profile of the Sample

The sample consists of 72 students. It is usual practice to classify people according to gender.

***Gender*:** Accordingly, students were classified into males and females. From the data, we find that, out of 72 respondents, 29 (40%) are males, while 43 (60%) are females (Fig. 3.1). Thus, we find that females dominate higher education in West Bengal. This finding is consistent with the findings of previous researches. (See Banerjee, 1991, 2003, and 2009).

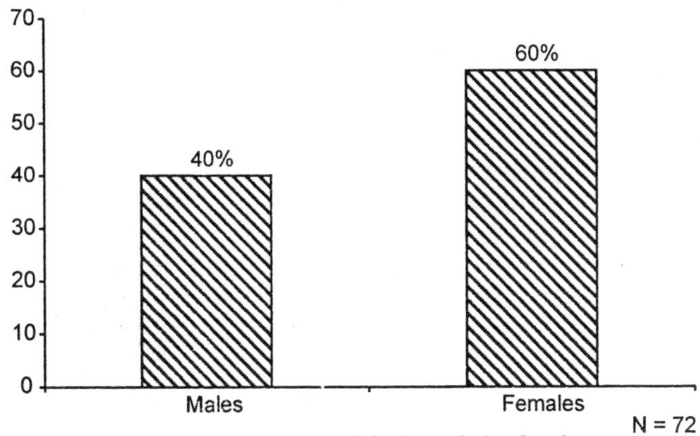

Fig. 3.1: Distribution of the Sample by Gender.

Source: Field data.

***Place of Origin*:** Rural, urban and suburban areas differ in their ecology and social characteristics. In this sample, 26 students (36% of the sample) hail from rural areas, 33 students (46% of the sample) are urban and 13 students (18%) hail from suburban areas. (Fig. 3.2). Thus, the sample is overwhelmingly urban in composition. Here also, we find that there is a consistency with previous studies (See Banerjee, 1991, 2003, and 2009).

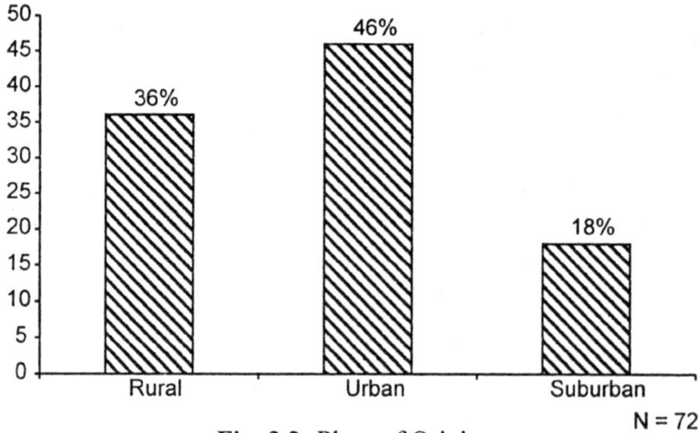

Fig. 3.2: Place of Origin.

Source: Field data.

***Family Income*:** Out of 72 respondents, 7 did not reply to this question, so our data is based on 65 respondents. We divided the respondents into three income groups—High, Middle and Low. 5 (8%) of the respondents come from High Income Group (Income Rs. 60,001+), 24 (37%) come from Middle Income Group (Rs. 20,001—60,000), 36 (55%) come from Low Income Group (below Rs. 20,000/-) (Fig. 3.3). Thus, the majority of the respondents come from the Low Income Group. This shows that despite globalization, higher education can still be afforded by the lower income groups, thanks to the state universities which make higher education affordable for the ordinary students.

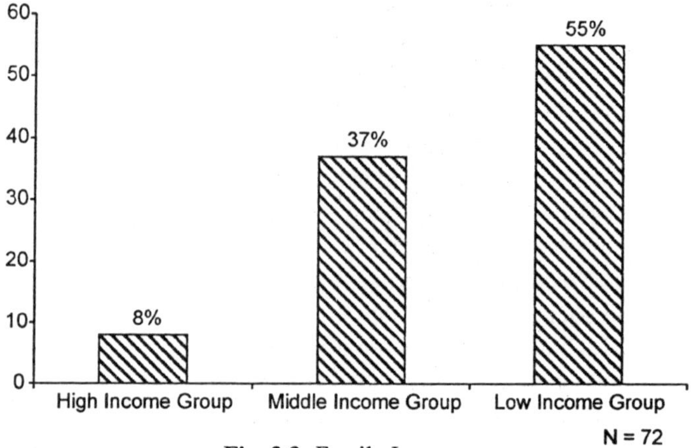

Fig. 3.3: Family Income.

Source: Field data.

MAJOR FINDINGS

Are Students Radical?

We will now answer one of our major queries—Are students in favour of radical social change?

From Fig. 3.4 we find that 38 per cent of the present sample is radical, 21 per cent are liberal and 32 per cent are conservative. Thus, we find that a minority of the students are radical. But if we combine the radical and the liberal we find that 59 per cent of the sample is either radical or left-wing liberal. Thus, we find that in spite of *parivartan*, a substantial section of the student community adheres to left-wing ideology.

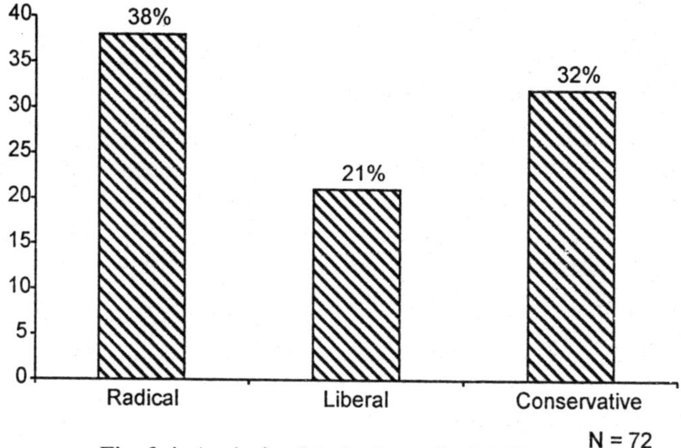

Fig. 3.4: Analysis of Attitudes to Social Change.

Source: Field data.

RADICALISM AND PLACE OF ORIGIN

Does, radicalism vary with the place of origin of the respondents?

From Fig. 3.5 we find that out of 26 rural students, 14 (54% of the rural students) are radical compared with 13 out of 33 (28%) urban students. 5 out of 13 suburban students (38%) are radical. We know that the Left Front carried out large scale land reforms in rural Bengal during its 34 year old rule. Naturally, its support base lay in rural areas. *Parivartan* has not changed the situation. Attitudinally, rural youth continue to remain leftist in orientation. This is consistent with previous findings (Banerjee, 1991: 169 and 2003: 151, 2009: 49).

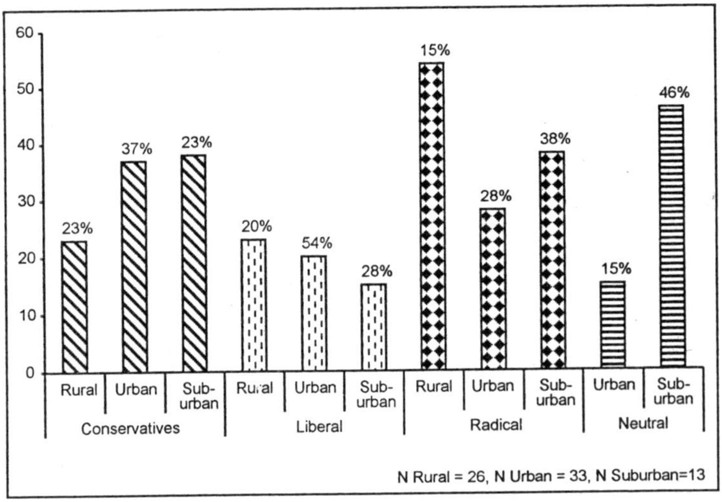

Fig. 3.5: Radicalism and Place of Origin.

Source: Field data. N Rural = 26, N Urban = 33, N Suburban=13

GENDER AND RADICALISM

Are males more radical than females? From Fig. 3.6 we find that this is indeed so.

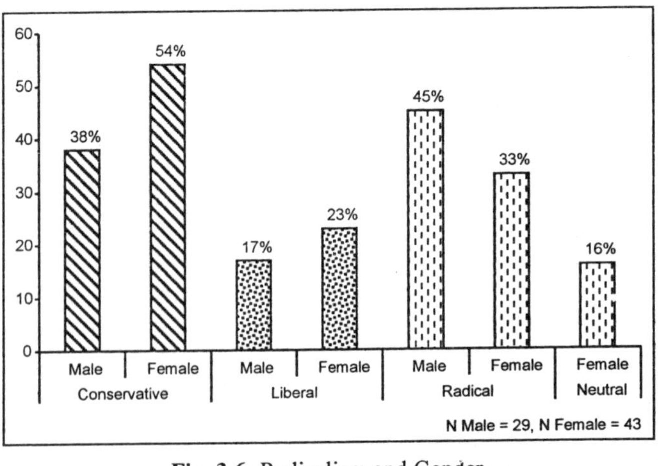

Fig. 3.6: Radicalism and Gender.

Source: Field data. N Male = 29, N Female = 43

Out of 29 males, 45 per cent are radical. In contrast, out of 43 females, 33 per cent are radical. I think that the socialization process contributes to a differential in the attitudes of males and females. While males are socialized to achieve, to change their existential circumstances, the females are socialized in terms of accommodation and adjustment. This contributes to a difference in attitudes. We find that more females (54%) are conservative compared to males (33%). Our findings are consistent with the findings of previous studies (Banerjee, 1991:165-167, 2003:149-150, 2009:49).

From Fig. 3.7 we find that students from the Lower Income Group are more radical. 16 out of 36 respondents (44%) are radicals. They are followed by Higher Income Group. 2 out of 5 respondents from the Higher Income Group (40%) are radicals. 9 out of 24 Middle Income Group students (38%) are radical. We find that there is little variation in attitudes in the three income groups. This shows that, in this case, economic status has little impact on attitudes. Previous studies (Banerjee, 1991 and 2003) show that there is an association between radicalism and economic status.

RADICALISM AND ECONOMIC STATUS

Does radicalism differ with economic status?

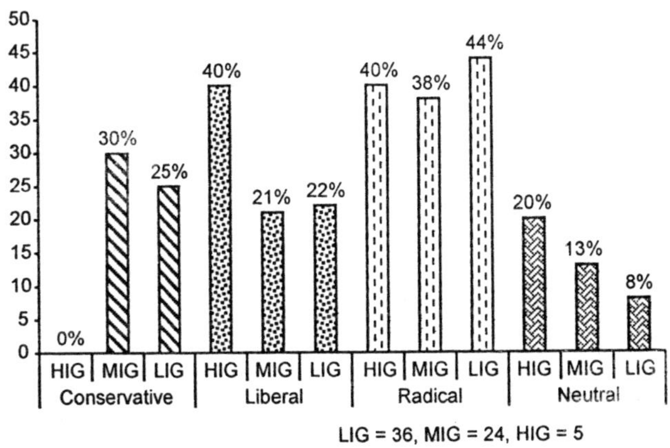

Fig. 3.7: Radicalism and Economic Status.

Source: Field data. LIG = 36, MIG = 24, HIG = 5

STUDENT RADICALISM AND POLITICAL PARTICIPATION

How far do radical attitudes have an impact on political participation?

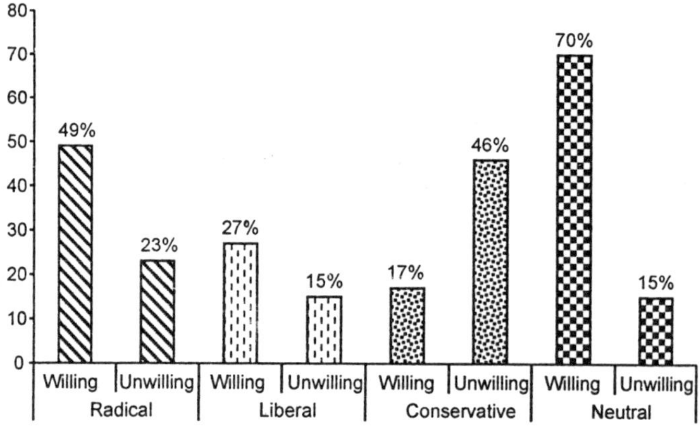

Fig. 3.8: Radicalism and Political Participation.

Source: Field data.

From Fig. 3.8 we find that out of 72 respondents, 41 students (56.94%) expressed willingness to participate in politics. 26 students (36.11%) were not willing to participate in politics. Five (6.94%) did not answer the question. Of the 41 students who expressed willingness to participate in politics, 49 per cent were radicals, 17 per cent were conservative, 27 per cent were liberal and 7 per cent neutral (Fig. 3.8). Conversely, more conservatives (46%) than radical (23%) were not willing to participate in politics. This clearly shows that there is an association between radicalism and political participation. This finding is consistent with findings of previous studies (Banerjee, 1991: 180-182, 2003: 159-160, 2009: 50).

IMPACT OF RÈGIME CHANGE ON STUDENT RADICALISM
(*See* Fig. 3.9)

Finally, let us have a look at the impact of règime change on student radicalism. Prior to the present study the author did another study on student radicalism (Banerjee, 2009). In this study, Calcutta University

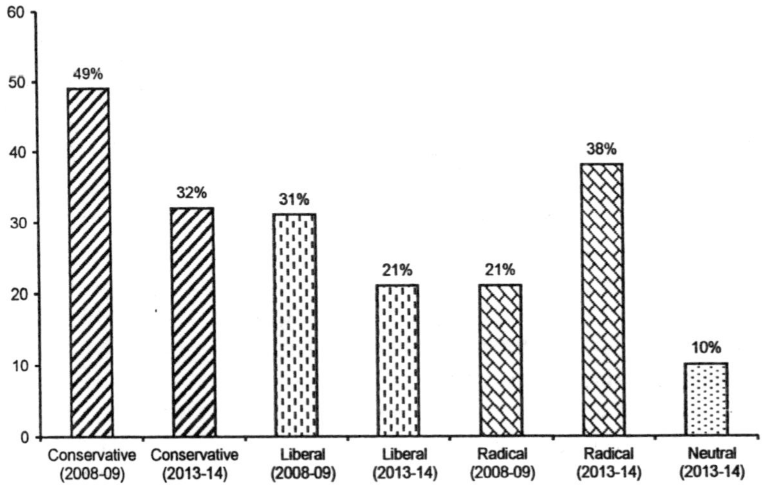

Field data (Session 2013-14)

Fig. 3.9: Règime Change and Student Radicalism

Source: A. Banerjee (Mimeo) Change and continuity in student radicalism (Session 2008-09).

Field data (Session 2013-14) N Session 2008-09 =150, N Session 2013-14=72

was considered to be a typical university of Bengal and its students representatives of Bengali university students. Comparing the two sets of data we find that:

(i) In the session 2008-2009—49 per cent of the 150 respondents were conservative. In contrast 32 per cent of the 72 respondents in the session 2013-2014 were conservative. Thus, conservatism declined.

(ii) Liberalism also declined. 31 per cent of the 150 respondents of session 2008-2009 were liberals. In contrast, 21 per cent of the 72 respondents of 2013-2014 session were liberals.

(iii) Radicalism has, however, increased. In the session 2008-2009, only 21 per cent of 150 respondents were radical. But in the session 2013-2014—38 per cent of 72 respondents were radical. Thus, we find that despite the apparent right-wing turn taken by Bengal post-May 2011, radical attitudes are held by a significant minority of the students.

CONCLUDING REMARKS

The main objective of our study was to examine the impact of règime change or political attitudes of the university students of Bengal. For examining this and related issues, we did an analysis of news reports and a pilot survey. We found that there was a right-wing deviation in the student movement. The student movement has lost its democratic moorings. It has become entrapped in adult power politics. Criminalization of student politics has occurred. So, the basic objective of conducting student union elections, namely to train students in democratic political participation has been defeated. Political considerations determine major administrative decisions in the field of education. Under our previous Education Minister, Bratya Basu, the Education Department sought to ensure a measure of transparency in college admissions by making centralized online admission in colleges mandatory from the session 2014-15. But he was removed just before the admission season and the portfolio was handed over to Partha Chatterjee. It was alleged in the media that he did a u-turn on the policy of online admission to please the leaders of the Trinamul Chattra Parishad who wanted to abolish this system. Their objective was firstly to maintain political control over students who are being admitted to colleges and secondly to retain the pecuniary benefits got by forcing aspiring students to pay hefty bribes to the students union to get themselves admitted to colleges.[8]

In this chapter we presented some tentative empirical findings based on the pilot survey. I am aware that since it is a non-random sample, there is a possibility of bias creeping in to vitiate the findings. But we now have some significant leads. We found that significant minority of the students to be radical. Previous studies (Banerjee, 1991, 2003, 2009, 2011-2012) also show that radicals are a minority. So, radicals have always been a minority. But they are a powerful minority. Prior to *Parivartan* we find that 49 per cent of the 150 students studied had become conservative, i.e., totally opposed to socialism. This was also reflected in the outcome of the Parliamentary elections (2009) where the Left could win only 15 seats out of 42 (Banerjee, 2011-2012). This indicated that the Left Front lost support from many sections of society including students and youth. After the 2011 elections, the Left lost power. The people had made their dissatisfaction with the Left known. This was hailed as *parivartan*. But two years after *parivartan*, it appears that left-wing radicalism is on the rise among university students. And the reason may be dissatisfaction with the prevalent state of affairs in Bengali society, polity and the educational institutions. We have also seen *interalia* that males are more radical than females. Rural students are more radical than urban students. Radicals are more willing to participate in politics than liberals and conservatives. My findings, which are based on the session 2013-14, have been corroborated by previous studies (Banerjee, 1991 and 2003; 2009 and 2011-2012).

To conclude most of our major research questions have been answered in the affirmative. We have found that a powerful minority of the students (38%) favour socialism. And, if we add the left-wing liberals (21%), we find that 59 per cent of the students are leftist in orientation. Therefore, règime change has not seen a right-wing shift in political attitudes among university students of Bengal despite the student movement being dominated by rightwing radicals. This study was a small Pilot Study. But it has thrown up interesting leads which we can follow to unearth the true state of student radicalism in post-Left Bengal. Here lies its significance and utility.

NOTES

1. Sen, Mrityunjoy (2012), "Sakale takiye siksha mantrir dike, Siksha mantra takiye nirbachan commissioner dike" in *Edutone*, **2(14),** 30 Pous, 1418, 15th January.
2. Vide *Ananda Bazaar Patrika*, 16 January, 2014.
3. Vide *Ananda Bazaar Patrika*, 29 January, 2014.
4. Vide *Ananda Bazaar Patrika*, 22 January, 2014.
5. Vide *Ananda Bazaar Patrika*, 20 January, 2014.
6. Menefee, Selden C. "Radical" (1958), in Henry Pratt Fairchild (ed.) *Dictionary of Sociology*, Vision Press, London, p. 47.
7. Marshall, Gordon, "Pilot Survey" (2007), in Gordon Marshall (ed.) *Oxford University of Sociology*, Oxford, New York, Fourth Impression, p. 496.
8. Vide Nijassha Sangbaddata (2014), "Adhipatya aar arther tagide kop sikshangane", *Ananda Bazaar Patrika*, Kolkata, 31st May, pp. 1 & 6.

REFERENCES

Banerjee, Anirban (1991), *Students and Radical Social Change* (Thesis submitted in partial fulfilment of requirements of Ph.D. dissertation under Calcutta University) Department of Sociology, Calcutta University, Supervisors: Prof. Surajit C. Sinha (Mimeo).

Banerjee, Anirban (2003), *Students and Radical Social Change*, The University of Burdwan, Burdwan.

Banerjee, Anirban (2009), *Change and Continuity in Student Radicalism* (Final Report of a UGC Major Research Project) Department of Sociology, The University of Burdwan, Burdwan (Mimeo).

Banerjee, Anirban (2011), *Student Radicalism in Hungary: A Survey of Corvinus University Students,* Institute of Sociology and Social Policy, Cornivus University, Budapest, Hungary (Mimeo).

Banerjee, Anirban (2012), "Change and Continuity in Student Radicalism" in *Socialist Perspective*, Vol. 34, Nos. 3-4, December 2011--March.

Henerson, Marlene E., Lynn Lyons Morris, and Carol Taylor Fitz-Gibbon (1987), *How to Measure Attitudes*, Sage Publications, Newbury Park, Beverley Hills, London, New Delhi.

Rez, Ashima (2008), *Paschimbanger Bampanthi Chattra Andolan O Rajniti: Bardhaman Jelar SFI er Ekti Samiksha* [Kalabibhage (Rashtrabijnan) Ph.D. degree janya Bardhaman bishwabidyalayer nikat upasthapita gabeshana patra) Nirdeshak: Dr. Nimai Pramanik, Professor of Bibhagiya Pradhan, Rashtrabigyan Bibhag, Bardhaman Biswabidyalay, Paschimbanga, Bharat (Mimeo).

4

Problems of Healthcare Facilities among the Tribals

A Case from Malda District in West Bengal

Arpita Ghosh

INTRODUCTION

The World Health Organization (WHO) has defined health as a "state of complete, physical, mental and social well-being and not merely the absence of disease or infirmity. The enjoyment of the highest attainable standard of health is one of the fundamental rights of every human being without distinction of race, religion, political belief, economic or social condition" (WHO, 1997). The Constitution of WHO which came into force on 7 April, 1948 became the first international legal document to contain an explicit right to the "enjoyment of highest attainable standard of health". The definition provided by WHO also implies 'health' to be a holistic issue that also includes accessibility to health institutions and healthcare facilities.

There is an inextricable link between health and human rights. Respect, protect and fulfilment bound human rights obligations can be achieved by promotion and protection of health and access to healthcare facilities is a necessary precondition for this.

TRIBAL HEALTH SCENARIO IN INDIA

The health situation of the tribals in India shows that with regard to access to and benefits from the public health system, the tribals have always remained at the receiving end of the system. The public health system has remained largely uneven and concentrated among the better endowed sections of the society. So, the socially disadvantaged sections of the society have always lagged in this respect and the tribals have remained excluded. This is particularly true for tribal women and children. The health indicators from National Family Health Survey-2 (NFHS-2) indicate high alarming figures for the Scheduled Tribes in all respects. Table 4.1 reflects the same.

Table 4.1: Showing the Variation in Health Status Among Different Socio-Economic Groups

Health Indicators	*Scheduled Castes*	*Scheduled Tribes*	*Others*
Infant Mortality/1000	83.0	84.2	61.8
Under-5 Mortality/1000	119.3	126.6	82.6
Children Underweight (%)	53.5	55.9	41.4
Children with diarrohea (%)	19.8	21.1	19.1
Women with anaemia (%)	56.0	64.9	47.6

Source: NFHS-2 (1998 -1999), M/o Health and Family Welfare, Government of India.

The tribal communities in general and the primitive tribal groups in particular are highly disease prone. The tribals in India have distinctive health problems depending on their habitat, difficult terrains and ecological conditions (Basu, 1993). In our country, the health issues of the tribals have not been given timely priority which has been further compounded by their poverty, illiteracy, ignorance about causes of diseases, hostile environment, blind beliefs, poor sanitation, lack of safe drinking water, lack of personal hygiene and health education. The chief causes of their diseases are chronic and poor nutritional status (Basu, 2000). Maternal mortality rates and infant mortality rates are also high among the tribes due to their poor nutritional status and traditional practices of child birth. Nutritional anaemia is a serious matter of concern among women of rural and tribal areas. Some of the common diseases that affect the Indian tribes are tuberculosis, malaria, filarial, gastroenteritis, respiratory diseases, tetanus, measles, whooping cough, night blindness, skin diseases especially scabies. Moreover, tribal diets are also grossly deficient in iron, calcium, vitamin A and vitamin C, riboflavin and animal protein (Basu, 2000). The tribals generally consume liquor which is another reason for their health problems.

Another significant problem has been persistent lack in health and medical care services in the tribal inhabited areas (Bhatt, 2008). The tribals are mostly afflicted by the inadequate access to health services and poor health delivery system and this in many cases prevent the tribals in availing western health facilities which also further influence their already poor health seeking behaviour.

Much of the health problems and dismal health conditions among tribals are responsible for their habitat, poverty, ignorance, malnutrition, absence of safe drinking water, insanitary living conditions, lack of personal hygiene, health education and poor maternal and child health (Basu, 2000).

The health indicators from National Family Health Survey-3 (NFHS-3) indicate high alarming figures for the Scheduled Tribes in all respects of child health (Table 4.2).

Table 4.2: Showing Some of the Health Indicators among Different Socio-Economic Groups in India

Indicator	*Infant Mortality/ 1000 Live Births*	*Under-5 Mortality/1000 Live Births*	*Child Mortality Rate*
India	57.0	74.3	18.4
SC	66.4	88.1	23.2
ST	62.1	95.7	35.8
OBC	56.6	72.8	17.3
Others	48.9	59.2	10.8

Source: NFHS-3, (2005-06) M/o Health and Family Welfare, Government of India.

Several researchers and authors have also contributed substantially towards the state of tribal health in India. Prominent among them are Hasan (1967) who pointed out that various social and cultural factors control the health situation and practices of the tribal communities. Basu (2000) indicated that the health problems among the tribals are mainly because of lack of health facilities, sanitation and access to safe drinking water. Singh (1981) pointed out that the tribal development programmes are largely plan based and target oriented and lesser attention is paid on the local felt needs of different eco-systems and communities and therefore, they are often not successful.

Menon (1985) noted that deforestation has a severe social and economic impact on the life of the tribal women. It has manifested into additional workload, reduced fuel and food supply, deterioration of their health condition and introduction of external values that result in their lower status.

Akram (2007) pointed out the long standing commitment to "Health for All" and the enormous health anomalies that continue to prevail among masses. He pointed out the problems related to judicious distribution of healthcare facilities as well as the limitation in choices in maintaining sustainable health conditions in which the marginalized tribal communities are the worst victim's.

As has been discussed earlier that the infant mortality rates among the Scheduled Tribes is more than other communities in India, it is nothing exception in West Bengal. Similarly, like the national trends maternal mortality, child and maternal malnutrition is rampant in West Bengal also. Although health intervention from both the Central and State Government are carried out in the tribal areas yet those are not enough to meet the deficiencies and proper access to health institutions and facilities still remains a distant dream. The tribal health in the state is also affected by their poor educational and socio-economic background of the tribals.

In this context, the present study is important to assess the state of the tribal's access to health facilities in the tribal dominated villages of one of the backward district in West Bengal.

OBJECTIVES

- To study the access to healthcare facilities among the tribals.
- To study the access to basic civic amenities that enhances the quality of health.
- To understand the situation of health infrastructure in the vicinity of tribal areas.

THE STUDY AREA

The present research has been undertaken towards understanding the access to healthcare facilities among the tribals in Malda district of West Bengal. The study was conducted in thirty one tribal villages in four tribal dominated blocks of the district covering seven hundred and eighty seven (787) families from five tribal communities namely Santals, Malpaharis, Mundas, Koras and Oraons.

SAMPLE

The present study constitutes of population from Kora, Malpahari, Munda, Oraon and Santal communities. A total of 787 families from the above named blocks and communities were included in the study. Of the total families there were 590 Santal families, 48 Malpahari families, 50 Munda families, 35 Kora families and 64 Oraon families. Among the families under the present study there were 3,567 individuals of which 1,797 were males and 1,770 were females.

METHODOLOGY

The village people were the major source of primary data. The secondary data were collected from the Block Development Offices and educational institutions. For collecting the primary data general observation of the villages was made and household information in Preliminary Schedule Form was conducted. The Preliminary Schedule was used for the purpose of the household census. Data analysis was done with the help of statistical software namely, SPSS V 16. In some cases Microsoft Excel and Microsoft Word was also used. The tabulated data were then analyzed with various correlates to highlight the thematic issues of the study and represented in the form of tables.

ACCESS TO HEALTH FACILITIES IN THE STUDY AREA

Universal access to healthcare is a prerequisite for achievement of health and human rights. Access to health facilities is a matter of serious concern in the rural areas across the country and more particularly in the tribal belts. In the present study, in order to understand the accessibility of the tribal families to health institutions, the distance of the sub-centres and the primary health centres were taken into account.

Table 4.3 shows the community-wise variation while accessing the sub-centres in the studied areas.

It is still a matter of concern as is evidenced from Table 4.3 that a total of 9.5 per cent families among the studied communities have to access sub-centres above 3 km distance and 57.2 per cent have access to sub-centres within 1-3 kms while 33.3 per cent have access within 1 km.

Table 4.3: Showing the Distance of the Sub-Centres (Community-wise) from the Studied Families

Distance (in km)	*Number of Families*											
	Santal		*Malpahari*		*Kora*		*Munda*		*Oraon*		*Total*	
	No.	*%*	*No.*	*%*	*No.*	*%*	*No.*	*%*	*No.*	*%*	*No.*	*%*
Within 1	223	37.8	0	0.0	18	51.4	21	42.0	0	0.0	262	33.3
1-3	328	55.6	48	100.0	17	48.6	8	16.0	49	76.6	450	57.2
Above 3	39	6.6	0	0.0	0	0.0	21	42.0	15	23.4	75	9.5
Total	**590**	**100.0**	**48**	**100.0**	**35**	**100.0**	**50**	**100.0**	**64**	**100.0**	**787**	**100.0**

Source: Field Survey.

As far as the community-wise variation in accessing health facilities is concerned, 37.8 per cent Santals access sub-centres within 1 km distance, 55.6 per cent have to access sub-centres between 1-3 kms and 6.6 per cent have sub-centres above 3 km distance.

Among the Malpaharis, 0 per cent have sub-centres within 1 km distance and above 3 km distance and 100 per cent Malpahari families have sub-centres between 1-3 kms distance.

Among the Koras, 51.4 per cent can access sub-centres within 1 km distance while 48.6 per cent families have to access sub-centres between 1-3 km distance and no families have to access sub-centres above 3 km distance.

Among the Mundas, 42 per cent can access sub-centres within 1 km distance and 16 per cent families have to access sub-centre facilities between 1-3 kms and 42 per cent families get access to sub-centres above 3 km distance.

Among the Oraons, the number of families who had sub-centre access within 1 km distance was nil while 76.6 per cent families had access to sub-centres between 1-3 kms and 23.4 per cent families had sub-centres facilities above 3 kms.

Thus, it is seen there that among the studied communities only the Koras had the maximum access to sub-centres within 1 km distance followed by the Mundas and the Santals. No Malpahari and Munda families got access to sub-centres within 1 km distance. Most of the Malpahari families got access to sub-centres between 1-3 km distance followed by the Oraons, Santals, Koras and Mundas. The maximum number of families that had access to sub-centre facilities above 3 km distance belonged mostly to the Munda community which was followed by the Oraons and Santals. No Malpahari and Kora families had to access sub-centres above 3 km distance and they remained better privileged on this than the other communities.

Table 4.4 shows the distance covered by the studied communities while accessing the first referral health units.

Table 4.4: Showing the Distance of the Primary Health Centres among the Studied Communities

Distance (in km)	*Number of Families*											
	Santal		*Malpahari*		*Kora*		*Munda*		*Oraon*		*Total*	
	No.	%	No.	%	No.	%	No.	%	No.	%	No.	%
Within 3	180	30.5	0	0.0	18	51.4	7	14.0	0	0.0	205	26.0
3-5	102	17.3	21	43.7	0	0.0	8	16.0	28	43.7	159	20.2
Above 5	308	52.2	27	56.3	17	48.6	35	70.0	36	56.3	423	53.8
Total	**590**	**100.0**	**48**	**100.0**	**35**	**100.0**	**50**	**100.0**	**64**	**100.0**	**787**	**100.0**

Source: Field Survey.

It is clear from Table 4.4 that among all the communities under study only 26 per cent had access to primary health institutions within 3 km distance while 20.2 per cent families had access to PHCs between 3-5 kms and large section, i.e 53.7 per cent families had PHCs above 5 km distance.

Among the Santals, 52.2 per cent families could get access to PHCs above 5 km distance, 30.5 per cent families got access within 3 kms and only 17.3 per cent families got access to PHCs between 3-5 kms.

Among the Malpaharis, 56.3 per cent families could get access to PHCs above 5 km distance and the rest 43.7 per cent families accessed it between 3-5 kms while there were no families who could access it within 3 km distance.

Among the Koras, 51.4 per cent families could get access to PHCs within 3 km distance while rest of the 48.6 per cent had to access above 5 km distance and there were no families who could access PHCs between 3-5 kms.

Among the Mundas, 70 per cent families had to access PHCs above 5 km distance, 16 per cent families had to access it between 3-5 kms distance and 14 per cent families got access within 3 km distance.

Among the Oraons, 56.3 per cent families had to access PHCs above 5 km distance and the rest 43.7 per cent families had to access it between 3-5 kms while there were no families who could get access within 3 km distance.

Thus, it is evident from Table 4.4 that within 3 km distance, the maximum number of families who accessed primary health centres belonged to the Kora community followed by the Santals and the Mundas while there were no Malpahari and Oraon families having PHCs within 3 km distance. The number of families who had access to PHCs between 3-5 kms belonged mainly to Malpahari and Oraon community followed by the Santals and the Mundas. The Koras did not have to access PHCs within this distance range. The number of families that had to access PHCs above 5 km distance belonged mostly to the Munda community followed by the Malpaharis, Oraons, Santals and Koras.

The tribals reported during the field study that they do not get regular medicines from the sub-centres and rural hospitals, the OPD and Emergency services are irregular as the doctors remain absent most of the times, the behaviour of the health personnels towards the patients and their relatives are not gentle. The sub-centres in most of the villages were run in rented houses which remained in dilapidated condition. The sub-centres remained closed for most of the times and the staffs were either absent or even if they were present, it was only once or twice a week.

The ward beds and toilets for in-house admitted patients in health centres were unhealthy, unhygienic. The villagers complained that due to lack of infrastructure, absence of doctors and nurses in the Emergency section of the hospital and due to the referral tendency of the doctors they have to shift their patients at odd hours of night to the District Medical College Hospital at Malda Town located very far away from the studied blocks like Gazole, Bamongola and Habibpur, where communication facilities are unavailable.

It was learnt from interviewing the villagers that the cost of diagnosis and treatment is another reason that pervades the villagers from accessing western medicines as they do not get free medicines from the hospitals. Hence, it is difficult for them to bear the cost of medicines required for treatment due to their low socio-economic status. Moreover, there are huge amount of fake medicines in the medicine shops which cost higher than the original medicines. The ignorant villagers often fall easy prey to this unscrupulous practice.

The family welfare services provided to the mothers, children and family planning programmes have failed to reach the anticipated level of success as the staffs in the sub-centre remain absent mostly.

ACCESS TO CIVIC AMENITIES

(a) Drinking Water Sources

Drinking water and sanitation are the two most significant indicators that shape the quality of health. In most tribal villages, safe drinking water was inaccessible and as a result, the tribal families had to depend on unhygienic water sources. It was a very common picture in the tribal villages for the women to fetch drinking water from sources that were even up to one kilometre away from their homes. Water scarcity was a common problem of the study area. Water tables remained low in these parts due to the topographic set-up. The problem of water was severe in the summer months when the water tables go deep down and the deep wells and ponds dry up. Sources of drinking water were not sufficient enough to meet the crisis. Another problem was that if a village tube well failed to work due to some mechanical fault, the concerned personnel from the local panchayats did not turn up timely to repair it and the villagers faced tremendous problem.

Table 4.5 shows the drinking water sources of the studied communities:

Table 4.5: Showing the Community-wise Drinking Water Facility

Sources of Drinking Water	*Number of Families of the Community*											
	Santal		*Malpahari*		*Kora*		*Munda*		*Oraon*		*Total*	
	No.	%	No.	%	No.	%	No.	%	No.	%	No.	%
Well	293	49.7	4	8.3	19	54.3	0	0.0	18	28.1	334	42.4
Tube Well	252	42.7	44	91.7	3	8.6	49	98.0	43	67.2	391	49.7
Water Supply	45	7.6	0	0.0	13	37.1	1	2.0	3	4.7	62	7.9
Total	**590**	**100.0**	**48**	**100.0**	**35**	**100.0**	**50**	**100.0**	**64**	**100.0**	**787**	**100.0**

Source: Field Survey.

Table 4.5 shows that among the studied communities, the Koras (54.3%), Santals (49.7%), Oraons (28.1%), Malpaharis (8.3%) and Mundas (0%) used well water for drinking and other purposes. Mundas (98%), Malpaharis (91.7%), Oraons (67.2%), Koras (8.6%), Santals (42.7%) used water from tube wells while Malpaharis (37.1%), Santals (7.6%), Oraons (4.7%), Mundas (2%) and Malpaharis (0%) used pipeline water supply.

The use of tube well for drinking water purposes was most among the Mundas followed by the Malpaharis, Oraons, Santals and Koras. Well water for drinking water purpose was mostly used by the Koras followed by the Santals, Oraons and Malpaharis. Pipeline water supply use was only limited to few families which included mostly Koras followed by Santals, Oraons and Mundas.

(b) Sanitation

Most of the tribal families are reluctant to use sanitary toilets because of their traditional beliefs that regard these amenities as impure. In some tribal areas some sanitary programmes were undertaken but they were unsuccessful.

Table 4.6 shows the sanitation facilities among the studied communities.

Table 4.6: Showing Community-wise Sanitation Facility

Sanitation Facility	*Number of Families of the Community*											
	Santal		*Malpahari*		*Kora*		*Munda*		*Oraon*		*Total*	
	No.	*%*	*No.*	*%*	*No.*	*%*	*No.*	*%*	*No.*	*%*	*No.*	*%*
Field	494	83.7	48	100.0	19	54.3	46	92.0	56	87.5	663	84.2
Non-Sanitary	38	6.4	0	0.0	0	0.0	2	4.0	4	6.3	44	5.6
Sanitary	58	9.8	0	0.0	16	45.7	2	4.0	4	6.3	80	10.2
Total	**590**	**100.0**	**48**	**100.0**	**35**	**100.0**	**50**	**100.0**	**64**	**100.0**	**787**	**100.0**

Source: Field Survey..

Table 4.6 shows that among the studied communities the Malpaharis (100%), Mundas (92%), Oraons (87.5%), Santals (83.7%) and Koras (54.3%) used field while the use of sanitary toilets was maximum among Koras (45.7%) followed by Santals (9.8%), Oraons (6.3%), Mundas (4%) and Malpaharis (0%). The rest, i.e. Santals (6.4%), Oraons (6.3%), Mundas (4%), Koras (0%) and Malpaharis (0%) used non-sanitary toilets.

It is seen that the use of sanitary toilets was most among the Koras followed by the Santals, Oraons and Mundas. The Malpaharis had no sanitary toilet facilities and all the families used the surrounding field or bushes as their natural toilet. The use of non-sanitary toilet facilities existed only among the Santal, Oraons and Mundas.

Thus, it is clear that the poor civic amenities in the tribal villages was another reason that compelled the tribal villagers to live an unhealthy lifestyle and fall prey to a number of diseases. The foremost among these are the lack of safe drinking water sources that makes them susceptible to seasonal and water borne diseases. The poor tribals depend on the tube wells and wells mainly under the supervision and maintenance of the local panchayats and block level offices for their primary source of drinking water and the villagers in some of the studied villages reportedly told that there is a substantial lack in the number of tube wells or wells in their villages and the ratio of tube wells to the number of families remain poor. As a result, the pressure is high on the village tube wells. In such situation they depend on the water of nearby ponds and ditches for drinking, bathing and washing which is extremely unhygienic. The problem aggravates when the tube wells goes out of order and the maintenance staff does not turn up for weeks or even months for repair. The crisis becomes acute in summer months when the water table goes down. Most of the wells and water bodies get dried up. The women and young tribal girls have to travel long distances to neighbouring villages to fetch water. This compels them to depend on unhygienic water sources for daily uses and drinking purposes which affect their health badly.

CONCLUSION

Scenario of Tribal health is basically different from their counterpart in the non-tribal fold. Tribal suffers more than the non-tribal areas in respect of health and health services. Generally, access to healthcare among the tribals is limited due to many factors which include poverty and lack of awareness among them.

Communication problems still remain in the remote villages which always hamper the timely accessibility of modern healthcare. Irregular attendance of medical staffs at village level health services is an impediment to the availability of healthcare which is badly needed by this poor tribal population.

Health personnels are not adequate to cater to the service of tribals who mostly live in relatively remote areas. Lack of goodwill and insensitivity on the part of a section of health staffs and doctors along with poor and inadequate health service remain as a major barrier in the proper outreach of health rights among the public in general and the studied communities in particular. It was noticed during visits to the rural hospitals that some doctors were busy with their private practice and devoted major time and effort for that rather than attending patients in the hospitals. Some doctors also remained absent in the hospital during duty hours and remained busy attending private patients in staff quarters and charged high fees from the patients which included patients from poor tribal families. During such situation if the villagers opt for private nursing homes going beyond their capacity, the private nursing homes refuse treatment or admission for critical patients and patients with low socio-economic backgrounds thinking that they would not be able to pay off medical charges. These creates delay in proper treatment at right time for critical patients and have to accept harsh realities in the delivery of health services and the health conditions either worsen or they have to go untreated.

It was also learnt from the patients and the villagers that while getting admission in Malda Medical College and Hospital they have to pay heavy amount to the local agents/brokers. Moreover, beds can be booked by special recommendations and influence of political leaders and the general public have to suffer for this. Reportedly, the behaviour of the nurses at duty in the wards, emergency department and outdoor services are inhuman and negligent in their duties and responsibilities. Since, the nurses are permanent employees of the State Government, they are not committed in their work and keep themselves busy in gossip while behaving rudely with the families of the patients. They do not even care for any higher instructions and live under the protective umbrella of their employees' union. The only work they do is that of maintaining official records of the patient while untrained and unrecognized sweepers and other Group D staffs carry out duties at the operation theatre, stitching, giving injections and other duties. Patients' parties have to engage special private caretakers for the patients. Even the hospital authorities are well aware about this practice and some of the officials who wanted to keep their name and designation confidential also admitted about the malpractices going around.

As they are very poor they expect the medicine from primary health centre at nominal prices or free of cost which is neither provided nor available in the health centre. Inadequate supply of medicine and infrastructure is very much absent and it aggravates the situation of healthcare in proper time of needs. Tribals on the one side are illiterate and non-aware about the health problems, but at the same time apathy of the local governmental support cannot also be ruled out.

After analysis of the above situation, it can be pointed out that to improve the accessibility of the tribals to healthcare facilities the actual medical services in the rural areas needs to be improved along with the infrastructural development. The referral systems at all the levels should be thoroughly revamped and properly developed so that the tribals receive proper treatment at the proper time. Basic amenities like safe drinking water and sanitation facilities also need to be improved for better health.

REFERENCES

Akram, M. (ed.) (2007), *Health Dynamics and Marginalized Communities*, Rawat Publications, Jaipur.

Basu, S.K. (1993), *Tribal Health in India,* Manak Publishers, New Delhi.

Basu, S.K. (2000), Dimensions of Tribal Health in India in *Health and Population – Perspectives and Issues*, Vol. 23, No. 2, pp. 61-70, New Delhi.

Bhatt, K.N. (ed.) (2008), *Population, Environment and Health Emerging Issues*, Rawat Publications, Jaipur.

Chaudhuri, B. (ed.), (1986), *Tribal Health: Socio-cultural Dimensions* Inter India Publications, New Delhi.

Chaudhuri, B. (2001), *A Bibliography of Tribal Studies in India*, Kolkata: CARID.

Chaudhury, S.K. (2004), *Constraints of Tribal Development*, New Delhi: Mittal Publications.

Government of India (2001), *Census of India,* New Delhi: Office of the Registrar General.

Government of India (2005), *Rural Healthcare System in India*, Ministry of Health and Family Welfare, New Delhi.

Government of India (2010), *Statistical Profile of Scheduled Tribes in India*, New Delhi: Ministry of Tribal Affairs, Statistics Division.

(Government of India, 2010), Annual Report to the People on Health, Ministry of Health and Family Welfare, New Delhi.

Government of West Bengal (2007), *District Human Development Report Malda*, Kolkata: Development and Planning Department.

Government of West Bengal (2011-2012), *Economic Review*, Kolkata: Development and Planning Department,

Hasan, R.A. (1967), *The Cultural Frontier of Health in Village India*, Manaktales, Bombay.

Menon, G. (1985), "Tribal Women: Victims of Development Process", in Walter Fernandes (ed.) *National Development and Tribal Deprivation*, Indian Social Institute, New Delhi.

Singh, B. (1981), "Tribal Development without much success: Review", in B. Chaudhuri (ed.) *Tribal Development in India: Problems and Prospects*, Inter India Publications, Delhi.

5

Corruption in India: Can the Hydra Headed Monster be Chopped!

Amal Mandal

INTRODUCTION

India is a land of contrast and paradox. In this country honesty, integrity and empathy in public and private life are upheld and glorified in the epics (like *Vedas, Upanishad*) and in religious books and precepts. Yet, India is one of the most corrupt countries in the world where grafts, bribery, kickback, embezzlement etc. rule the roost.[1] Indian people are overtly religious and here *Bhakti* is one powerful cult in private lives. But the religious tradition is somewhat hallowed where the blessing of God is supposed to be bought. People make it a point to propitiate the chosen God with expensive jewellery, gorgeous structure or hefty amount of donation etc.[2] While almost every form of corruption is haunting the state and society, trifling little has been done to curb the menace. Apparently, people are indignant at the cancerous growth and spread of corruption, they engage in animated debate on the corruption phenomenon, but they tend to be resigned with the conviction that the cancer has spread every nook and corner and it is almost beyond redemption. The recent anti-corruption movement—spearheaded by civil society and social media—created a hype that one strong Ombudsman type *Lokpal* would clear up the scourge, yet all tended to have ended in a whimper.

As per Corruption Perception Index (CPI), 2012 of Transparency International (TI), India stood at 94th position, one notch above than its rank in 2011. In the survey of 1000 Indian urbanites—undertaken by TI—51 per cent respondent reported that they paid bribe in the preceding year—the quantum more than double of the world's average—and 74 per cent believed that corruption had worsened compared to the preceding three years. Even though CPI and methodology of TI are not beyond reproach[3], the disclosures demonstrate quite a higher level of incidence and frequency of corruption in India.

Corruption is more like a multi-focal, multi-variate and mutli-dimensional eternity of Indian socio-political system. It seems to have no bounds, is endless as eternity, universal as the cosmic system, constant as the polar star, permanent as the galaxy and perennially saltish as sea water. Governed by unalterable rules of moral turpitude and backed by a decadent and remorselessly shameless law-enforcement agency, the sentinels of public interest are enveloped in the thick fog of putrid depravity and feel emboldened to continue with their public depredations with impunity. Corruption is not one single individual's cloistered virtue, but a multilateral effort of innumerable participants who together receive their spoils that make it institutionalized and market worthy.[4]

The swindle and frauds like 2G Spectrum, Indian Premier League, Commonwealth Games, Adarsha Housing, Santa Land, Citibank, Insurance, Palmolive, Land (Yediyurappa), Sorpene Submarine, Stamp Paper, Hawala, Satyam, Stock Market (Harshad Mehta), Madhu Koda, Mundra, Prasar Bharati, National Human Rights Commission (NHRC) and Coal-gate are of recent cases [5] that are of grand nature—involving thousand of crores and immense media attention. What is ominous is that together with Ministers, senior politicians, top brass of military, top businessmen, involved are the top watchdog bodies like Central Vigilance Commission, Central Bureau of Investigation (CBI), NHRC and judges of Supreme and High courts. Obviously, only few are out in the open and many others are either covered up or yet to be unearthed.[6] If and when the local level petty cases are taken into consideration, the situation can only aggravate. Thus, "Corruption is the most endemic and entrenched manifestation of poor governance, so much so that it has almost become an accepted reality and a way of life".[7]

DEFINITION AND DYNAMICS

For quite a while corruption has attracted ample attention from academics and activists. Consequently, whopping volumes of scholarship and commentaries have proliferated and those have enriched our understanding of the nuances of corruption, its dynamics, effects, implications all of which help in grasping its nature, dimension and thereby the formulation of countervailing initiative. However, how to conceptualise corruption has remained one enigma.

Corruption has become one of the most important notions of social discipline—the testimony being huge volume of literature. The trend is mainly rooted in Western intellectual debate over the relationship of the state and the society, the state and market, formal-informal, legal-illegal and black and white practices etc. Theorisation attempts have followed significant paradigm shifts—moving from evolutionary concern for the historical forms of corruption to its influence on political parties, its anti-normative and functional role in the political system, its nexus with democracy, civil society and development.

Following the postulate of the World Bank and Transparency International, corruption has, for long, been conceptualised as "the misuse of public office for private gains". This somewhat simple definition connotes the improper and unlawful act and behaviour of public officials and politicians who do have the opportunity and who do usurp or divert money and assets from the public coffer to themselves and to their accomplices.

Abuse of public office definition is rooted in firm dichotomy between public/impersonal and private/personal spheres and keeps the two separate, largely in line with the celebrated Weberian notion of rational-legal bureaucratic organization. However, it needs emphasis that Weber himself had asserted that his ideal type might not be found empirically anywhere in the world.

However, this definition is too narrow and parochial; it implies as if corruption is confined exclusively to public office and it is all about private gains. This straightway excludes the private and social spheres. In private enterprises—of whatever nature—corruption is no less rampant. Corruption does exist also in private activities regulated by the government. Moreover, the abuse of public offices does not necessarily for private gains—more often the benefits go to one's caste, friends and to a significant extent to finance the activities of the political parties.

Almost in the same vein, yet another simple formula has dominated many literature; C = M + D–A, where corruption equals monopoly plus discretion minus accountability. The postulate is equally non-encompassing, excluding private and social spheres. This formula is rather apt for only political dimension of corruption, particularly when discretion and accountability are involved.

Series of corruption and scandal—Enron for instance—have prompted rethinking of the popular definitions. TI and others now refer to the "abuse of trusted authority for private gain". This new definition yet again relies on simplified distinction between public and private spheres and includes only the private gains. Such narrow ambit cannot account for the magnitude and reality in most countries.

Such contracted political conceptualization may seem to be somewhat deliberate. It is the political variety of corruption that evokes public outcry, it serves the interest of the donor agency and it is more amenable to substantiation. When the money involved is massive and above all, reforms measures, if taken or implemented, will have deterrent impact on other forms of corruption.

Dictionary meaning of corruption implies change or deviation from the expected or ideal form; it is all about dishonest, illegal or immoral act or behaviour especially of someone having power. *Concise Oxford Dictionary has* furnished one comprehension definition; the dishonest act in return for money or personal gain.

In another plain, corruption refers to those transactions which involve undue benefits to some people who do not deserve or are not entitled to those. Such transactions make some people recipient of financial benefits, physical and social resources that make these people capable of exhorting power over others and controlling the rewards and punishment for others.

Corruption should better be positioned on private, socio-cultural arenas as well and it should be regarded more as social peril rather than purely political perversion. After all, corruption is not absent in usual social interaction/transaction. For substantiation with common practices from academic field, there are several instances where teachers force students to take private tuition with the caveat that otherwise they would not qualify the examination in the subject concerned. Not infrequently, teachers indulge in manipulation of marks of their 'own' students. Leaving aside pecuniary benefits, teachers mobilize group of students whenever they find themselves in a tight corner or spot of bother. Still more, abuse of religion for propagating or fomenting communal clashes is not uncommon in many Indian states. Would not those abuse or deliberate acts come under the compass of corruption?

One may prefer holistic conception of corruption. And paraphrasing the illustrious concept of Rawal, corruption can be seen as the manifestation of *unfairness*. It can be any and every human act or activity whereby someone is illegally, unethically or unwarrantedly made to suffer or victimised for financial, political, social gains and benefits. Broader definition—unfairness or abuse of political, economic and social power and position in whatever manner and purpose—is important for grasping the dimensions and nuances of corruption. It is still more imperative for planning and devising apposite intervention strategy. Admittedly, such wider definition would be unwieldy to handle the phenomenon in a rigorous manner. Yet, in order to understand and consequently palliate the spectre of corruption one has to be aware of every conceivable dimensions of corruption.

In essence, corruption is a two way process. Everywhere there is giver and taker, victim and victimizer. It has demand and supply side. In many analyses the demand side receives inordinate emphasis. The takers are branded as the culprits. There has been thunderous silence on the supply side of corruption, the choking of which can have constricting impact on demand side. There are several interrelated factors which determine the elasticity of demands and supply function in a given context and every analysis and reform initiative should better attend to those aspects.

People with contrasting background, interest, stake and standing differ in their perception and consequences of corruption. The politicians, bureaucrats and businessmen tend, in general, to define corruption in a rather slender and legalist sense. Conversely, journalists, judges and academic take a broader and moralist standpoint. While the former group accepts somewhat minimal consequences, the later one regards it as the scourge having horrifying consequences.[8] It is equally worth mentioning that the so-called educated middle class seems to regard it as the scar or blot that requires sweeping surgical operation. The raging controversy and anti-corruption movement also make the middle class even more critical about the practice and phenomenon of corruption.

Corruption takes insidious forms in daily engagements of people in most countries including India. Few common instances will vindicate it. From any bus stand or railway station if one intends to go to the destination by auto/three wheeler etc. the drivers will invariably refuse to follow the official rate (or meter rate) and will charge extra, more so if it is late night. Almost all drivers will stick to the non-official rate. One will have no option but to accede to the rate laid down by the drivers. By paying more than the legitimate rate, does not one indulge in some sort of bribery, even if indirectly? Almost all fish/meat vendors cheat their customers—either by price, quality or weight. What one must take note is that the same driver or vendor is to regularly pay subscription etc. to their Union and police. This way one tacit as well as symbiotic relationship between the individual bribe taking and collective bribe giving develops.[9]

Corruption may, broadly, be grand/mega and petty/retail in nature. In the scholarship grand or high profile political corruption—involving important politicians and media frenzy—usually receive intensive attention. The cases of corruptions indulged by private enterprises/businessmen—without having track with public affairs—are seldom discussed and debated. Those incidents occurring at social sphere are often ignored or shunted to the genre of social problem, even though the dividing line between problem and corruption is practically blurred.

Grand corruption is that which entails political leaders, usually massive amount of embezzlement, becomes sensational news, receives media interest and offers scope for mud-slinging. Petty/retail corruption is just the reverse; it envelops lesser mortals, smaller amount/magnitude and scant public glare. Ironically, ordinary people encounter more frequently the petty cases in their everyday lives and almost everyone remains impervious to the recurring plight. Petty cases impinge more on the poor people. For instance, slum dwellers of Bangalore had to pay an average bribe of Rs. 850 for getting municipal services.[10] Given the income of the slum dwellers, the amount is no less inflicting. However, grand and petty corruptions are interrelated; mega corruption encourages or spurts petty corruption—after all a fish rots from the head first (one Turkish proverb)—or one adept in petty cases will surely recycle those into grand scale provided opportunity.

In the literature corruption has been typified into several categories. In fact, the *modus operendi* is one substantial reason why it is difficult to identify and measure the magnitude and intensity of corruption in comprehensive sense and terms.

(i) ***Collusive/transactive***: This refers to the willing and deliberate cooperation between giver and taker, where mutual agreement to the advantage of and activity pursued by both actors are evident. Most political corruptions—award of contract/favour—are of this type.

(ii) ***Extortive***: Here those in a position or having authority extort bribe/other favour from those who seek certain services/decision. The obvious point is that the bribe givers are entitled to the services/ decision but, are forced to shed extra bit either for speedy disposal or for following engrained practice in the organization concerned (telephone, passport, private tuition).

(iii) ***Investive/anticipatory***: Here gift, money or indirect favour (admission of offspring to reputed school) is presented in anticipation or tacit request of favourable decision/reward in future.

(iv) ***Nepotistic/parochial***: In this variety ties such as kinship, caste, affection and so on determine the access to or incidence of decision or favour.

(v) ***Market type***: Here the highest payers receive the rewards.

(vi) ***Systemic***: This is mostly socio-political in nature, where the office holder—bureaucrats, politicians—seek to expand the illicit benefits through official channels and where the upper caste people despise and discriminate the lower rung.

Regarding the most visible players of the game of corruption, the observation of N. Vittal, former Central Vigilance Commissioner, may be worth reproducing. To him there are five specific players who collectively strengthen and entrench the vicious cycle of corruption; the *Neta* (corrupt politicians), the *Babu* (corrupt officials), the *Lala* (corrupt businessmen), the *Jhola* (corrupt NGOs), and the *Dada* (criminal/thug).[11]

PROGNOSIS OF PROLIFERATION

Over the years, corruption—more so its political variety—has thrived phenomenally. It has gained legitimacy and indulgence, has been defended shamelessly and has evaded reform initiatives. Common believe is that corruption has become a way of life in every sphere of state and society. Thus, the question survives; how to account for its growth and sustenance. There are many explanations regarding the proliferation of corruption, specifically its political *avatar*.

There is a temptation to accept corruption as a fact of life rooted in the frailties of human nature. Aristotle long ago realized; men are always wanting something more and more and never contended until they get to infinity. Kautilya had observed that it is "impossible for one dealing with government fund not to take at least a bit of the King's wealth...it is impossible to find out which government servants misappropriate money".[12] However, there is unanimity that systemic corruption is ingrained in certain form of socio-economic inequality.

Corruption is seen as function of a particular kind of culture. Poor countries are poor because they have a culture that accepts corruption. In poor countries the distinction between gift and bribe is diffused because people lack the capacity to differentiate between private and public sphere. Thus, Ackerman[13] postulates that corruption is prevalent when it is accepted as a part of the culture. However, she is also aware that people are often frustrated with corruption and their expression of tolerance sometimes reflects both resignation and fear of reprisal against those who complain. While exploring the origin of corruption in India, Myrdal concluded that corruption represented a heightened form of reciprocal system present in rural society that had been distorted as rapid urbanization and new form of politics emerged after Independence. Similarly, Johnston has submitted that corruption is one of the constellations of interrelated development problems endogamous to society and changes they experience or undergo.[14] However, the survey results of Widmalm reveal that Indian respondents are averse to the cultural thesis. They do not support corruption and favour a rule governed bureaucracy within a democratic setting irrespective of whether the society is plagued by corruption or not.[15]

Central Vigilance Commission once published *Citizens' Guide to Fight Corruption* where it identified few social causes of corruption. These are as follows:

- Indian society is chiefly based on caste and kinship. Caste and nepotism have become the basis of distribution of patronage.
- Indian culture of tolerance is one important social root of corruption. Person after leading a life of sin can easily get redemption by taking the name of Lord of choice. In social terms, such salvation is generously accepted and the sinner is embraced in the mainstream.
- Extreme attachment to family breeds nepotism and corruption. When a person feels that s/he should earn enough not only for oneself but also for other family members—wife, children or even generation—s/he tends to earn as maximum as possible. Such motive lies behind the enormous accumulation of wealth by the corrupt.

- The corrupt persons were once castigated and ghettoised. Now, such ethos is gone and we have reached such a cynical stage where ill-gotten money or wealth is not only taken for granted but also the capacity of such fortune maker receives applause.
- Dowry system also promotes corruption. Everyone wants to make sure that the daughter is married off well. This may be one reason why otherwise honest/clean officials become susceptible to corrupt practices during later part of service.
- Social pressure of giving children best education is yet another motive. When the pressure of competition is getting intense and education has become commercialised, parents tend to scramble for required money from all possible sources.
- The cult of consumerism and desire for an ostentatious life style tempts many to go after money by hook or by crook. The extravagant consumption or up stair-down stair status syndrome and consequent jealousy among the deprived leads to crime even.
- Power is best demonstrated by its misuse. Somewhere amassing as much wealth as possible is seen as a macho-demonstration of the competent. When it is the attitude, those having no share in the pie tend to rationalise that if they ever get opportunity they must misuse power and accrue wealth in whatever means, thus a vicious cycle of corruption may set in.
- Indian society is largely illiterate one where emotion dictates politics. When in Indian democracy politics is the route to power and where politics is based on caste etc., corruption tends to get firmly entrenched as well as tolerated.

Political corruption is often seen as one common and harmful feature of the developing countries. For instance, Huntington argued that the presence of corruption correlates with rapid social and economic modernization. In countries where large scale bureaucratic structure has been implanted, there may exist divergence between the aims, attitude and methods of the government and society. Modernization can enlarge government very swiftly, widening its scope of intervention and regulation well beyond the capacity and all those can multiply the opportunity for corruption.

However, poverty, culture, modernization or democratic hypotheses are not incontrovertible. The contention that traditional societies with hierarchy, strong family value, poverty and culture are more prone to corruption does not fit in the states like Rwanda, Ghana etc. It is not clear which way poverty causation goes. Few rich countries are obviously least corrupt, but Qatar is one super rich, but not super clean state. Democracy *per se* does not have much to do with corruption. Non-democratic Hong Kong and Singapore are not considerably corrupt. Following neo-liberal ideology some tend to argue that government's deep involvement in the economy is one contributing factor. Where there is fewer resources and service, bureaucrats are less likely to resort to corruption. But the relationship is not iron-clad. Bahrain and Mauritius are grossly free market economy, but they have formidable corruption problems.

At the abstract level, there are few specific factors that help flourishing (political) corruption. Scarcity of goods and service, red tape, complicated rule and procedures, lack of transparency in decision making, legal cushion of safety (innocence until proved guilty, anticipatory bail) and 'tribalism' among the corrupts who protect each other.

The Santhanam Committee[16] identified many procedural causes like red tape, administrative delay, unnecessary regulation, scope of personal discretion, cumbersome procedure, scarcity of goods and services and lack of transparency. When officials engage private companies to perform public works/services, when discretionary power is conferred to persons with specialized skill/knowledge (defence, IT) corrupt practices can flourish. Lack of transparency, obscure, ambiguous and technically complicated regulations also spawn corruption.

As the governments buy and sell goods and service (including below market price), disburse subsidy, award contract for mega projects, allow concession to private operation (infrastructure) and resort to disinvestment, there are every opportunity for corrupt practices. Moreover, when governments impose regulations, levy taxes and enforce criminal laws, the officials can delay and harass or even impose cost selectively, all may lead to extortive corruption.

Governments do have monopoly over many regulatory and delivery of services. In essence, governments control and engage in many activities, allocation and choice that are beyond the reach of anyone else. Absence of competition tends to create opportunity for corruption, as by restricting supply deliberately or by withholding information. Without alternative way, people become vulnerable to the pressure of monopolistic regulations which create fertile ambience for arbitrary decisions and corrupt practices that citizen cannot easily avoid or fight.

Lack of effective accountability in government's functioning is another contributing factor. Except presenting audited (formal) accounts and report to Parliament/Assembly or answering few questions, officials are not otherwise accountable to anyone. When there is collusive tendencies and when those expected to supervise the subordinates are themselves party to the collusion, the enforcement of accountability tends to be mockery. The problem aggravates due to the difficulty in measuring the performance and outcome of the decision of the officials.

Wade[17] concluded that elective institutions have amplified pressure towards corruption and have made corruption more systemic because of spiralling cost of fighting elections and nursing constituencies. Another account[18] argued that the legal-rational apparatus during British rule worked wonderfully because politics and administration was kept separate. But after Independence such distinction has been abolished; subsequently politicization of bureaucracy has rendered the Indian system one of the most corrupt one.[19] From horse's mouth[20], one can get hold of the account how senior politicians interfered in administration and how senior officers became helpless spectators to the degeneration of the system. Thus, the sole objective of politicians was to subvert bureaucracy and use it for personal/political gains. Politicians were obsessed with controlling in posting and transfer—or "transfer industry"—of the bureaucrats for political purpose.

Few recent eventualities have accelerated the dimensions and intensity of (political) corruption. Indian politics has seen a new breed of politicians.[21] Politics has come to acquire the character of a big business where fund rising capacity/quality attracts larger premium. In every party emphasis is now on the capacity of members to raise fund in any manner or by any means. When a party assumes power, such fund risers get plum posts from which compensation is to be paid to the contributors. One clear consequence of this process is to "mortgage much of the political system to money power".

At the same time, elections have become the fountainhead of public corruption in India. Almost all political corruption flows from and sustained by the imperative of enormous fund necessary for meeting elections related expenses. The legal limits in election expenses are flouted with impunity. The cost of getting elected in a multi-party democracy is skyrocketing. In conservative estimate, the per capita cost of parliamentary election is more than $ 50,000. Fund the contesting candidates seek or raise requires to be repaid more often in the form of allotting contracts to the 'banker' as and when the candidates win or retain power. The recent glamour and glitz of elections spectacle of Narendra Modi is one testament of how massive is the election expenses and from where the funds land![22]

With the disintegration of the 'Congress System', India has plunged into an era of coalition politics and this has led to competitive populism. Different political formations have their own vote-bank— not in customary communal sense. Rush is on to appease and accommodate those vote-banks through doling out largesse or offering political post having power and pelf. Moreover, in the coalition politics, the alliance partners do not always have the altruistic attitude; they often get hell bent to extract maximum pound of flesh which the coalition cannot resist for its survival sake. All these have virtually opened the floodgate of corruption.

CAN THE HYDRA HEADED MONSTER BE CHOPPED

Dr. Radhakrishnan, speaking on the historic night of 14-15th August, 1947, observed somewhat passionately, "Unless we destroy corruption in high places, root out every trace of nepotism, love of power, profiteering and black marketing which have spoiled the good name of our country, we will not be able to raise the standard of efficiency in administration as well as in production and distribution of necessary goods of life".[23]

Has the warning been heeded or have we seen downward turn of all those spoilers? The most ardent optimists would perhaps not deny that the overall situation is getting from bad to worse. Corruption is ballooning, corrupts are getting more daring. Lamentation is that corruption is worsening poverty and inequality, is breeding welfare mafia, the stealing of scare resources is dragging India's development drive down and it is fomenting other social banes. As the Supreme Court (in Niranjan Hemachal Sashittal *Vs.* the State of Maharashtra, 2013) has succinctly held: "corruption mothers disorder, destroys societal will to progress, accelerates undeserved ambitions, kills the conscience, jettisons the glory of institutions, paralyses the economic health of a country, corrodes the sense of civility and mars the marrows of governance." Yet, the state and society are being impervious or loath to take the hydra-headed monster head on.

Common urge is to fight and defeat the omen once and for all. When anti-corruption movements have been internationalized, Indian people have, over the years, gone quite frenzy about corruption in socio-political spheres. In many cases high profile corruption sparked public eruption.[24] Eventually, three different strands of praxis have come to the forefront: proactive role of civil society with grassroots activism, indispensability of ombudsman type powerful *Lokpal* and *Lokayukts* and simplification and transparency of decision making as through E-governance.

Undoubtedly, corruption must be smashed and there must not be an iota of encouragement to corruption. However, have those suggested praxis contributed in diminishing the spectre of corruption in all embracing sense? The answer is by and large in the negative. Thus, the question survives; can corruption ever be cured or eradicated.

In its holistic conception and from objective standpoint, corruption can at the utmost be contained and controlled, but its outright elimination is almost next to impossible! At least that is the lesson of history, worldwide. And there are several reasons accounting for why the war can be half won.

One should proceed from the premise that corruption is very complex and dynamic in nature and it has several layers, multiple actors and contributors, its dimensions are vast and variegated, context is subjective and roots are embedded in human traits, culture and economy. Every dimension of corruption cannot be addressed by legal measures alone.[25] Problem is that one cannot stem the tide by putting finger in the dyke. If one head of the monster is chopped, another will surface, possibly in more subtle or complex form. After all, India does have an array (though not adequate) of anti-corruption laws and agencies.[26] Yet, the incidences and magnitude of corruption have not come down appreciably.

Inadequacy of legal intervention has led to another insistence that harps on mass struggle to get the legislation implemented or enforced consistently and robustly. Strong, sustained movement by civil society organization is ardently expected to be the most important bulwark against rampaging corruption and it will have the potential to change the socio-economic habit. Indeed, forces of corruption are firmly embedded in society. And they will not give up without tough fight. These are powerful enough to frustrate and resist the intervention. However, two specific points—intrinsic incapacity of civil society organization and imminent backlash of the corrupt forces—merit mention.

Transparency International admits that civil society is typically the major victim of corruption and thus it should have strong incentive to dismantle the very system. Nevertheless, TI itself confesses that civil society's response has been fragmented in general and ineffectual in particular. One specific hurdle of civil society relates to the reluctance of the key actors to engage in confrontation.

Klitgaard (1991: 97)[27] has identified few factors which account for poor track records of civil society. It is rather difficult to form a political constituency for anti-corruption effort. Well organized citizen group has a clear stake in combating corruption. It is possible to launch anti-corruption campaign during the spurt of mega-corruptions, but institutionalising public concerns is rather problematic.

Few Indian instances evince that there is strong incentive among individual citizen to support corrupt practices as by paying bribe—whether out of necessity or to avoid inconvenience. Any fledging anti-corruption movement faces the stumble of sustaining the movement which simultaneously demands details of complex cases of frauds as well as intensive confrontation with the authority. The problems compound when the group is exclusively composed of poor and socially excluded.

Jenkins[28] has elaborated on the dilemma of forest dwellers' demand for greater transparency in forest affairs. Many dwellers are implicated in corruption; their source of livelihood is determined by public forest policy. Many occupants of forest land are illegal encroachers, who remain there by paying off forest and land revenue officials. Such illegality leaves the participants vulnerable and they might be unwilling to risk exposure to what is illegal behaviour and acts.

However, there are few instances of success. *Mazdoor Kisan Shakti Sangathan* (MKSS) in Rajasthan has successfully fought for access to official expenditure records of local governments and has undertaken cross-check of those through people's audit. In the process MKSS has exposed several frauds and has deterred further malfeasance. Several other civil society organizations reportedly share

MKSS concerns of empowerment of village people, but almost none has so far been able to replicate the effort. The fear of backlash from the government—chocking of fund flow or detection of procedural/ financial lapse—is one disincentive that explains their inability to undertake participatory audit like that of MKSS.

How powerful, brutal and innovative are the forces of corruption can be guessed from few concrete instances.

One assertion is that corruption is basically an individual act of aberration.[29] Exposure and punishing those individuals will help in weeding out corruption and here individual initiative will go a long way. No doubt, the corrupt individuals must be brought to book but individual (also collective) efforts will be rudimentary in general and risky at worst. Fate of few fighters will vindicate it.

Mr. S.K. Dubey, Deputy GM of National Highway Authority of India's Golden Quadrangle Project in Bihar sent written letter complaining about corruption in the construction works to the Former Prime Minister A.B. Vajpayee. Though Mr. Dubey specifically requested not to disclose him name, his letter was tossed around various Departments including Ministry of Road, Transport and Highway. In the process, the identity of the whistleblower was made public. Eventually, Mr. Dubey was shot dead by the contract killer. Moreover, Mr. Abhijit Ghosh, former GM of Central Bank of India, quipped in disgust; is fighting corruption in India a corrupt act in itself? If not then why are the ones I raised voice against sitting comfortably and it is me who is running from pillar to post?[30] When such was the fate of highly placed whistleblowers, the destiny of ordinary fighter is not beyond comprehension.

Right to Information (RTI) Act 2005, is often touted to usher in new era of governance in India and Indian states. This statutory right can become one significant tool to fight corruption of many varieties and to make governance still more transparent and accountable. Notwithstanding its huge potential, many individual activists who sought to use this route had been mowed down and hundreds were either assaulted or harassed simply for seeking specific information or poking in the hornet's nest.[31]

Nobody should ignore or undermine the organized strength of the corrupters. When someone alleged that the Custom officials at Delhi Airport were corrupt, the outcome was awful. The Custom department went on strike bringing the Airport services to grinding halt. Whenever specific organization or service provider is painted as corrupt, their organized onslaught is imminent. As every public department has stranglehold on the government, such blackmailing is not inescapable.

Still more, charges against powerful politicians often turn terrible, if not repulsive. The jail term for Jayalalitha, CM of Tamil Nadu for disproportionate assets, has evoked strong public fury that brought the state to standstill, precipitating law and order problems. Similarly, Fodder Scam involving Lalu Prasad Yadav, former CM of Bihar, is another intriguing example. Besides encouraging his supporters to go berserk, Lalu went on to demand snap poll, so as to get popular verdict on his alleged involvement in the case. Implication was that if he were elected, he would have come clean in the court of people. Few other politicians also took recourse to this dubious route. However, such manoeuvre is dangerous as well as preposterous. Nobody accused of corruption charges can escape the clutches of laws. Winning elections must not prove innocence of anyone. Rather, charge of corruption should in the first place debar everyone from contesting elections.

Another argument emphasises on transparency in decision making and placement of all information records in the public domain. Delay is one contributing factor to bribe; so also secrecy and discretion. E-governance is seen as the viable option and its benefits will include transparency, convenience, cost-effectiveness, speed and all these will lessen corruption. To the Transparency International literature, it is supposed to be simple, accountable, responsive etc. Two specific initiatives—reservation of railway ticket and registration of transfer deeds of immovable property—are cited as the successful efforts that have combated corruption.

Most possibly, E-governance will lessen the scope and incidence of corruption particularly when the access is universal, information is in public domain, thus open for public scrutiny. Surely, sandals and extortions in reservation of railway ticket have diminished. But not entirely. Indian people are ingenious; they are capable of 'inventing' avenues to subvert even the revolutionary technology. When confirmed ticket is not available in railway counter/portal one can still get it from touts/agents with extra money. One wonders from where and how the confirmed ticket is arranged. Still more, Tatkal ticket is beyond the reach of ordinary mortals. Allegation is that during the two hour duration of Tatkal booking the general access is virtually snapped by slowing down the speed of the Server and in railway counter it is the rampage of the touts.[32]

It is not enough to establish anti-corruption institution/agency or to reform existing institutions etc. If history is any indicator, imperative is the firm political will that will back well meaning measures and will initiate 'big bang' reforms.

Take the instance of Rwanda, one poorer, conservative and autocratic state in Africa. Rwanda stood 83rd in CPI ranks 2005. But it jumped to 50th position in 2012. The 'miracle' came about because of serious reforms introduced by just one man, President Paul Kagane. His government pushed ahead anti-corruption reforms, declared extortion, bribery, money laundering as criminal offence. The government slashed the number of public officials, sacked judges and set-up powerful bodies to audit the public services. Almost similar was the case of Georgia under President Saakashveile, who assumed reign after Rose Revolution, 2003. He arrested many corrupt officers, fired all traffic police, overhauled regular police force, cut the number of public officials by half, simplified tax laws and cleaned up custom officers etc. If the two aforesaid cases are non-sustainable attempts of individual leaders who were more engrossed with making own imprint, the cases of Singapore and Hong Kong will authenticate how far the political will can be one clinching factor in the war against corruption. The determination of the political class in the tiny states is reflected in the higher per capita expenditure, favourable staff position and non-interference in the working of the Independent Commission Against Corruption (Hong Kong) and Corrupt Practices Investigation Bureau (Singapore).

Anti-corruption agencies in a country can indeed be as effective as the incumbent government wants it to be.[33] Mere establishment means nothing. Nor can it be the magic bullet in eradicating all forms of corruption within a whiff. In general, anti-corruption agencies fail to reduce public venality in all but a few specific circumstances.[34] More ominously, such agencies can be double edged sword that can be used either for good or for evil purpose (victimising political foes, allegedly the role being played by CBI in India).

Is strong and positive political will against corruption perceptible or impending in India? Even taking the risk of overstatement, one can say not much really! The apparently innocuous statement of Indira Gandhi that corruption was a "worldwide phenomenon" heralded the first big boost that coincided with the flourish of whooping black money and emergence of "money politics" as the major factor in public life. Later on, the insistence on or recourse to "coalition *dharma*" by

Manmohan Singh put virtual public approval to organized looting of public coffer and natural resources. Bogey of capitalists' ploy by the Left Front Government and branding of "trifling matter" by Mamata Banerjee have helped in proliferation of the propensity and act of corruption in West Bengal.

In the war—not battle—against corruption political parties hold the key. Obviously, they are the principal abettors to corruption. Yet, it is equally true that they are the major surgeons capable of controlling the cancer. However, their track records and obsessive mudslinging, hypocrisy and blame game etc. bode ill to the optimists even. So far, who are the parties interested in enforcing the existing anti-corruption laws and regulation? Which are parties willing to shed criminals/ corrupt elements from their rank and file? Who are ready to make their property and assets properly audited and placing those in public domain? Who are committed to take apposite strategy to deal with administrative, political and social forms of corruption? Besides rhetoric, what have they done to combat corruption? Have not the leaders and parliamentarians of most parties amassed enormous wealth and resorted to parochial form of corruption? When almost all parties are virtually silent on tangible strategy on corrupt what can be their credibility in upholding moral stand the parties usually take in public proclamation? And how can the ordinary mortals be enthused about the future breakthrough?[35]

THE FUTURITY

Dilemma is that almost everyone is indignant but seems to be used to the corrupt practices and takes the peril in one's stride. Most are reluctant to go the extra length to root out and this trend actually perpetuates the incidence of corruption. Citizens, in general, are ambivalent; they decry it, but indulge corruption. Many wage protest against corruption in high offices, but remain unperturbed about petty cases in everyday life. Very often, civil society movements languish for lack of mass support, their scaling up of the momentum often stumbles and more importantly, these are cleaved by internal contradictions. Sometimes, public anger or revulsion erupts, but collective and sustained attempt is seldom seen. Political parties, at least publicly, proclaim their opposition to corruption, engage in mudslinging. Yet, they pamper or promote corruption after assuming the reign. Laws are there but these are hardly enforced fairly and squarely. Few anti-corruption agencies are in place, but without requisite power, personnel and prop from the leadership.

Any pragmatic intervention strategy must accede that corruption is complex phenomenon, fairly endemic in human society. The fight cannot critically be waged at individual level. One must also concede that corruption entails both givers and takers or it has demand and supply dimensions. Some are there to pay and some others are eager to offer something. In the background, there is the state in its entirety of actions and activities carried through numerous agencies and institutions. And it is the state that creates through its policies and decisions the ambience and it offers incentives that can either prevent or promote corruption depending on the context, ideology, policy and commitment of the ruling leadership.

NOTES

1. However, aggregate picture does not disclose everything. There are critical variations across Indian states (Kerala being the more notable exception). See for details Bussell Jennifer, 2012. *Corruption and Reform in India*. Cambridge University Press; Nicholas Charron 2009, *Correlates of Corruption in India: Analysis and Evidence from the States*, Working Paper Series 2009:11, Department of Political Science, University of Gothenburg.
2. From the cognition that God's blessing is purchasable, it follows that the blessing of politicians can also be bought—may be with higher price. Another bizarre manifestation is that even many educated persons worship the political leaders like other abstract Gods (mainly in South Indian states) and few have sacrificed lives for their revered leaders.
3. CPI is popular, it offers composite world scenario and collates views of top echelon of corporate, politicians and social strata. However, CPI in particular and conception and methodology of TI are not beyond contestation.

   (i) The conception of TI is narrow, it focuses only on political variety and takes on the takers and not givers. (ii) The survey respondents are typically educated, articulated ones whose world view is different from majority of ordinary people. (iii) CPI remains a measure of perception and corrupt practices seldom get consideration. (iv) Ranking of countries is somewhat ambivalent. (a) Few Central East European countries move up and down, losing or gaining 12th to 16th position within 1-2 years. Do those countries become less or more corrupt within such a short span? (b) Japan consistently ranks among the top 20 countries. But Japan is said to be inherently corrupt in its informal, legal and political practices. Sardonically, Japan government issues anti-corruption manuals for public officials.

4. Shekhawat, Vibhuti Singh (2005: 399). "Corruption in India: An Exercise in Perpetuity". *The Indian Journal of Political Science*, Vol. 66, No. 2, pp. 395-404.
5. Besides the recent ones, series of scam/frauds etc. surfaced soon after Independence. The first high profile case was Jeep Scandal, 1948. Then Mudgal, 1951, Mundra Deals, 1957, Malaviya and Sirajuddin, 1963 scams came out. AD Gorwala Committee—to suggest governance improvement measures—observed rather bluntly; quite a few of Nehru's ministers were corrupt and government went out of its ways to shield those corrupt ministers. Another recent mega scam involving more than Rs. 2 lakh crore is food-grain scam (during UPA regime) that has been elaborated by Ghandy Kobad, 2011. Corruption a Mere Symptom; the Disease is Unbridled Greed. *Mainstream*, April 23.
6. Most public exposures of corruption are motivated by partisan political interests. In many of the developing nations outcries and mobilizations against corruption and anti-corruption rhetoric are to deflect attention from its own economic difficulties (Balachandrudu, K., 2006). "Understanding Political Corruption". *The Indian Journal of Political Science*, Vol. 67, No. 4, pp. 809-816.
7. *National Human Development Report*, (2002: 122). Planning Commission and Oxford University Press, New Delhi.
8. Pavarala, Vinod, 1997. *Interpreting Corruption: Elite Perspectives in India*. Thousand Oaks: Sage Publications.
9. Banerjee, Sumanta, 2011. "Anna Hazare, Civil Society and the State". *Economic and Political Weekly*, 3 September.
10. Paul, S. and Shan, M., 1997. "Corruption in Public Service Delivery", in Guhan, S. and Paul, S. (eds.) *Corruption in India: Agenda for Action*, New Delhi: Vision Books.
11. Vittal, N., 2000. "Combatting Corruption", Seminar, no. 485. Elsewhere he wrote: "It is intense selfishness which is perhaps characteristic of not only humans, but all life. Intense selfishness leads to greed which is the fountain-head of corruption. That is why, many poor people are honest, many rich people and high officials are corrupt". "Corruption in India", *IASSI Quarterly*, January-March, 2012, pp. 1-7.
12. Kautilya listed 40 ways in which revenue officers embezzled money—from creating obstacles to outright stealing—and worked out cruel ways to punish the culprit.
13. Ackerman Susan Rose, (1999). *Corruption and Government: Causes, Consequences, and Reform*. Cambridge: Cambridge University Press.
14. Johnston, Michael, (1996), "The Search for Definitions: The Vitality of Politics and the Issue of Corruption", *International Social Science Journal*, Vol. 48, No. 3.
15. Widmalm Sten, (2005). "Explaining Corruption at the Village and Individual Level in India: Findings from a Study of the Panchayati Raj Reforms", *Asian Survey*, Vol. 45, No. 5, pp. 756-76.

16. Cited in Kashyap, Subhash (1982: 16). *The Ministers and Legislators*, Metropolitan, New Delhi.
17. Wade, Robert, (1982), "The System of Administrative Corruption in Canal Irrigation in South India", *The Journal of Development Studies*, Vol. 18, pp. 378-79.
18. Das, S.K., (2001), *Public Office, Private Interest: Bureaucracy and Corruption in India*. New Delhi: Oxford University Press.
19. However, the contention of Das (2001) that corruption was absent during British rule and watertight compartmentalization was maintained is contested propositions.
20. Hota, P.C., (2011), "Corruption in Public Service". *Dialogue*, Vol. 13, No. 2.
21. Jain, R.B., (1994), "The Craft of Political Graft in India: An Analysis of Major Scams", *The Indian Journal of Political Science*, Vol. 55, No. 4, pp. 335-52.
22. One documentary account informs that Rs 1.04 crore was the expense for just one small election rally in remote Manipur addressed by Modi. This rally was one of total 5827 (of which 437 were bigger) public events of Modi during Parliamentary elections, 2014. The question is when one small rally costs so much, what was the total amount incurred for all 5827 events? How much was spent by other BJP leaders in the elections? And how was it all funded? (*Source*: *The Statesman*, 11 October, 2014).
23. *Constituent Assembly Debates*, (1947), Vol. V, 14 October.
24. Bong, Sasha, *et al.*, (2012), *Analyzing Social Media Momentum, India's 2011-12 Anticorruption Movement,* available at www.lafollette.wisc.edu/publications/workshops/2012/India.pdf.
25. Corruption and serious economic offences cannot be curbed either by law or code of conduct or by sporadic preaching of moral values (Mukherjee, Arun Prasad, (2011), "Combating Corruption: the Indian Experience", *Dialogue,* Vol. 13. No. 2).
26. Few provisions/Agencies are Prevention of Corruption Act, 1988, Prevention of Money Laundering Act, 2001, Right to Information Act, 2005, Indian Penal Code [dealing particularly with disproportionate asset as in section 109, 120/b]; Central Vigilance Commission, Comptroller Auditor-General, Central Bureau of Investigation, Lokpal and Lokayukta Act, 2013.
27. Klitgaard, Robert (1991), "Political Corruption: Strategies for Reform", *Journal of Democracy*, Vol. 2, No. 4, pp. 86-100.
28. Jenkins Rob and Goetz Anne Marie, (1999), "Constraints on Civil Society's Capacity to Curb Corruption: Lessons from the Indian Experience". *IDS Bulletin*, October.
29. Paul Samuel, (2001), "Corruption as Spectator Sport". *Economic and Political Weekly*, 31 March.
30. For many other details see website of fightcorruption.com; tinyuri.com; cleanias.wikidot.com.

31. So far 25 RTI activists have been killed, the latest being Sanjay Tyagi in Meerut (*Source*: Wikipedia).
32. For recent scams in Railways see Singh, Shiv Kumar, (2010), "It is Always Spring Time for Corruption", *The Statesman*, 15 December; "When Cost and Price Are Unrelated", *The Statesman*, 29 June, 2010.
33. Quah Jon St. *Defying Institutional Failure; Lesson from the Experience of Anti-Corruption Agencies in Four Asian Countries*. Available in www.jonstquah.com.
34. Heilbruun John R. (2011), *Anti-corruption Commissions: Panacea or Real Medicine to Fight Corruption*? The World Bank and IMF, Washington.
35. As an illustrative case, the press interview of Nitin Gadkari, former President of BJP (now Union Minister of Rural Development), is worth pondering. Gadkari admitted that "one can promise not to take bribe but cannot assure of not giving money to get a job done". He rejected that only politicians are involved in illegalities. Rather corruption is a social problem and not one political problem. He went on to contend that it is not possible to give election tickets only to clean people. When asked if India will ever be corruption free country, Gadkari averred: "wrong thins will continue in the society. *It can be lessened but not eradicated"* (emphasis added).

6

Globalization, Development induced Displacement and the Livelihood Issues of Tribal

A Case of Mineral-based Industries in India

Notan Bhusan Kar

INTRODUCTION

Development means different things to different people. According to Laufee (1967), "It means dams and factories, roads and canals, bush-cleaning, electrification, soil improvement, Universities, secondary schools, primary schools, sanition, research and a multitude of other activities and achievements. But above all, the preparation and activation of people is the cause of economic and social development" (*cf.* Mehta, 1984)[1]. Morris (1975)[2] defined "development in terms of improvement in the quality of life of people". Liu (1975)[3] stated, "quality of life has multiple dimensions ranging from economic to social, environmental, political, cultural, psychological and philosophical aspects". According to United Nations Development Programme Report, the definition of development is "to lead long and healthy lives, to be knowledgeable, to have access to the resources needed for a decent standard of living and to be able to participate in the life of the community" (UNDP, 2010)[4].

In ordinary parlance, most of the common man denotes developments means, the construction of large size industries, highways, setting up of shopping malls, dams etc. Conversely, to some people implies development is economic growth of one country or society. On the other hand, the concept of development is also associated with a series of social changes, though it should equally be conceded that social changes are directly interrelated with social conflicts. Therefore, when we think or talk about development of a particular country, it should as well be considered what types of socio-economic conditions are existing among the major population of the country concerned. If we take India as an example we see over a billion populations where around 60 crores live in villages and most among them depend almost exclusively upon agriculture for their subsistence. Apart from them, around 8 per cent or about 9.5 crores indigenous and tribal (aboriginal) people mostly live in forest and depend on natural resources for their livelihood. Thus, any approach or policy for development cannot be proper excluding marginalized section of the society. So, emphasis and priority should be given on how to improve the living standard of those specific segments of population.

But what type of development paradigm was adopted by our development planners and policy-makers after Independence? In the year of 1951, India had introduced five year plan which tended to have combined capitalist and socialist models of planned development in a mixed economy framework. The Planning Commission initially laid stress on grounding and building of many development projects such as dams, large industries, irrigation projects thermal power plants, townships, large roads and highways, ports, and airports etc. No doubt, this type of development model had helped the country to emerge as a strong economic and political power in the world, but it has come at the cost of the weaker sections of the society. Now, it is proved that this type of development model has generated wider socio-economic inequalities across the people of the country.

LPG DEVELOPMENT MODEL AND TRIBAL DISPLACEMENT

Since the onset of the current era of economic liberalization, privatization and globalization (LPG) in India, the sustainable subsistence livelihood of the tribal people is now under threat and as a result the large scale displacement of tribals from their habitats is occurring in the name of 'development' or economic growth in India.

When the New Economic Policy was adopted in India in the year of 1991, after a short break a New Mining Policy was also enforced by Central Government in 1993 and cleared many obstacles for the big industrialists and corporate houses to allow them mining of the natural resources in India. India is a mineral-rich country.

Fortunately or unfortunately, most of India's minerals are situated in the tribal belts. 90 per cent of all coal and around 50 per cent of the remaining minerals are in their locales and also the forest, water and other sources abound in their habitat (*update*)[5]. In recent years the phenomenon of displacement has become more intensified due to the conditions created by globalization and economic liberalization.

In post-Independence during 1951 to 2004 in India, "around 60 million or 6 crores people were displaced due to various development projects. Among them 40 per cent were tribal and 20 per cent are dalit attesting that 60 per cent displaced people come from the group of marginalized and weaker communities" (Fernandes, 2008)[6].

"The MNCs in the developed countries of the world are almost at the verge of exhausting the non-renewable mineral resources. Fortunately for them, the LPG model of development has opened avenues for the MNCs to locate their mineral and metal processing activities in India at the cheapest possible price for both the land (natural resources) and the local labour they need. As a result, in recent years the regions inhabited by indigenous peoples are involuntarily displaced from their lands and homes without any sincere efforts being made for their proper rehabilitation and integration into the modern development process" (Blaser, 2004)[7].

Now, we will look into some revealing figures on violent displacement of the *adivasis*:

- Between 1950 and 1991, mining displaced about 26 lakh people—the second highest toll among all development projects (dams have displaced the maximum numbers). Of these, not even 25 per cent have been resettled. About 52 per cent of those displaced were tribals (CS&E, 2008)[8].
- In 4 states, i.e., Jharkhand, Chhattisgarh, Odisha and Andhra Pradesh, during the past 10 years, number of people displaced due to various development projects is over 1.6 million. Amongst them, 7,49,555 people were displaced for various dam projects, 3,04,698 for industry, 5,39,351 for mining and 22,050 for defence establishments, among them 50 per cent are tribal communities and 20 per cent are backward communities (*www.minesandcommunites.org*)[9].

The following data also shows the conditions of tribals in India:

- More than 40.1 per cent of the tribals are displaced throughout India.
- 45.86 per cent of the Scheduled Tribes (STs) population lives below the poverty line (BPL) in rural areas alone and at national level this rises to 55.2 per cent.
- 63.71 per cent of *Adivasis* are classified as living in extreme poverty conditions with no access to land, poor cultivation and poor health service provision, resulting high incidence of communicable and non-communicable diseases.
- Over 63.5 per cent of the tribal households do not have access to electricity.
- About 53.1 per cent of the tribal households do not have an accessible source of safe drinking water.
- Almost 83 per cent of the tribal population do not have access to a sanitation facility.
- Average Monthly Consumption Expenditure of the tribal communities is Rupees 388/- only. (PESA Act)[10].

MINING AS A FUEL OF WAR

Tribal areas are extremely rich in high quality of bauxite in India. Hence, the Multinational Corporations with Indian Big Corporate are rushing madly to these areas to control the reserves of bauxite which is the 'strategic metal' of modern war.

> "In Britain and the US, a regular, guaranteed supply of aluminium at the cheapest possible rate is a matter of highest concern, since, it supplies one of the arms industry's basic resources, and 'aerospace/defence' is central to both nation's economy. This is why aluminium is classed as a 'strategic metal' by the US administration, meaning its supply is to be guaranteed and stockpiled" (Padel and Das).[11]

The authors also quoted a significant, but not readily available document from 1951 called "Aluminium for Defence and Prosperity." The author Dewey Anderson, a US government official, notes: Aluminium has become the most important single bulk material of modern warfare. No fighting is possible, and no war can be carried to a successful conclusion today, without using and destroying vast quantities of aluminium" (Anderson, 1951).[12]

PESA ACT: TRIBALS RIGHTS AND LIMITATIONS

The fundamental spirit of the Panchayat Extension Scheduled Areas Act (1996) for tribal areas under the 5th Schedule is that it devolves power and authority to Gram Sabha and Panchayats rather than delegation; hence, it paves the way for participatory democracy. The provision under Constitution and the composition under this act call for every legislation on the Panchayat in the 5th Scheduled areas are in conformity with the customary law, social and religious practices and traditional management practices of the community resources.

It also directs the State Government to endow powers and authority to make Gram Sabha and Panchayats function as Institutions of Local Self-Governance, specifically on matters of enforcing prohibition of sale and consumption of intoxicant; ownership of minor forest produce; power to prevent alienation of land and restoration of unlawfully alienated land, management of village markets, control over moneylending, etc. PESA also empowered Gram Sabha of the Scheduled Areas to approve plans, programmes for social and economic development, identify beneficiaries under poverty alleviation programmes, certify utilization of funds by Gram Panchayats, protect natural resources, including minor forest produce and be consulted prior to land acquisition.

PESA Act clearly mentioned that non-tribal or outsiders cannot purchase their lands. But often we see the Government mostly is ignoring the law consciously to help the corporate and outsiders.

A limitation of the PESA law is that it is applicable only to those areas which are legally regarded as Scheduled Areas. A significant number of tribals living outside the Scheduled Areas are not covered by this legislation.

The State Government should incorporate provisions in the Panchayat Extension to Scheduled Areas Act (PESA) that would enable proper resettlement of tribals and prevent future displacements.

But overall, it is fact that lack of willpower, honesty and farsightedness of the Central and State Governments, the aims and objectives of PESA Act have been vanished into the blue. The bureaucratic state machinery has kept intact the self-interest with the corporate. Hence, the *adivasi* people never got either the real freedom or sovereignty from the clutches of implementation of PESA Act. Under these circumstances, the 5th Schedule of the Constitution of India could not be safeguard to the *adivasi* communities of their own rights.

IMPACT OF DEVELOPMENT PROJECT ON DISPLACED TRIBALS

Tribals are the worst sufferers since most developmental projects such as dams and industries are located in inaccessible tribal areas. The following social impact assessment on tribal communities may be seen to the impact of developmental projects:

1. ***Decline in Joint Family System*:** Both tribal and non-tribal families showing the same trend of breaking down of joint family to nuclear families. This is a general feature noticed in most of the development projects.
2. ***Landlessness*:** India, being a farm dominated society with agriculture as the main occupation, displacement from land, removes the main foundation on which people's productive systems, commercial activities and livelihood are based. Unless this foundation is reconstructed elsewhere or replaced by steady income-generating employment, landlessness sets in and the affected families are impoverished. In most of the cases/projects, "land for land" norm could not be followed. But cash compensation is inadequate to make up for the loss of land.
3. ***Joblessness and Increase in the Proportion of Workers*:** When people are displaced from their habitat, they lose their means of livelihood. Creation of new jobs or alternative sources of income for them becomes very difficult since the oustees do not possess any skill to learn new methods of earning their livelihood. Hence, those who were owners of the means of production before displacement have now become daily wage earners.
4. ***Homelessness*:** Loss of house and shelter remains a permanent feature for most of the displaced families.
5. ***Food Insecurity*:** Forced displacement increases the risk of chronic food insecurity. In India, crops are grown to provide food to the family while vegetables are grown in the kitchen gardens that take care of the food needs of the family. Surplus

is also sold in the market. But forced displacements deprive the oustees from their former resource of livelihood rendering them landless. As a result, the displaced families have to buy everything including food items from the market.

6. ***Loss of Access to A Common Property*:** For the oustees, particularly, the landless and poor people, loss of access to common property (forest lands, water bodies, grazing land, etc.) leads to a major deterioration in their income and livelihood levels. As a result, the resettler do not get fuel wood and other minor forest produce, which they used to collect from the forests in their old habitat.
7. ***Social Disintegration*:** Forced displacement has made production systems dismantled, kinship groups and family systems are often scattered and cultural identity of the people is under threat. Social and community networks that help people to cope with poverty through exchange of food and clothing, mutual help with farming, building houses and caring children are disrupted.
8. ***Increased Morbidity and Mortality*:** Loss of ancestral and homestead land, less or no access to health care facilities, the psychological trauma caused thereby and the food insecurity together often leads to serious diseases. In fact, lack of food, safe drinking water, unhygienic living and environmental degradation has a serious impact on the health of the oustees.

LIVELIHOOD AND RESISTANCE MOVEMENT

Tribal people live customarily in forest and mountainous regions or in the vicinity of nature. The economy of the tribals has been primarily hunting, fishing, cultivation etc. More than 90 per cent of the tribal depend on forest and forest resources for their subsistence. The large scale land transfers to non-tribal culminated in armed tribal uprisings many times in the late nineteenth and early twentieth centuries in India. The forest laws since the British period have been curtailing the rights and movement of tribal in forest regions.

Anthropologist, Felix Padel, and the Social activist, Samarendra Das, in their book *Out of this Earth* provide a comprehensive analysis of the social and environmental impacts of the mining boom in the tribal belts in India. The authors show how companies split tribal communities by bribes and coercion, such that a division emerges between 'accepters' and 'refusers'. They documented the extensive collusion, between politicians/bureaucrats and the private companies, which has displaced scores of tribals from their land they inhabited for ages.

Odisha, for instance, has the highest percentage of India's total deposits of chromites, bauxite, graphite, manganese, iron ore, dolomite and other rich minerals. It has 24 per cent of India's reserves of coal, 17 per cent of its iron ore, 98 per cent of chromite, 51 per cent of bauxite and 35 per cent of manganese. The State Government has entered into signing of 46 Memorandum of Understandings with different MNCs expecting of an investment of two lakh and fifty thousand crores of Foreign Direct Investment (FDI). Simultaneously, the Government has invited Hindalco (Birla Group), Alcan (Canada), Vedanta (UK), BHP Billiton (UK), Rio Tinto (UK), POSCO (South Korea) and many other big corporate with an investment of nearly 53,000 crore and permitted 7,330 lakh tonnes bauxite extraction of total deposit from the state. All these projects would displace nearly 2.5 lakh families or 10,00,000 people (*Update*).[13]

The leading newspaper '*The Hindu Business Line* (July 24, 2006)' reports that the State has received private investment worth Rs. 4,00,000 crore in mineral based industries. It boasts the presence of all the big names. Several multinationals and leaders in the mining sector POSCO (Pohang Iron and Steel Company), Arcelor Mittal, Rio Tinto and ALCAN have already acquired mining leases here or are in the process of doing so.

The leading Odia newspaper '*Dharitri*' (October 9, 2012) also reports that by December 2011, the State Government had MoUs with 94 industrial units, which have been given 11,187 acres of government land and 25,345 acres of private land.

When resistance against these forceful displacements is increasing, the response of the government is highly repressive. In Kalinga Nagar 13 tribals gave their life because of their opposition to the Tata Project. Recently, the resistance struggles against MNC Vedanta by *Kondh* tribals of Niyamgiri region of Odisha has widely been reported by media, newspapers etc. In the Niyamgiri hill Vedanta Company intends to set-up a mining industry which will be polluting the environment of that region and will uproot the tribal community. Tribals are against the setting up of the industry. After continued and protracted movement of tribal people [common people] the Odisha Government has been forced to withhold its approval of the project along with POSCO project.

Jharkhand is an important State from the viewpoint of *Adivasi* population. As per the Census 2011, the *Adivasi* population in the state was 70,87,068 including 35,65,960 male and 35,21,108 female, which consists 26.3 per cent of the total population (2,69,45,829) of the State though they were more than 50 per cent before the Independence of India. The growth of the *Adivasi* population is steadily declining. It was 17.3 per cent in 2011, which is lower by 6 per cent if compared with the growth (23.3%) in 2001. The state has a total of thirty two (32) sub-communities of the *Adivasis*. Among them Santal, Oraon, Munda, Ho and Kharia are the major *Adivasi* groups in the state. The major *Adivasi* populations (91.7%) reside in villages and merely 8.3 per cent have shifted to the urban areas. The rapid industrialization is one of the major reasons for population declination of the *Adivasis*.

Jharkhand region is rich of natural resources in India. The State contains 40 per cent of India's precious minerals like Uranium, Mica, Bauxite, Granite, gold, silver etc. Forests and woodlands occupy more than 29 per cent of the state which is amongst the highest in India. Many multinational companies have been offered leased land to build number of factories, extracting natural resources and build for other industries. The State has signed 102 MoUs (memorandum of understanding) for establishing steel factories, power plants and mining industries with the estimated investment of Rs.4,67,240 crore, which require approximately 2,00,000 acres of land which directly means the displacement of approximately 1 million people (*update*).[14] Arcelor Mittal intends to invest $ 8.79 billion to set-up one of the world's biggest steel plants for which 12,000 acres (49 sq. km) of land is required and this proposed industry is likely to be displaced not less than 40 (forty) tribal villages. Apart from causing massive displacement, the project will also destroy the forests in the region. It will also have an adverse impact on the water sources and ecosystems, thereby threatening the environment and the very source of sustenance for indigenous peoples. The tribal people's slogan here "we will not give an inch of our land".

The Government, the Industrialists and the Media are putting hard efforts to convince the people by propagating the messages that the industrialization is only way to develop the young Jharkhand therefore the villagers must surrender their land for the development projects, which would provide them jobs, infrastructure and boost the economy of the state. But the *Adivasis* are not convinced with the ideas as 91.7 per cent of them still rely on agriculture, forest produces and livestock for their survival. They are resisting against displacement, attacking the company's officials and not allowing them to enter into the villages. Consequently, the Government is unable to execute most of the MoUs at the grassroots.

The tribals have protested against the implementation of "Koel Karo" hydroelectric project by National Hydroelectric Corporation over the Koel and Karo rivers. The project, if implemented, would submerge as many as 256 villages involving 50,000 acres of forest area, 40,000 acres of agricultural land and 300 forest groves, 175 churches and 120 temples.

There has been turmoil against displacement in the state. On 1st of October, 2008, the villagers attacked on the Kohinoor steel plant near Jamshedpur, seized 70 trucks and stopped the work. They alleged that after acquiring their agricultural land, the company neither compensated nor gave them jobs as promised and the company is also causing huge environmental affect in agriculture, water sources and public health therefore they would not allow the company to destroy their livelihoods. In another case, the villagers declared for not giving their precious land to the Bhushan Company.

The corporate houses are in anxiety, worried and uncertain about their future in Jharkhand therefore they are putting pressure on the Government for taking action against the displacement activities.

The fundamental question is why *Adivasis* do not want to give their land for the development projects, which can provide them jobs? In every project approximately 80 to 90 per cent *Adivasis* and local people were displaced but merely 25 per cent of them were halfway rehabilitated and no one has any idea about the rest 75 per cent displaced people. The benefits of these development projects were highly enjoyed by the Landlords, Project Officers, Contractors, Bureaucrats, Politicians and Outsiders, and those who sacrificed everything for the sake of the "development" are struggling for their survival.

Secondly, the people were betrayed in the name of rehabilitation, compensation and jobs. The promises were not fulfilled and the jobs were given to the outsiders. In the present era, the technologics are mostly used in the companies therefore job opportunities and job security have declined by the corporate. For example, when the Tata Steel was producing 1 Mt steel, the workforce was 70,000 in 1995. The growth of the Tata Steel went up to 7 Mt in 2008, but the workforce declined to 20,000. Similarly, in the Heavy Engineering Corporation, Ranchi there were 23,000 employees at the beginning, but it declined to 3000 in 2009.

In the case of Chhattisgarh there are 28 varieties of valuable minerals available now. The state has one-fifth of the country's iron ore deposits and one of the best quality iron ore deposits in the Bailadila mines. Similar like Odisha and Jharkhand, the tribal people of Chhattisgarh are losing their sustainable means of subsistence due to the opening of mines and setting up of many mineral-based industries in the state. The state's Mineral Policy 2001 has facilitated large-scale private sector investment in the mining sector and this has had its fall out effects on the tribal people and other marginalized people. In the coal bearing zones of Sarguja, Raigarh and Bilaspur districts, more than 72,000 acres of land have been granted on lease to South Eastern Coalfields Ltd. (SECL), a subsidiary of CIL. Similarly, in the Bailadila and Dalli-Rajhara which is in the districts of Bastar and Durg respectively more than 20,000 acres of land have been occupied for mining. Apart from these areas, the state has reportedly given on lease 18,652 acres of land for various mining purposes and 26,410 acres for the setting up of various industries such as cement, steel, Ferro-alloys, re-rolling mills and rice mills. That means the total 1,37,062 acres of land have been leased by the state for mining and mineral based industries (Goldy, 2004).[15]

After 'Independence', particularly during 1990-2008 period more forest lands had been snatched away from *adivasi*-hands for the so-called development and industrialization programmes: "The maximum diversion took place in the last decade approximately 55 per cent of the total diversion of forestland occurred from 2001 to 2008". In Odisha 295 projects were approved, diverting 331.36 sq. kms of forestland. 27479.65 hectares of forestland was diverted from January 1989 to December 2006, out of which 11,242.08 hectares were cleared for 115 mining projects in the State. About 7,375 hectares of forestland was diverted for irrigation projects while 2,551 hectares of forestland was diverted to industrial projects. In Chhattisgarh, the total forestland diverted from 1980 to 2003 was 17,166.50 hectares, of which 67.22 per cent was diverted for mining (GoI, 2009).[16]

At this juncture, tribal and marginalized communities of mineral rich and forests based regions of the country have revolted against their forced eviction. But the Central and State Governments are very much adamant to stop such tribal movements and favouring corporate. They almost thoughtlessly, perceive these as movements led by the Maoist and they habitually brand these as anti-development. At the same time, they frequently and unabashedly deploy para-military forces for combating the confrontation. A chart submitted in connection with Public Interest Litigation in the Supreme Court shows almost 548 killings, 99 rapes and more than 3,000 burnt house by the Salwa Judum in Chhattisgarh in last three years (Choudhary).[17]

Few years back, the Indian Government launched 'Operation Green Hunt' overtly to combat Maoist insurgency, but covertly to root out the tribal resistance struggles. The security forces comprising hundreds of thousands of paramilitary forces along with scores of police forces are now engaged in a full blown war in the villages of terrains, hills and jungles of central and eastern India. The Operation being waged is gushing in across eight states of the eastern and central-eastern India including Jharkhand, Andhra Pradesh, Odisha, Bihar and West Bengal.

Displacement of people from traditional habitats causes much trauma to the affected persons. Compulsory acquisition of land for construction of dams and roads, quarrying and mining operations, industries and reservation of forests for National Parks and environmental protection forces people to leave their traditional abodes and land—their main sustenance. Thus, development projects have often become a major threat to the people whom they deprive of their traditional livelihood without alternatives. Now-a-days, conflicts between weaker sections and the State are increasing due to forceful acquisition of land, forest, mines etc. Tribals, the weaker section of the society are fighting and resisting in order protecting their lands, forests etc. and ultimately, these conflicts are resulting in bloody war between the Tribals and State. The *Adivasis* have lost their faith in the state machinery, Constitutional authorities and judiciary, therefore, they have firmly decided not to allow the corporate development model over their graves.

CONCLUSION

LPG development model has created increasing divides and conflict between natural resource dependent peoples and the 'police' State. The tribal and marginalized people are fighting to defend their traditional and sustainable forms of subsistence and the later are forcibly trying to acquire their assets in the name of development programmes. Thus, bloody conflict between peasants-tribal-marginalized people and para-military forces has become a daily feature in central region of India. In this circumstance, if mining, SEZs or technology based industries are allowed, the inequalities and poverty of the country will aggravate further. The mega-development project can only benefit the economic elite class who are hell bent on profit maximization. The development projects should be planned and designed, so that, it will help the poor people to uplift their socio-economic status.

Secondly, it is necessary not only to identify, avoid and mitigate risks in each development project that entails displacement, but also to focus on benefits over and above compensation and rehabilitation for damages as well as benefit sharing arrangement. A prudent approach demands long term commitments, financial and institutional guarantees and the use of professional approach in dealing with the issues of social development of indigenous people. Constant monitoring by technically competent independent observers can go a long way in ensuring more effective resettlement and rehabilitation arrangements in case of the displaced families.

Thirdly, the Ministry of Tribal Affairs must undertake an immediate extensive project-wise survey of number of displaced as well as affected tribals across the country. It should order a fact finding inquiry as to why tribal laws such as the PESA, 1996 and The Forest Rights Act of 2006 remain subservient to other laws and come up with suitable amendments to make them unbreakable in the Schedule V and VI areas.

Finally, one should understand that the displacement is not just shifting people from one place to another, but it is destruction of their livelihood resources, culture and identity which they develop by nourishing for the ages. The life cycle of the *Adivasis* is based on the natural resources, therefore, their co-existence with the nature cannot be questioned. Hence, it is need of the hour to rethink on the present development model. The unjust development process cannot be carried on as the *Adivasis* also have similar rights to life with dignity, freedom and equality guaranteed by the Constitution of India.

NOTES

1. Mehta, S.R. (1984). *Rural Development Policies and Programmes,* New Delhi: Sage Publications.
2. Morris, David (1975). *Measuring the Conditions of World's Poor, the Physical Quality of Life Index*. Oxford: Oxford University Press.
3. Liu, B.C. (1975). "Quality of Life: Concept, Measures and Results", *Americal Journal of Economics and Sociology*, 34(2):27-38.
4. WWW. Undp.or.id/faq.asp#HDR1
5. *Update Journal* (2010), page-11, Series-18, published from Salt Lake, Kolkata-64.

6. *E-Journal: Indian Tribes after Sixty Years—A Study*—Prof. Walter Fernandes, *Sanhati*—November, 27-2008. (http://sanhati.com/articles/1094/)
7. M. Blaser, Feit, H.A. and McRae, G. (eds.) (2004). *In the Way of Development, Indigenous People, Life Projects and Globalization*, London and New York: Zed Books.
8. "Rich Lands Poor People, Is Sustainable Mining Possible"? (2008), Centre for Science and Environment—New Delhi.
9. www.Minesandcommunites.org/article.php?a=8377&highlight= displacement,in, india.
10. PESA Act, 1996, pp. 4-5, http//:socialissuesindia.wordpress.com.
11. Felix Padel and Samarendra Das, "Anthropology of a Genocide: Tribal Movement in Central India against Over-Industrialization", http://Sanhati.com/literature/915).
12. Dewey Anderson, "Aluminium for Defence and Prosperity", Washington, US Public Affairs Institute, 1951; quoted in "Anthropology of a Genocide: Triabl Movement in Central India against Over-Industrialization", by Felex-Padel and Samarendra Das, http://sanhati.com/literature/915
13. *Journal 'Update'* Series No. 18, p. 42, March (2010), published from Salt Lake, Kolkata-64.
14. *Journal 'Update'* Series No. 18, p. 55, March (2010), published from Salt Lake, Kolkata-64.
15. George, Goldy, M. (2004), "Mining to Destruction and Hijacking Their Rights to Submission'. [Accessed 28th February, 2004 (http://www.countercurrents.org)]
16. National Land Reforms Policy, Committee on State Agrarian Relations and Unfinished Tasks of Land Reforms, Ministry of Rural Development, Government of India: http://www.rd.ap.gov.in/IKPLand MRD_Committee_V_01_Mar_09.pdf)
17. Salwa Judum: *Strategy that backfires*, Shubranshu Choudhary, 19.06.08. http://www.rediff.com/news/2008/jun/19guest.htm

BIBLIOGRAPHY

Dr. B.D. Sharma, (2007), "Unbroken History of Broken Promises: Indian State and the Tribal People", Freedom Press, New Delhi.

Prof. Raj Kishor Meher (2009), "Globalization, displacement and livelihood issues of Tribal and agriculture dependent people—The Case of Mineral Based Industries in India", Nabakrishna Choudhury Centre of Social Development, Bhubaneswar. Sage Publications, vol. 25 (4): 457-480.

Prof. Ratan Khasnobis "Development induced Displacement-2007, University of Calcutta, Department of Business Management, *e-Journal 'Macroscan'*.

Socio-Economic Journal 'Aneek'—autumn number (September.-October)-2007. Published by Peoples Book Society, Kolkata.

7

Maternal Mortality and Associated Risk Factors: A Study in Kolkata Metropolitan Area of West Bengal, India

Partha De

INTRODUCTION

According to the report of WHO, UNICEF, UNFPA, and the World Bank in 2010, eleven countries accounted for almost 65 per cent of global maternal deaths and India has the largest (63,000) share of deaths (WHO, UNICEF, UNFPA and The World Bank, 2010). India also accounts for the largest number of births per year (27 million) and 20 per cent of all global burdens of maternal deaths (WHO, 2007). Though India has achieved rapid economic growth and a stable economy, still its maternal mortality is high due to lack of political will and administrative and managerial failures rather than absence of expertise. Lack of management capacity in the health system has led to poor quality services and slow progress (WHO, 2008). Accesses to health services are only helpful when pregnant mothers are able to make use of them during obstetric emergencies. If obstetric care is poor, there the lifetime risk of maternal death is very high. In India since 1990s, Emergency Obstetric Care (EmOC) has been recognized as an important cost effective instrument for reduction of maternal mortality. Several health care programmes like, Child Survival and Safe Motherhood Programme (CSSM), Reproductive and Child Health Programmes (RCH), National Rural Health Mission (NRHM) etc. have been implemented during last three decades in India, where top priority has been set for providing EmOC services to pregnant women. But still due to lack of focus and limited management capacity not all EmOC facilities are fully functional.

The Millennium Development Goal Number 5 (MDG 5) has set the target of achieving 109 maternal mortality ratios by 2015. There are two targets for assessing the progress of maternal health under MDG 5: reducing the maternal mortality ratio (MMR) by three quarters between 1990 and 2015, and achieving universal access to reproductive health by 2015. The Central Statistical Organization (CSO), Government of India has provided future estimates of MMR up to 2015. The report shows that, given to achieve an MMR of 109 per 1,00,000 live births by 2015, India tends to fall short by about 26 points as it tends to reach MMR of about 135 per 1,00,000 live births in 2015 (CSO, 2009). Several national socio-demographic goals to safe motherhood for 2010 are specified by the National Population Policy (NPP) adopted by the Government of India during the year 2000. The goals were that, 80 per cent of all deliveries should take place in institutions, 100 per cent of deliveries should be attended by trained personnel, and the maternal mortality ratio should be reduced to a level below 100 per 1,00,000 live births (MoHFW, 2000). But according to the CSO report, unless improved drastically, the existing rate of increase in deliveries by skilled personnel is expected to take the coverage only to 62 per cent by 2015. It has also pointed out that, the slow progress in skilled attendance to deliveries is mainly due to poor progress in institutional deliveries (CSO, 2009). A significant portion of the delivery is still conducted by traditional birth attendants (TBAs) at home in both the urban slums and rural areas in India.

According to available information, obstetric complications are the most frequent causes of maternal mortality in the country like India (RGI, 2006). Thus, it is also important to know about the relative importance of various direct and indirect obstetric causes of maternal deaths specifically the impact of different indirect obstetric causes like, anaemia, viral hepatitis and other infectious diseases on maternal mortality. For example, anaemia is the second most common cause of maternal death in India. It is accounting for 20-40 per cent of total maternal deaths in the country (Pandit and Mehta, 2010). A study in Indian rural hospital has observed that post-partum hemoerrhage is the leading direct cause while infective hepatitis is indirect leading cause for maternal deaths (Vidyadhar *et al.*, 2011). Another hospital-based study from North India showed that, the causes of deaths were sepsis 23.84 per cent, eclampsia/pregnancy-induced hypertension

17.69 per cent, haemorrhage 13.84 per cent, hepatitis 13.84 per cent, anaemia 13.07 per cent, respiratory infections 8.46 per cent, other indirect obstetrical causes 6.15 per cent, and unrelated causes 4.61 per cent (Puri *et al.*, 2011).

In West Bengal, the Maternal Mortality Ratio was 145 in 2007-09, lower than the National average of 212 at that time. West Bengal has brought down the maternal mortality rate from 303 (in 1998) to 145 (in 2009) during a span of twelve years period (CSO, 2009; RGI, 2011). The pregnant women in this state having a lifetime risk of 0.3 per cent, compared to 0.6 per cent, at National level in the year 2009 (CSO, 2009). "Life time risk" is the estimated risk of an individual woman dying from pregnancy or childbirth during her lifetime, based on maternal mortality and the fertility rate in the country.

The available studies related with maternal mortality in India are mainly based on hospital records. However, findings from hospital-based studies are not truly representative of a particular area or community, but only the segment that sought care at the hospital. In our country still a significant portion of the delivery is done by Traditional Birth Attendants (TBAs) at home in both the urban slums and rural areas resulted in high maternal mortality. This leads the present study to collect information directly from the households where maternal death happened. It collected direct information from the households among the weaker sections in Kolkata Metropolitan Area (KMA) of West Bengal. The main objective of the study is to determine the epidemiological risk factors and its related causes associated with maternal mortality. So, the entire study may be segregated as follows:

- to determine the utilization pattern of available health care facilities by deceased women during pregnancy and at the time of death;
- investigation about the morbidity characteristics experienced by the deceased women during different stages of pregnancy and at the time of delivery; and
- determination of socio-economic, cultural and biological correlates of maternal mortality representing the women belonging to poorer section of population in a big metropolitan area like Kolkata.

The findings of this study would be useful in undertaking further studies and to plan intervention programmes to improve access in health facilities and use of emergency obstetric services in order to reduce maternal mortality in the metropolitan slum areas of the country.

STUDY DESIGN AND METHODOLOGY

In order to determine the important causes of maternal deaths in a large metropolitan area of India, particularly among the vulnerable population, the present study conducted a survey in Kolkata metropolitan area of West Bengal, India. This study collected information from the beneficiaries covered under Indian Population Project VIII (IPP-VIII) and Integrated Child Development Services (ICDS) Project under Kolkata Metropolitan area (KMA) covering the entire district of Kolkata and part of the districts of North 24 Parganas, South 24 Parganas, Howrah, Hooghly and Nadia. These two projects are nationally funded initiatives to reduce infant, child and maternal mortality and, improve health and nutrition in vulnerable groups in the above said areas. These programmes in any locality are, in effect, carried on at the field level by the Honorary Health Worker (HHW) and Anganwadi Worker (AWW) for IPP-VIII and ICDS projects respectively. These projects target the most vulnerable groups (i.e., families living below the poverty line) of population within the poorest of the poor families in the country.

This study included households where at least one maternal death has occurred in three years preceding the date of survey. In order to get information about the deceased's household, first the name of the Health Administrative Unit's (HAU) of IPP-VIII or the Anganwadi Centre under ICDS within 'Kolkata Metropolitan Area' (KMA) is identified from the Government official records where maternal death happened. Following identification of the area, 'Sub-Centre' (SC) under IPP-VIII or 'Anganwadi Worker Centre' (AWC) under ICDS is also located. Now, socio-economic and demographic particulars about the household where maternal death happened are noted from the household registrar maintained in the centre under ICDS and IPP-VIII schemes. Finally, the interviewer visited the house of deceased woman to collect detailed information. Along with official records snowball sampling technique, a special non-probability sampling method is also applied to indentify the households other than the above where maternal deaths happened (Kaplan *et al.*, 1987). This is done by asking question to household members about a similar event (maternal death) happened in the locality during last three years before the survey. A pre-tested and properly designed questionnaire is used to collect the detailed information on maternal death cases. The interview is conducted with the household members, in particular with the husband if present at the time of interview. They are interviewed after the objective of the study is explained and verbal informed consent is obtained. Sub-centre staffs like HHW and AWW are also consulted in this regard. The information investigated and received during verbal autopsy are maternal, environmental and health system characteristics. Lastly, gynaecologist has consulted to assign the cause of death on the basis of information collected through verbal autopsy. A total of 187 maternal death cases are collected from the study area, which occurred during last three years before the survey.

The study included 'maternal death' which may be defined as the death of a woman while pregnant or within 42 days of termination of pregnancy, irrespective of duration and site of the pregnancy, from any cause related to or aggravated by pregnancy or its management, but not from accidental causes (WHO, 2000; WHO, 2007). Maternal mortality can be classified in terms of direct obstetric, indirect obstetric and non-obstetric causes. Direct obstetric deaths are those resulting from complication of pregnancy, delivery or their management. Examples of such conditions are abortion, ectopic gestation, pre-eclampsia and eclampsia, ante-partum and post-partum haemorrhage and puerperal sepsis etc. Indirect obstetric deaths are those resulting from previous existing disease or disease that developed during pregnancy and aggravated by the physiological effects of pregnancy. These include anaemia, cardiac disease, diabetes, thyroid, viral hepatitis etc. Similarly, non-obstetric causes include accidents, malaria and other infectious diseases. The present study has followed the above said definition and classification of maternal death. Again, considering the time of death, maternal deaths can be classified into: (i) death during pregnancy, (ii) death during delivery, and (iii) death during 42 days following delivery. So, the maternal deaths during above said periods are evaluated with different maternal, health care and environmental characteristics to identify the risk factors associated with maternal mortality. One point should be noted here that medical information collected about the deceased women is based on verbal autopsy and from the available medical records.

The questions are asked by the investigator to the relatives and health workers about the pregnancy related problems (like, blurred vision, night blindness, convulsions, swelling of the hands and feet, anaemia, vaginal bleeding etc.) experienced by the deceased women in different periods of pregnancy. Supportive available medical reports of the diseased woman are also consulted for collecting morbidity and mortality characteristics. For analytical convenience, women are classified into three broad categories like, those who are alive during antepartum, intra-partum and post-partum periods. Conventionally, morbidities are classified as obstetric (direct, indirect) and non-obstetric (Graham and Campbell, 1990). Actually different researchers classified maternal morbidities differently. Some preferred to categorize based on its severity and others based on duration. Srinivasan and others have classified maternal morbidity based on severity as 'life threatening', 'serious', and 'mild' (Srinivasan *et al.*, 1997). The classification of morbidity is important for planning of intervention programmes. However, in the present study, following the above said classification, mainly the 'potentially life threatening' and 'serious' morbidities are reported. The classification is done with the assistance of expert Obstetrician and Gynaecologist.

To ascertain the main causes of maternal mortality in KMA, the present study collected information about the possible reasons for the death and which is assigned by the appropriate medical personnel. It is well known that, women in lower economic class often arrive at the hospital very late and they also receive antenatal care facilities which are available not in due time. In many urban slums high-risk cases often are delivered at home, a situation, which often results in foetal complications. As mentioned earlier cause of maternal death may be classified into three categories—direct, indirect and others. There also may have some unrelated causes, like physical injury during pregnancy that aggravates health problems and may lead to maternal death. The important direct causes of maternal death are: haemorrhage, infections, induced abortion, obstructed labour etc. But in most cases causes may overlap with one another. For example, haemorrhage which results from a ruptured uterus or severe infection could be happen associated with prolonged or obstructed labour. Among the indirect causes anaemia, viral hepatitis, heart and lung diseases are important.

For bivariate statistical analysis, Chi-square or Fisher exact tests are used to evaluate difference in proportions between different groups and any p value <0.05 is considered significant. Relationships between the prevalence of each cause of maternal death and various socio-economic, demographic and maternal care characteristics are evaluated using Chi-square test. Now, bivariate analysis of causes of maternal death by several background characteristics has been performed to examine the nature of association between these factors and causes of death. But, bivariate association between two variables does not necessarily imply a significant causal relationship between them. Thus, a multi-variate approach has applied to determine which background characteristics best explain different causes of maternal death. For multi-variate analysis, logistic regression has employed. Here, the outcome variable is a cause of maternal death, which is one if a mother died in that cause and zero if not. Now, all independent variables used in the analysis are categorical in nature. Independent variables are included in the analysis on the basis of their influence in maternal death as described by the bivariate analysis and past studies in this area. Data have been analyzed with the statistical package STATA, ver.10.

RESULTS

Reproductive and Child Health Programme recommends that antenatal care should include—two doses of tetanus toxoid injection, adequate amounts of iron and folic acid tablets or syrup for the prevention of anaemia. Other measures include at least three ANC check-ups, which include blood pressure checks and other detection procedures to understand complications of pregnancy (MoHFW, 2005; MoHFW, 2006). The number and the place of ANC check-ups are important for the health of the mother and the outcome of the pregnancy. Utilization of the existing health care and other related facilities by the deceased woman during pregnancy and child birth are presented in Table 7.1. Among the women who died, 94.7 per cent received ANC check-up during pregnancy. Thus, only very few deceased women (5%) did not receive antepartum care. The deceased women mainly received ANC from Government Institutions and health workers. But a significant portion of women also received it from private Institutions and doctors.

In India, an important cause of death in child birth is tetanus. But two doses of tetanus toxoid (TT) vaccine given one month apart during early pregnancy are nearly 100 per cent effective in preventing tetanus among both newborn and their mothers (IIPS, 2000; IIPS & Mac. Int., 2007). A significant percentage (19%) of women in this study who died on maternal reasons has deficiency in receiving TT injection during pregnancy. At the same time, only 50.2 per cent of those who died received 100 and more tablets of Iron and Aolic Acid (IFA).

Consumption of a wide variety of nutritious foods is important for pregnant women. The present study after consultation with dietitian, mainly grouped four types of food intake like, animal protein, plant protein, green vegetables and fresh fruits as an indicator of 'adequate' food intake during pregnancy. Now, in absence of consumption of foods like protein or green vegetables or fresh fruits are considered here as 'inadequate' nutritional level attained during pregnancy. In this study, it has been observed that 40.7 per cent women, who died during pregnancy, did not receive adequate foods during pregnancy. Thus, nutritional deficiency might have some positive contribution in aggravating heath problems during pregnancy.

It is well-known that poor maternity care leads to unsafe motherhood. Thus, any pregnant woman can experience sudden and unexpected complications during pregnancy and childbirth or following delivery. In West Bengal, during childbirth near about 52 per cent women give birth with the help of an untrained traditional birth attendant or a family member or others. Only 44.3 per cent women received post-partum check-up within two months of birth (IIPS & Mac. Int., 2007). These are the background reasons, for which majority of maternal deaths, which occur after childbirth and are mostly within 24 hours of delivery. The study observed that, about 32.5 per cent of the deceased women delivered in home and 22.3 per cent deliveries are assisted by the untrained *Dais* (traditional birth attendant) at home (Table 7.1). Now, at the time of detachment of umbilical cord new razor blades are utilized in case of 27.7 per cent cases of the deceased women who delivered at home.

Near about 24 per cent deceased women who delivered outside home had to travel (by any vehicle) at least one hour to reach any health facility and only 54 per cent among the deceased women who delivered outside home availed bus, car, taxi, auto rickshaw etc. Distributions of maternal deaths are shown according to the age at death and periods of pregnancy (i.e., antepartum, intra-partum and post-partum) classifications (Table 7.2). This table clearly shows that majority (65.2%) of maternal death happened during the post-partum period. Only 20.9 and 13.9 per cent maternal death happened during 'before delivery' and 'during delivery' periods respectively. Again a high percentage of death (about 57%) happened with the age group '20-29 yrs'.

Table 7.1: Utilization of Health Care Facilities by the Deceased Women in Kolkata Metropolitan Area, West Bengal, India

Maternal Health Care Characteristics		*Women*	
Category	*Group*	*No.*	*%*
Number of ANC check-up	None	10	5.3
	1	7	3.7
	2	23	12.3
	3 or more	147	78.7
Place of ANC check-up	No ANC check-up	10	5.3
	Govt. Institutions and HHW	142	75.9
	Private Institutions and doctor	29	15.5
	Other health professionals	6	3.3
Iron and Folic tablets received	Less than 100	69	36.9
	100 and more	94	50.2
	Received no such tablet	24	12.9
No. of T.T. injection	One	17	9.1
	Two or More	147	78.7
	Don't know	5	2.6
	None	18	9.6
Nutritional Level during pregnancy	Adequate	111	59.3
	Inadequate	76	40.7
No. of deceased women receive Antenatal Care:		**187**	
Place of last Delivery	Home	48	32.5
	Govt. Institutions	86	58.1
	Priv. Institutions	14	9.5
Delivery Assistance	Doctor	99	66.9
	Dai (trained) / Nurse	9	6.1
	Dai (untrained) at Home	33	22.3
	Others at home	7	4.7
Umbilical cord detached with	Blade (Home Delivery)	41	27.7
	Knife/Caesurae (Hospital Delivery)	90	60.8
	Others	2	1.4
	Don't know	15	10.1
Time to reach any health facility before delivery (outside home)	Walking distance	33	22.0
	Less than 1 hr. from home by bus/train	80	54.0
	More than 1 hr. from home by bus/train	36	24.0
Mode of Transport used to reach health facility before delivery (outside home)	Van / Rickshaw	38	26.0
	Auto / Taxi / Car	80	54.0
	Others	30	20.0
No. of deceased women who delivered:		**148**	

Source: Compiled from the primary data collected (2005-06) for the present study.

Table 7.2: Percentage of Maternal Deaths during Ante-Partum, Intra-Partum and Post-Partum Periods According to Age at Death in KMA, India

Age at Death	*No. of deceased women*	*Percentage of maternal deaths during*		
		Antepartum	*Intrapartum*	*Postpartum*
15 - 19	19	21.1	10.5	68.4
20 - 24	57	28.1	10.5	61.4
25 - 29	49	4.1	20.4	75.5
30 - 34	35	28.6	5.7	65.7
35 and Above	27	25.9	22.2	51.9
Total	**187**	**20.9**	**13.9**	**65.2**

Source: Compiled from the primary data collected (2005-06) for the present study.

MORBIDITIES SUFFERED BY THE DECEASED WOMEN IN DIFFERENT PERIODS OF PREGNANCY

Starting with the antenatal problems, the percentage of deceased women those who suffered from different diseases/symptoms during their pregnancies are presented in Table 7.3. Among all types of morbidities, 'anaemia' had the largest share (49%). Anaemia is defined during pregnancy as an haemoglobin (Hb) level below 110 gr/L (World Health Organization, 2008). Acute onset of anaemia during pregnancy greatly increases the risk of death during childbirth (Brabin *et al.*, 2001; Gupta *et al.*, 2007). Moderate to severe anaemia in pregnancy also has been associated with low birth weight (Murphy *et al.*, 1986, Renee *et al.*, 2005) and prematurity (Zhou *et al.*, 1998). Among the women those who died during pregnancy and before delivery, more than half of them (20 out of 39 cases) suffered from anaemia. Other important antepartum life-threatening morbidities extremely suffered by the deceased women are 'haemorrhage' (31%) and 'eclamptic fit' (27.2%). Haemorrhage remains one of the most serious maternal health problems—causing high proportion of all maternal deaths. Anaemia before haemorrhage increases the risk of death. On the other hand eclamptic fit is characterized by very high blood pressure and convulsions. This can be life threatening for both mother and baby. Serious morbidities suffered by the women are "swelling of hands and feet" (43.9%), "fever for last three days" (27.3%), "high blood pressure" (23%), "severe vomiting" (22.5%), "heart disease" (15%), "jaundice or liver disorder" (13.4%) etc.

Table 7.3: Number of Deceased Women who Suffered from various Morbidities during different Stages of Pregnancy in KMA of West Bengal, India

Period	*Severity of the morbidity**					
	Life threatening	***No.***	***%***	***Serious***	***No.***	***%***
Ante-partum	Anaemia	92	49.2	Heart disease	28	15.0
(Total Cases = 187)	Eclamptic fit	51	27.2	High Blood Pressure (HBP)	43	23.0
	Mild Anaemia	16	8.6	Jaundice/Liver disorder	25	13.4
	Haemorrhage	58	31.0	Asthma/Lung Disease	19	10.2
				Diabetes	2	1.1
				Fever for last 3 days	51	27.3
				Swelling of Hands and Feet	82	43.9
				Severe Vomiting	42	22.5
Intra-partum	Haemorrhage	47	48.0	Twin/Multiple birth	14	9.5
(Total Cases = 148)	Fits or Convulsions at delivery	23	15.5	Labour >18 hrs. for 1st parity women	17	3.4
	Abnormality in baby's position at delivery	8	5.4	Labour >8 hrs. for the woman having parity>=2	19	14.9
	Placenta is low at delivery	30	20.1			
Post-partum	Haemorrhage	25	20.5	Pus formation in tears	7	6.0
(Total Cases = 122)	Fits / convulsion	33	26.9	Fever more than 3 days	27	22.4
				Fainted for more than 15 minutes	25	20.9
				Foul smelling discharges	2	1.5
				Pain in Pelvic region	18	14.9
				Painful burning feeling while urinating	4	3.0
				Piles	4	3.0

Note: *Any woman can suffer from multiple morbidities.

Source: Compiled from the primary data collected (2005-06) for the present study.

In the same table, morbidities experienced by the deceased women during delivery (i.e., intra-partum period) and after delivery (i.e., post-partum period) are presented. During intra-partum period, haemorrhage is observed to be highest (48%) among morbidities experienced by the deceased women under study. Second important morbidity or complication is "placenta was low at delivery", which is 20.1 per cent for the women who are still alive during intra-partum period. Among other life threatening morbidities, the problems of "fits or convulsion" and "abnormality in baby's position at delivery" are important factors to be noted. Serious morbidities suffered by the women during intra-partum period of pregnancy are, "labour more than 8 hours" (for the deceased woman with parity greater than equal to 2) and "twin or multiple births" etc. During post-partum period, "haemorrhage" and "Fits/convulsion" are observed as dominant life threatening morbidity. Within serious morbidity, "fever more than 3 days", "fainted more than 15 minutes" and "pain in pelvic region" are found important.

CAUSES OF MATERNAL DEATH

The information about causes of maternal death for the state of West Bengal is available through the State Government (State Bureau of Health Intelligence, 2003). According to this report, anaemia (22.2%) and toxaemia (27.5%) are responsible for nearly half of total maternal deaths. In addition to these two important causes, haemorrhage (16.1%) is found to be a major cause of maternal death. Particularly, post-partum haemorrhage has observed to be an important cause of maternal death. The present study observed that, haemorrhage accounted for 18.7 per cent of maternal deaths making it as the major cause of death (Table 7.4). Haemoerrhage is the single most common cause to claim 35 lives and majority of death caused by haemorrhage happened during post-partum period. These women had morbidities during their pregnancy like, bleeding followed by anaemia and swelling of hands and feet. Eclampsia resulted in 25 (13.4%) deaths and for them antepartum morbidities are: high blood pressures, swelling of hands and feet with severe vomiting. Infection resulted in 17 (9.1%) deaths where fever more than 3 days duration and anaemia are the important conditions present during their antepartum stage of pregnancy.

In case of death due to retained placenta (12.8%), majority of women had anaemia along with haemorrhage and fever in their antepartum period. Severe anaemia is responsible for 20 (10.7 %) deaths

Table 7.4: Main Causes of Maternal Death in KMA of West Bengal, India

Main cause of maternal death	Maternal Mortality	
	No.	Per cent
Direct Obstetric Causes:		
Haemorrhage	35	18.7
Eclampsia	25	13.4
Infection	17	9.1
Prolonged Labour	9	4.8
Retained Placenta	24	12.8
Anaesthetic Complications	2	1.1
Indirect Obstetric Causes:		
Anaemia	20	10.7
Viral Hepatitis	18	9.6
Heart Disease	14	7.5
Lung Disease	7	3.8
Other Causes *	6	3.1
Unrelated Causes **	10	5.3
Total sample	**187**	**100.0**

Note: * Malaria, uterine and blood cancer, diarrhoea, high blood sugar etc.
** Injury.

Source: Compiled from the primary data collected (2005-06) for the present study.

and they suffered due to anaemia and oedema of hands and feet during antepartum period of their pregnancy. However, retained placenta is responsible for 24 deaths and home delivery is done (71%) for majority of these cases. Viral Hepatitis (VH) brought about 18 (9.6%) deaths. This is especially dangerous as a pregnant women infected with hepatitis has greater risk of dying during her pregnancy. Viral hepatitis continues to be a major public health problem in India. It has been observed that, pregnant women in their second and third trimesters get infected more frequently (12-20%) than men and non-pregnant women (1-2%). Hence, the mortality rate is higher among pregnant women who develop hepatitis, than in the general population affected with hepatitis (Kar, 2007). Now, out of 18 deaths in VH, 6 and 12 women died during antepartum and post-partum periods respectively. During pregnancy all these women were also suffering from VH and had the morbidities like anaemia, frequent fever for more than three days, swelling of hands and feet, severe vomiting etc. Among the other indirect causes, prolonged labour caused 9 (4.8%) deaths and 14 (7.5 %) deaths are due to heart disease. Other causes (3.1%) include malaria, uterine cancer, blood cancer etc. Overall, direct causes are responsible for death in 60 per cent cases, indirect causes in 35 per cent cases and unrelated in 5 per cent cases. It is also noted that 76 (41%) deaths occurred within 24 hours of delivery.

DETERMINANTS OF MATERNAL MORTALITY

Causes of maternal death are basically reflections of the existing social, economic and cultural factors, which influence the health seeking behaviour of the women and also depend on the availability, accessibility and quality of reproductive health services for emergency and essential purpose. This study has concentrated on three types of characteristics namely, demographic, socio-economic and health care. Attempts are made to correlate those characteristics with the causes of maternal death to understand the risk factors behind their death (Table 7.5).

Among the demographic characteristics "maternal age" undoubtedly plays an important role in pregnancy and in the later periods. The analysis shows that, within '15-19' years' age group death due to haemorrhage and eclampsia are quite high. For the age group of '20-29' years, death due to haemorrhage, eclampsia, retained placenta and viral hepatitis are comparatively higher than the other causes of death. Similarly, the problem of haemorrhage, retained placenta, anaemia and heart diseases are contributed much for maternal death of '30 plus' age group. The frequency of eclampsia significantly decreased with maternal age (Chi-square [1 df]= 9.24; p=0.002), whereas the frequency of heart disease increased with age (Chi-square [1 df]= 4.62; p=0.03).

In case of birth order, deaths due to eclampsia are quite high for birth order 'one'. As birth order increases death due to eclampsia also decreases (Chi-square [1 df]= 8.85; p=0.002). Again, the number of death increases due to the problems of anaemia (Chi-square [1 df]= 3.51; p=0.05) and retained placenta (Chi-square [1 df]= 7.89; p=0.005) as birth order moves from lower to higher. Maternal deaths caused by eclampsia (Chi-square [1 df]= 7.46; p=0.006) and prolonged labour (Chi-square [1 df]= 4.71; p=0.03) are negatively related to parity, but positively related to the problem of retained placenta (Chi-square [1 df]= 7.89; p=0.005). Compared to other castes, SC has more death from viral hepatitis (Chi-square [1 df]= 4.30; p=0.03). Similar effect is also observed for Hindu than Muslim in case of death caused by viral

Table 7.5: Distribution of Main Causes of Maternal Death by the Selected Background Characteristics in KMA of W.B., India

Causes of Maternal death	Age at death							Birth order							Parity				
	15 to 19 yrs		20 to 29 yrs		30 yrs and above		P Value	One		2 to 3		4 and Above		P Value	One		2 or more		P Value
	N	(%)	N	(%)	N	(%)		N	(%)	N	(%)	N	(%)		N	(%)	N	(%)	
Haemorrhage	4	(21.1)	19	(17.9)	12	(19.4)	0.980	15	(18.8)	13	(19.7)	7	(17.1)	0.860	15	(18.8)	20	(18.7)	0.990
Eclampsia	7	(36.8)	14	(13.2)	4	(6.5)	0.002	17	(21.3)	7	(10.6)	1	(2.4)	0.002	17	(21.3)	8	(7.5)	0.006
Infection	1	(5.3)	12	(11.3)	4	(6.5)	0.700	8	(10.0)	5	(7.6)	4	(9.8)	0.880	8	(10.0)	9	(8.4)	0.700
Prolonged Labour	0	(0.0)	7	(6.6)	2	(3.2)	0.960	7	(8.8)	0	(0.0)	2	(4.9)	0.170	7	(8.8)	2	(1.9)	0.030
Retained Placenta	2	(10.5)	13	(12.3)	9	(14.5)	0.600	4	(5.0)	11	(16.7)	9	(22.0)	0.005	4	(5.0)	20	(18.7)	0.005
Anaesthetic Complications	0	(0.0)	1	(0.9)	1	(1.6)	0.530	1	(1.3)	1	(1.5)	0	(0.0)	0.590	1	(1.3)	1	(0.9)	0.830
Anaemia	2	(10.5)	10	(9.4)	8	(12.9)	0.590	5	(6.3)	8	(12.1)	7	(17.1)	0.050	5	(6.3)	15	(14.0)	0.890
Viral Hepatitis	0	(0.0)	13	(12.3)	5	(8.1)	0.720	9	(11.3)	7	(10.6)	2	(4.9)	0.300	9	(11.3)	9	(8.4)	0.510
Heart Disease	0	(0.0)	6	(5.7)	8	(12.9)	0.030	6	(7.5)	5	(7.6)	3	(7.3)	0.970	6	(7.5)	8	(7.5)	0.995
Lung Disease	0	(0.0)	3	(2.8)	4	(6.5)	0.130	1	(1.3)	3	(4.5)	3	(7.3)	0.080	1	(1.3)	6	(5.6)	0.121
Other Indirect Causes	1	(5.3)	1	(0.9)	4	(6.5)	0.270	2	(2.5)	2	(3.0)	2	(4.9)	0.500	2	(2.5)	4	(3.7)	0.635
Injury	2	(10.5)	7	(6.6)	1	(1.6)	0.080	5	(6.3)	4	(6.1)	1	(2.4)	0.420	5	(6.3)	5	(4.7)	0.636

Table 7.5 (*Contd.*)

Causes of Maternal Death	Caste					Religion					Education						
	SC		Others		P Value	Hindu		Muslim		P Value	Illiterate		Middle Sch. complete		High Sch. and above		P Value
	N	(%)	N	(%)		N	(%)	N	(%)		N	(%)	N	(%)	N	(%)	
Haemorrhage	8	(14.8)	27	(20.3)	0.384	19	(15.6)	16	(24.6)	0.132	10	(14.9)	21	(21.6)	4	(17.4)	0.521
Eclampsia	6	(11.1)	19	(14.3)	0.564	16	(13.1)	9	(13.8)	0.889	7	(10.4)	15	(15.5)	3	(13.0)	0.536
Infection	5	(9.3)	12	(9.0)	0.959	11	(9.0)	6	(9.2)	0.961	6	(9.0)	7	(7.2)	4	(17.4)	0.436
Prolonged Labour	3	(5.6)	6	(4.5)	0.763	7	(5.7)	2	(3.1)	0.419	3	(4.5)	4	(4.1)	2	(8.7)	0.559
Retained Placenta	7	(13.0)	17	(12.8)	0.973	12	(9.8)	12	(18.5)	0.011	12	(17.9)	12	(12.4)	0	(0.0)	0.033
Anaesthetic Complications	0	(0.0)	2	(1.5)	0.366	2	(1.6)	0	(0.0)	0.300	0	(0.0)	1	(1.0)	1	(4.3)	0.110
Anaemia	5	(9.3)	15	(11.3)	0.686	13	(10.7)	7	(10.8)	0.980	7	(10.4)	12	(12.4)	1	(4.3)	0.639
Viral Hepatitis	9	(16.7)	9	(6.8)	0.038	16	(13.1)	2	(3.1)	0.020	10	(14.9)	8	(8.2)	0	(0.0)	0.028
Heart Disease	3	(5.6)	11	(8.3)	0.523	10	(8.2)	4	(6.2)	0.610	3	(4.5)	7	(7.2)	4	(17.4)	0.680
Lung Disease	3	(5.6)	4	(3.0)	0.406	6	(4.9)	1	(1.5)	0.247	5	(7.5)	2	(2.1)	0	(0.0)	0.048
Other Indirect Causes	1	(1.9)	5	(3.8)	0.503	4	(3.3)	2	(3.1)	0.940	3	(4.5)	2	(2.1)	1	(4.3)	0.709
Injury	4	(7.4)	6	(4.5)	0.426	6	(4.9)	4	(6.2)	0.721	1	(1.5)	6	(6.2)	3	(13.0)	0.030

Note: $p<0.05$ indicates significant variable and p-values are calculated using chi-square or Fisher exact test. N-number of women.

Table 7.5 (*Contd*)

Causes of Maternal death	Foods taken at pregnancy					Delivery Assistance									Place of last Delivery				
	Adequate		Inadequate		P Value	Doctor		Dai (trained)/ Nurse		Dai (Untrained)		Others		P Value	Home		Institutions (Govt. and Priv.)		P Value
	N	(%)	N	(%)		N	(%)	N	(%)	N	(%)	N	(%)		N	(%)	N	(%)	
Haemorrhage	20	(18.0)	15	(19.7)	0.778	17	(17.2)	1	(11.1)	5	(15.2)	3	(42.9)	0.490	9	(18.8)	17	(17.0)	0.794
Eclampsia	20	(18.0)	5	(6.6)	0.024	18	(18.2)	1	(11.1)	3	(9.1)	1	(14.3)	0.255	5	(10.4)	18	(18.0)	0.234
Infection	11	(9.9)	6	(7.9)	0.638	12	(12.1)	0	(0.0)	2	(6.1)	1	(14.3)	0.448	3	(6.3)	12	(12.0)	0.279
Prolonged Labour	6	(5.4)	3	(3.9)	0.648	4	(4.0)	0	(0.0)	1	(3.0)	0	(0.0)	0.564	1	(2.1)	4	(4.0)	0.547
Retained Placenta	13	(11.7)	11	(14.5)	0.580	6	(6.1)	3	(33.3)	15	(45.5)	0	(0.0)	0.001	17	(35.4)	7	(7.0)	0.001
Anaesthetic Complications	2	(1.8)	0	(0.0)	0.240	2	(2.0)	0	(0.0)	0	(0.0)	0	(0.0)	0.346	0	(0.0)	2	(2.0)	0.325
Anaemia	8	(7.2)	12	(15.8)	0.050	11	(11.1)	1	(11.1)	4	(12.1)	0	(0.0)	0.710	5	(10.4)	11	(11.0)	0.915
Viral Hepatitis	8	(7.2)	10	(13.2)	0.176	10	(10.1)	1	(11.1)	1	(3.0)	0	(0.0)	0.142	2	(4.2)	10	(10.0)	0.225
Heart Disease	11	(9.9)	3	(3.9)	0.129	7	(7.1)	0	(0.0)	1	(3.0)	1	(14.3)	0.769	2	(4.2)	7	(7.0)	0.501
Lung Disease	2	(1.8)	5	(6.6)	0.091	2	(2.0)	2	(22.2)	1	(3.0)	0	(0.0)	0.725	3	(6.3)	2	(2.0)	0.181
Other Indirect Causes	4	(3.6)	2	(2.6)	0.711	3	(3.0)	0	(0.0)	0	(0.0)	0	(0.0)	0.247	0	(0.0)	3	(3.0)	0.227
Injury	6	(5.4)	4	(5.3)	0.966	7	(7.1)	0	(0.0)	0	(0.0)	1	(14.3)	0.417	1	(2.1)	7	(7.0)	0.217

Note: $p < 0.05$ indicates significant variable and p-values are calculated using chi-square or Fisher exact test. N-number of women.
Source: Compiled from the primary data collected (2005-06) for the present study.

hepatitis (Chi-square [1 df]= 4.89; p=0.02). Deaths from viral hepatitis (Chi-square [1 df]= 4.77; p=0.02) and retained placenta (Chi-square [1 df]= 4.51; p=0.03) are higher for the illiterate women. Inadequate food intake during pregnancy resulted in more death cause by anaemia (Chi-square [1 df] = 5.07; p=0.05). Most important observation is that, delivery assistance by "untrained *dai*" resulted in 33 deaths and majority of those deaths are caused by retained placenta (Chi-square [1 df] = 15.6; p=0.001). These traditional birth attendants mostly do their job at home and hence in this study "home delivery" also shows highest percentage death due to retained placenta.

Multivariate logistic regression model is used to see the joint effect of various background characteristics upon the important causes of maternal death like, haemorrhage, eclampsia, infection, retained placenta, anaemia, viral hepatitis and heart disease. These important causes of maternal death are used separately as dependent or explaining variable in logistic regression analysis to identify their risk factors from different socio-economic and maternal health care covariates or predictor variables (e.g., mother's age at death, birth order, caste, religion, education, consumption of food during pregnancy and delivery assistance). Each indicator or dependent variable has two values, if the response is 'yes' (i.e., died in a particular cause) then the value is considered as 'one' and if it is 'no' then the value is 'zero'. Seven important socio-economic and other predictor variables are included in the analyses which are categorical in nature on the basis of their importance in maternal health. Many variables are excluded due their similar effects in the model.

The results of the multiple logistic regression analyses are presented in Table 7.6. The odd ratios for different dependent variables against selected categorical independent variables are described in the table. Results show that the risk of maternal death due to haemorrhage is more among Muslim women and who received delivery assistance from the 'others' (i.e., relatives and neighbours). Eclampsia is negatively related with age at death and birth orders. Death due to eclampsia is slightly higher among Muslims compared to Hindus. The risk of death associated with retained placenta is higher for higher birth orders and among untrained *dais*. Similarly, death due to anaemia is two and three times higher for birth orders '2 to 3' and '4 and above' respectively compared to birth order 'one'. Consumption of inadequate food during pregnancy had serious effect in death due to anaemia. However, due to small numbers in many

Table 7.6: Odds Ratios of Different Causes of Maternal Death according to Selected Background Characteristics in KMA of West Bengal, India

Background Characteristics	Categories	Cause of death						
		Haemorrhage	*Eclampsia*	*Infection*	*Retained Placenta*	*Anaemia*	*Viral Hepatitis*	*Heart Disease*
Age at death	15 to 19 yrs	1.00	1.00	1.00	1.00	1.00	1.00	1.00
	20 to 29 yrs	0.65	0.38 **	0.98	0.72	0.89	0.98	0.95
	30 yrs and above	0.54	0.49 **	0.93	0.48	0.45	0.95	0.92
Birth order	One	1.00	1.00	1.00	1.00	1.00	1.00	1.00
	2 to 3	0.67	0.37 *	0.80	1.96 *	2.03 **	0.70	0.61
	4 and Above	0.48	0.47 **	1.65	4.10 *	3.41 ***	0.19	0.78
Caste	SC	0.98	1.03	0.88	1.27	0.46	1.59 *	1.18
	Others	1.00	1.00	1.00	1.00	1.00	1.00	1.00
Religion	Hindu	1.00	1.00	1.00	1.00	1.00	1.00	1.00
	Muslim	2.47 **	1.65 *	0.83	0.82	0.29	0.50	0.96
Education	Illiterate	1.00	1.00	1.00	1.00	1.00	1.00	1.00
	Middle Sch complete	2.05	0.64	0.51	0.96	2.93	0.31	2.15
	High Sch and above	2.18	0.38	1.27	0.46	0.49	0.29	3.45 *
Foods consumed at pregnancy	Adequate	1.06	0.94	1.43	0.76	0.29 **	0.89	0.89
	Inadequate	1.00	1.00	1.00	1.00	1.00	1.00	1.00
Delivery Assistance	Doctor	1.00	1.00	1.00	1.00	1.00	1.00	1.00
	Dai (Trained)/ Nurse	0.93	0.51	0.49	2.04 *	0.87	0.62	0.97
	Dai (Untrained)	0.96	0.59	0.44	4.13 ***	0.80	0.25	0.69
	Others	2.77 *	0.89	1.05	0.98	0.59	0.32	0.59

Note: '***' Significant at 1% level; '**' Significant at 5% level; '*' Significant at 10% level. N.A.-Not Applicable.
Source: Compiled from the primary data collected (2005-06) for the present study.

categories created inability to show significant level in 'odds ratios' and hence do not exhibit meaningful conclusions. This type of analysis may be done in future studies with sufficient sample sizes.

CONCLUDING REMARKS

Maternal Mortality Ratio (MMR) is the most important index for monitoring the progress of safe motherhood programmes. However, the level as well as the distribution of causes of maternal mortality varies from region to region or place to place in India depending on socio-economic factors and religious beliefs, with availability and extent of utilization of health care services, and in general, state of health of the community. From this study, it has been observed that the leading causes of maternal deaths in the Kolkata metropolitan areas are haemorrhage, eclampsia, retained placenta, anaemia, and viral hepatitis in pregnancy. Among them, haemorrhage is the highest cause to claim 35 lives (18.7%) and majority of death due to haemorrhage happened during post-partum period. Another important cause like, retained placenta are responsible for 24 deaths and home delivery is done (71%) for majority of cases. Similarly, viral hepatitis which is a major public health problem in India brought about 18 deaths (9.6%) in the study. It is also noted that, 76 deaths (41%) occurred within 24 hours of delivery.

Important socio-economic factors indirectly responsible for the maternal death are: pregnancies in the youngest and oldest reproductive age groups, higher birth order, woman's illiteracy, inaccessibility in health care services and delivery by untrained birth attendants at home. Particularly, higher birth order increases the risk of death due to retained placenta and anaemia. Similarly, risk of death due to eclampsia is higher for the women aged 20 years and above. The chance of death due to haemorrhage and eclampsia are comparatively high for Muslim women than Hindus. The most important finding of this study is that, the risk of death due to delivery assistance by the 'Untrained Dai' is 4 times higher than the assistance by the doctor. In the present study, 33 deaths occurred during delivery by the TBAs and out of that 15 cases are caused by retained placenta.

The findings of the present study suggest that the preventive and health promotional measures related with maternal health are not sufficient to tackle multifarious causes for maternal death. Again, it is difficult to predict obstetric complications in advance. So, the emergency obstetric care services might be available and also accessible to all women at the time of emergency. An emergency service would help to reduce the number of deaths. Similarly, adequate antenatal and post-natal cares can reduce maternal mortality significantly. The prompt diagnosis and adequate treatment of infections due to liver disorder and other infectious diseases during ante-partum and post-partum periods may have major impacts on maternal death.

It has been observed from the present study that, heavy bleeding after giving birth (Postpartum Haemorrhage, PPH) is one of the main causes of women's death. The most effective intervention for preventing PPH is active management of labour, which includes using an uterotonic drug after the baby's birth. In a home birth, it is possible to prevent PPH in most of the cases if such drug is used just after the child has been born. Other preventive measures which would help to lower maternal mortality are: mass education among the women about the need for antenatal as well as post-natal cares, stable arrangement for good obstetrical service, provision of quick transport in emergency situation, adequate staffing of hospitals, and arrangement of emergency blood transfusion service. One of the important measures to fight against maternal mortality is the possible service of the most knowledgeable personnel for monitoring the labour and for this regular mandatory training course for birth attendants and other allied medical personnel is very much important.

The main limitation of the present study is that, the results only reflect a particular socio-economic class (i.e., vulnerable population) and not representing the wider community. Again, it is conducted in urban areas and hence the contribution of different causes of maternal death might differ from those observed in the rural areas.

REFERENCES

Brabin, B.J., Hakimi, M., and Pelletier, D. (2001). An analysis of anaemia and pregnancy-related maternal mortality, *The Journal of Nutrition*, Vol. 131, No. 2, pp. 604S–614S.

CSO (2009). *Millennium Development Goals, India Country Report 2009, Mid-Term Statistical Appraisal.* Central Statistical Organization (CSO), Ministry of Statistics and Programme Implementation (MoSPI), Government of India (http://www.mospi.nic.in).

Graham, W.J. and O.M.R. Campbell (1990). *Measuring Maternal Health:*

Defining the Issues Maternal and Child Epidemiology. Unit Publication. London: London School of Hygiene and Tropical Medicine.

Gupta, K., F. Arnold, S. Kishor, and S. Parasuraman (2007). Concern on prevalence of anaemia in pregnant and lactating women in India. *Indian Journal of Medical Research* 125(1):99-101.

IIPS and Macro International (2007). *National Family Health Survey (NFHS-3), 2005–06: India: Volume I*, International Institute for Population Sciences, Mumbai (IIPS), India, p. 220.

Kaplan, C.D., Korf, D., Sterk, C. (1987). Temporal and social contexts of heroin-using populations. An illustration of the snowball sampling technique. *The Journal of Nervous and Mental Disease*, September, 175(9):566-74.

Kar, P. (2007). Viral hepatitis—is it still a challenge in the Indian subcontinent? *The Indian Journal of Medical Research*; 06/2007; 125(5):608-11.

MoHFW (2000). *National Population Policy, 2000*. New Delhi: Department of Family Welfare, Ministry of Health and Family Welfare (MoHFW).

MoHFW (2005). *Annual Report 2004-2005*. Ministry of Health and Family Welfare (MoHFW), New Delhi.

MoHFW (2006). *National Rural Health Mission (2005-2012), Mission Document*. Ministry of Health and Family Welfare (MoHFW), New Delhi.

Murphy, J.F., J. O'Riordan, R.G. Newcombe, E.C. Coles, and J.F. Peason (1986). Relation of haemoglobin levels in first and second trimesters to outcome of pregnancy. *Lancet* 1(8488):992-994.

Pandit, Niraj, Mehta, Rajesh. (2010). Anaemia—A simple community based diagnostic tool, *Healthline*, Volume 1, Issue 1, July-December, pp. 53-55, ISSN 2229-337X.

Puri, Alka, Indra Yadav and Nisha Jain (2011). Maternal Mortality in an Urban Tertiary Care Hospital of North India, *The Journal of Obstetrics and Gynaecology of India*, May/June, pp. 280-285.

Renee Larocque, Martin Casapia, Eduardo Gotuuzzo and Theresa, W.G. (2005). Relationship Between Intensity of Soil-transmitted Helminth Infections and Anaemia during Pregnancy. *The American Journal of Tropical Medicine and Hygiene*, Vol. 73, No. 4, pp. 783-789.

RGI (2006). *Maternal Mortality in India: 1997-2003, Trends, Causes and Risk Factors*, Registrar General of India (RGI), New Delhi.

RGI (2011). *Special Bulletin on Maternal Mortality in India, 2007-09*. Sample Registration System, Registrar General of India (RGI), New Delhi.

Srinivasan, D.K., Narayan, K.A., Oumachigui, A. and Roy, G. (1997). *Prevalence of Maternal Morbidity in a South Indian Community*. Report of a Ford Foundation Study, Department of Community Medicine, Jawaharlal Institute of Postgraduate Medical Education and Research, Pouducherry; pp. 1-20.

Vidyadhar, B. Bangal, Purushottam, A. Giri and Ruchika Garg (2011). Maternal Mortality at a Tertiary Care Teaching Hospital of Rural India: A Retrospective Study, *International Journal of Biological and Medical Research*, Vol. 2, No.4, pp. 1043-1046.

WHO (2000). Maternal Mortality in 2000: Estimates Developed by WHO, UNICEF and UNFPA.

WHO (2007). Maternal Mortality in 2005: Estimates developed by WHO, UNICEF, UNFPA, and the World Bank. World Health Organization, pp. 15-16.

WHO (2008). Achieving Millennium Development Goal 5: is India serious? Mavalankar D., *et al.*, *Bulletin of the World Health Organization*, Vol. 86, No. 4.

WHO, UNICEF, UNFPA and The World Bank. (2010). *Trends in Maternal Mortality: 1990 to 2008*. Estimates developed by WHO, UNICEF, UNFPA and The World Bank. World Health Organization.

World Health Organization (2008). *Worldwide Prevalence of Anaemia 1993–2005*. Geneva: World Health Organization (WHO). http://whqlibdoc.who.int/publications/2008/9789241596657_eng.pdf.

Zhou, L.M., W.W. Yang, J.Z. Hua, C.Q. Deng, X. Tao, and R.J. Stoltzfus (1998). Relation of haemoglobin measured at different times in pregnancy to preterm birth and low birth weight in Shanghai, China. *American Journal of Epidemiology* 148:998-1006.

8

Status of Women in East India: Its Measurement and Determinants

Chaiti Sharma Biswas

INTRODUCTION

Within patriarchy, women are commonly treated as the backward section of the society and are not properly included in the development process. But as a vital part of the society, their role in the development process cannot be denied. Therefore, mainstreaming of women becomes the main focus of various developmental policies and programmes formulated by Government and Non-Governmental Organizations. As a process of mainstreaming, various policy-makers recommended to empower women. As empowerment is a multi-dimensional aspect; so empowerment in one sphere of life does not necessarily ensure empowerment in other spheres of life. It is to note that empowerment is linked with the concept of power and is *defined as the expansion of people's ability to make strategic life choices in a context where this ability was previously denied to them* (Kabeer, 2001).

Despite earnest effort of the policy-makers, it is observed that the achievement level of women empowerment remains well behind the third MDG goal (empower women) in India. Both social and economic factors are responsible for this lag. This demands a minute enquiry to locate the exact causes of failures or successes that affect the achievement level of women empowerment.

Present study is confined to Jharkhand because from development point of view this state lags in many aspects. It will assess the status of women empowerment in Jharkhand and identify the causal factors responsible for the lag (if exist) in achieving MDG goal based on the data extracted from Third National Family Health Survey (NFHS-3) conducted during 2005-06.

PAST STUDIES ON EMPOWERMENT

It is established that women are treated as a deprived section in the society; consequently they are denied from various advantages thereby leading to gender inequality. Also, it is said that women are the poorest of the poor because as a poor, male faces a number of disadvantages and exclusion. Female of these families are abused both as female and poor and have less empowerment. Many scholars advocated that absence of economic freedom is the main reason for low empowerment of women in the society (Mikkola & Miles, 2007, Kabeer, 2003). According to this school of thought empowerment of Indian women depends on their economic freedom. In this direction, several studies examine the effect of micro-finance on women empowerment (Goetz & Gupta, 1996; Hashemi, Schuler & Riley, 1996; Amin, Becker & Bayes, 1998; Kabeer, 2001, 2005b; Holvoet, 2005; Pitt, Khandker & Cartwright, 2006; Bali & Walletin, 2009). Though, economic independence helps women to gain power, but cannot always ensure empowerment to the expected (Sharma Biswas, 2008) level. This indicates that besides economic factors, women empowerment is determined by some other factors also. Various studies show that social factors are stronger than economic factors in a society and it varies directly with its nature of conservativeness. Alsop, Bertelsen and Holland (2005) prove that any intervention to improve agency and enhance opportunity structures can increase people's capacity to make effective choices.

Some of the studies on empowerment show its impact on health, education, fertility, development so on (Kabeer, 1999, 2005a; Jejeebhoy, 2000; Jejeebhoy & Sathar, 2001; Mason & Smith, 2003; Klassen, 2006; Schuler, 2006; Choudhuri & Nosheen, 2009). Another study (Chakraborty & Sharma Biswas, 2012) pointed out the simultaneous relationship between empowerment and the determining factors. They show that increase in women empowerment enhance children's education, better health condition so on. On the other, the factors like higher education, better income and health condition or better life contributed positively to enhance women empowerment, which ultimately enriches development.

DATA AND METHODOLOGY

Data

Present study is based on the household level data extracted from National Family Health Survey (NFHS-3), 2005-06. Current study considers women's decision making power as a measure of their level of empowerment. In addition to empowerment related informations, there are some socio-economic factors which are used as explanatory or causal factors (Table A2). Except a few, the variables are qualitative in nature.

Methods

In order to measure the status of women empowerment this study first develop an empowerment index then classify it as low, medium and high, and lastly a regression analysis is performed to identify the determinants of empowerment.

Construction of Empowerment Index (EI)

As a measure, an Empowerment Index (EI) is constructed using all the available decision-making variables provided by NFHS-3 (Table A1). All these variables are classified into four broad decision making groups namely—*(1) access to money* (AMI), *(2) spending money decisions (SPI), (3) routine household decisions (RHDI)* and *(4) mobility freedom (MI)*. The variables grouped under these groups are:

(1) *AMI*: Have (i) money for her own use, (ii) bank or savings account, (iii) knowledge of loan, and (iv) been given loan.
(2) *SPI*: Right to (i) spend money, (ii) spend husband's earned money, and (iii) make large purchases decisions.
(3) *RHDI*: Right to take decisions for (i) health care, (ii) daily purchases, (iii) visit relatives'/friends' houses, and (iv) using contraception.
(4) *MI*: Freedom to (i) visit market, (ii) outside village/ community, and (iii) for health facility. Specific scores are then assigned to different responses according to the intensity of the scale. Score '3' is assigned if the response is "Yes/

Alone", score '1' if the response is "No" and score '2' if the response is "Joint decision".

An Empowerment Index (EI) is developed and is constructed for each respondent combining all the categories mentioned above. Initially, for each respondent a ratio is estimated dividing sum of the recorded responses by total number of queries in each of the categories, namely access to and spending money decisions, routine household decisions and freedom of mobility. Then they are summed up to get the total value of the composite index. After computing EI, it is classified as *low, medium* and *high.*

In the last step, a multiple regression analysis is performed to identify the determinants of empowerment. In this regard, EI is regressed on various socio-economic factors like religion, caste, media-exposure, age, education, occupational and marital status of the respondent, her type of earning, relationship to the household head, household structure (joint or nuclear), and household's wealth index.

PROFILE OF JHARKHAND

Number of women covered in Jharkhand is 2,983 (Table 8.1). Sex-ratio is very poor in Jharkhand where number of female per thousand male is only 947 (Census 2011). Majority of the women in Jharkhand are Hindu; presence of Muslim and other religion women are relatively less.

In Jharkhand, 45 per cent of the Hindu belongs to Other Backward Castes (OBC) and 23 per cent are from ST population. Most of the women in Jharkhand are illiterate women (53%). Among the literate (47%), majority attain middle level education (31%), and a noticeably small percentage of women are found to be highly qualified (6%). Though TV appears as the only popular medium of exposure to outer world surprisingly 40 per cent women in Jharkhand still remain ignorant about the outer world. Obeying Indian social norms, majority of the Indian women choose to remain unemployed but surprisingly Jharkhand exhibits just an opposite trend where percentage of employed women (51%) is larger than that of unemployed (49%) women. Majority of the employed women in Jharkhand are engaged in manual or unskilled jobs (44%) while very few are engaged in medium (5%) and high (2%) level jobs.

Table 8.1: Socio-Economic Features of Women from Jharkhand, 2005-06

Items					
No. of Respondent (2011)		2983	Sex-ratio (census, 2011)		947
Religion (%):	Hindu	72.5	Ethnicity (%):	SC	11.5
	Muslim	15.3		ST	22.7
	Others	12.2		OBC	44.7
				General	21.1
Literacy rate:			Level of Occupation:		
	Illiterate	53.0		Unemployed	49.15
	Low	10.5		Low	43.68
	Middle	30.6		Medium	5.03
	Higher	5.9		High	2.15
Employment Status (%):			Exposure to Media:	No	40.15
	Unemployed	49.15		Yes	59.85
	Employed	50.85			

Source: Extracted data from National Family Health Survey, 2005-06, Census of India, 2011.

FINDINGS

On an average, the estimated EI (sum of the components AMI, SPI, RHDI and MI) at India level is 7.42 and Jharkhand (7.21) failed to achieve this level (Table 8.2).

Among various components of EI mobility index occupy the major share (2.39) and spending index the minimum share (1.53). This is also true for average Indian women. The index value of AMI is same for both Jharkhand and India. An important indicator of empowerment is spending rights of women (SPI), in this regard women from Jharkhand are little bit advanced than Indian women. Women of this state (1.70) have relatively less command on routine household decisions (RHDI) with respect to Indian women (1.84). Compared to Indian women (2.48), women of Jharkhand (2.39) have relatively less freedom of mobility (MI).

After construction, EI is classified as low, medium and high. By and large, 79 per ent of women in Jharkhand accomplish medium level of empowerment (Table 8.2). Notable fact is that that not only percentage of highly empowered women is found to be small in Jharkhand (9%), but percentage of low empowered women (12%) is also very little here. Compared to India, percentage of low empowered women is found to be more in Jharkhand and percentage of high

Table 8.2: EI of Women by its Component and Distribution of Women by their Level of Empowerment in Jharkhand, 2005-06

	Jharkhand	*India*
EI	7.21	7.42
AMI	1.58	1.58
SPI	1.53	1.52
RHDI	1.70	1.84
MI	2.39	2.48
Level of Empowerment:		
Low	12.2	9.16
Medium	79.3	76.96
High	8.5	13.88
Total Number of women	2294	87815

Source: Data Extracted from NFHS-3, 2005-06.

empowered women is less here. Also, percentage of low empowered women is more than that of highly empowered women in Jharkhand.

Above findings ascertain that very few women attain high level of empowerment in Jharkhand, majority of the women is endowed with medium level empowerment, but these women rarely have control over financial matters. Hence, it is necessary to investigate the reasons that restrict women to achieve high level of empowerment. To identify the factors that help to shape the level of women empowerment, estimated EI is regressed on various socio economic factors mentioned above.

Study demonstrates that respondent's *self-confidence* and *awareness generating* factors (level of education, exposure to media, and participation in economic activities) play significant role in determining the level of women empowerment. More specifically, women's religion, caste, media exposure, education, occupation, higher income compared to their husband, age, relation to household head, and household structure have influence on empowerment of women (Table 8.3). Besides, their husband's age and occupation also have significant influence on women empowerment.

All of these factors enable women to be endowed with power and with enhancement of these factors their level of empowerment increases.

In Jharkhand religion has some influence on women empowerment while caste factor becomes important only in Jharkhand. Here, it is observed that Muslim and other religion women

Table 8.3: Influence of the Factors on Women Empowerment in Jharkhand, 2005-06

Causal Factors	*Jharkhand*	
	B values	*Directions*
Religion	.158*	↑
Caste	—.069**	↓
Media exposure	.213*	↑
Respondent's education	.219*	↑
Respondent's occupation	.365*	↑
Husband's occupation	.039	X
Respondent's age	.644*	↑
Husband's age	.217*	↑
Relation to household head	—.190*	↓
Household structure	—.216*	↓
Type of earning	—.022	X
Higher income compared to their husband	.356*	↑
WI	.188	X

Source: NFHS-3 extracted data.

Note: (i) *Implies significant at 1 per cent level and (ii) ** implies significant at > 5 per cent level.

↑ = positively significant and ↑ = negatively significant at.01 per cent level.

x = not significant, ⇑ = positively significant and ⇓ = negatively significant at. 05 per cent level.

are more empowered than Hindu women and among Hindus, general castes women are less empowered than backward castes women. Other factors namely respondent's *education, age* and *higher earning* have positive significant contributions, relation with head has negative significant contribution on women empowerment. Husband's occupation, their type of earning and economic status (WI) has no influence in explaining the variation in level of women empowerment.

ANALYSIS/DISCUSSION

Data depicts that majority of the Indian women are Hindu by religion. Few of the respondents belong to Muslim and other religion. Majority of the Hindu respondents are from backward classes. Consequently, most of them are characterized by medium or low level of literacy, but have acquaintance with media (mainly TV). Incidence of unemployment is observed in high rate in every state, however, majority of the employed (few) women are engaged in manual or unskilled jobs.

Average value of Empowerment Index (EI) is found to be 7.42 for Indian women, and Jharkhand failed to achieve this rate. One has to make various decisions in daily life which can be classified into four different broad groups namely Access to Money (AMI), Spending Money decisions (SPI), Routine Household Decisions (RHDI) and freedom of Mobility (MI). All these four components together form EI, all of which has different level of influence on EI. It is assumed that SPI is a crucial decision-making factor; therefore, a female who has control over financial decisions seems to enjoy high level of empowerment in the family. In addition to spending decisions capacity, mobility freedom also plays a significant role in achieving high level of empowerment. MI consists of the factors like visit to market, hospital and outside villages. Though restriction is imposed on visiting places outside the village, they are allowed to visit market and hospitals in order to carry on daily life activities. Relatively, AMI has the lowest impact in shaping one's EI among the four components because keeping money or having bank account or the knowledge of loan programme does not effectively influence the daily life activities, although this component has some control on EI.

In Jharkhand women has more access to money for their own use and mobility freedom compared to other components.

Around 79 per cent women are observed to have medium level of empowerment in Jharkhand and very little women are found to have both low and high level of empowerment. Probably, women are discouraged from having no or low empowerment in order to protect family interest and to carry on the regular routine household activities.

In search of reasons it is unveiled that as a whole, *self-confidence* and *awareness generating* factors are the main determinants of women empowerment. Some of these confidence generating factors are women's education, exposure to media, job, higher income than their husband, and their stay in nuclear family instead of joint families.

Respondent's education appears as a significant factor for empowerment of women because it generates self-confidence among women which in turn helps to gain power. Women's exposure to media plays fairly significant role on their empowerment as it enhances one's awareness about self and surrounding thereby generating self-confidence among them. It is to note that though employment rate of women is highest in Jharkhand, still it has no impact on their empowerment because women are mainly attached with manual or unskilled jobs. Rather women's high-level jobs, higher earning relative to their husband enhance their control on household decision making. Family structure (nuclear/joint family) is found to be an important factor for women empowerment because women living in nuclear family have more control on household decision making than those who live in joint families and sharing many things with other family members.

There exist some other factors, which also regulate women empowerment, like their own and husband's age as well as relationship to household head. It is observed that with age, women achieve relatively higher empowerment may be due to the fact that, with age they learn to cope with various household problems. Similarly, empowerment of women seemed to be enhanced with increase in their husband's age, may be, with increase in age, the male members (husbands) gradually becomes busy so they are forced to allow their wives to take some decisions in the family. In Odisha husband's age do not contribute to EI. Headship position (functional) of a woman enhances her agency to a great extent thereby increasing her empowerment. Religion and caste also act as a determinant of women empowerment. General castes women are always less empowered than the backward castes women may be due to economic reason, backward castes women contribute more in the family expenditure, which enhance their say in family decision makings relative to their general castes counterpart.

CONCLUSION

Current study depicts that Indian women in general have medium level empowerment in the family. A small percentage of women have high level of empowerment, which is normal in Indian society, but surprisingly percentage of women having low level of empowerment is also modest. Level of women empowerment (EI) in Jharkhand lies far below India average. This happens probably due to lag in confidence generating factors like education, employment etc. Each mainstreaming policy therefore aims to create confidence among the backward section. Among several factors, education is found as the most important factor for building confidence which in turn helps them to be empowered.

Women in this state mainly have medium level education that filed to earn higher level of empowerment for women because most of the respondents are engaged in manual or unskilled jobs. This indicates that Indian social norms are so rigid that medium or higher education failed to involve Indian women in the job market. Thus to ensure higher level empowerment, women must be engaged in higher level jobs which in turn requires higher qualification of women. Both higher qualification and higher level job of women can fetch them empowerment to the targeted level. Moreover, if they earn more than their husband then their level of confidence increase to a great extent, which in turn increase their control on household decision making. Besides, attempts should be taken to enhance women's self-esteem, awareness about self and surrounding. All these increase their self-confidence and awareness about social issues.

REFERENCES

Alsop, R., Bertelsen, M.F., and Holland, J. (2005), "Empowerment in Practice: From analysis to implementation", Book, World Bank Publications ISBN-10 0821364502, ISBN-13 9780821364505

Amin, R., Becker, S. and Byes, A. (1998), "NGO-promoted micro-credit programme and women's empowerment in rural Bangladesh: Quantitative and qualitative evidence". *The Journal of Developing Areas,* 221-236.

Bali, Swain, R., and Wallentin, F.Y. (2009), "Does Micro-finance empower women?" *International Review of Applied Economics, 23*(5): 541-556.

Chakrabarti, S., and Sharma, C. (2012), "An exploratory analysis of women empowerment in India: A structural equation modelling approach". *Journal of Development Studies, 48*(1): 164-180.

Choudhary, I.S., and Nosheen, F.(2009), "The determinants of women empowerment in southern Punjab (Pakistan): An empirical analysis". *European Journal of Social Sciences, 10*(2): 216-229.

Goetz, A.M. and Gupta, R.S. (1996), "Who takes the credit? Gender, power and control over loan use in rural credit programmes in Bangladesh". *World Development, 24* (1): 45-63.

Hashemi, S., Schuler, S.R. and Riley, A. (1996), "Rural credit programmes and women's empowerment in Bangladesh". *World Development, 24*(4): 635-653.

Holvoet, N. (2005), "The impact of micro-finance on decision-making agency: Evidence from South India". *Development and Change, 36* (1): 75-102.

Jejeebhoy, S. (2000), "Women's autonomy in rural India: Its dimension, determinants and the influence on context". In H.B. Presser and G. Sen (eds.), *Women and Demographic Processes—Moving beyond Cairo (*pp. 204-238). Oxford University Press, New York.

Jejeebhoy, S.J., and Sathar, Z.A. (2001), "Women's autonomy in India and Pakistan: The influence of religion and region". *Population and Development Review, 27*(4): 687-712.

Kabeer, N. (1999), "Resources, agency, achievements: Reflections on the measurement of women's empowerment". *Development and Change, 30*(3): 435-464.

Kabeer, N. (2001), "Reflections on the measurement of women's empowerment". *Discussing Women's Empowerment—Theory and Practice,* SIDA: Swedish International Cooperation Agency.

Kabeer, N. (2003), "Gender equality, poverty eradication and the millennium development goals: Promoting women's capabilities and participation". Retrieved from http://www.unescap. org/esid/committee2003/genderequality.pdf.

Kabeer, N. (2005 a), "Gender equality and women's empowerment: A critical analysis of the third millennium development goal". *Gender and Development, 13*(1): 13-24.

Kabeer, N. (2005b), "Is micro-finance a 'magic bullet' for women's empowerment? Analysis of findings from South Asia". *Economic and Political Weekly, 40*(44, 45): 4709-4718.

Klasen, S. (2006), "UNDP's Gender related measures: Some conceptual problems and possible solutions". *Journal of Human Development 7*(2): 243-274.

Mason, K.O. and Smith, H.L. (2003), "Women's empowerment and social context: Results from five Asian countries". Gender Development Group, *World Bank,* Washington, DC.

Mikkola, A., and Miles, C.A. (2007), "Development and Gender equality: Consequences, Causes, Challenges and Cures". Discussion Paper No. 159, Institute for the Studies of Religion at Baylor University.

Pitt, M.M., Khandker, S.R., and Cartwright, J. (2006), "Empowering women with micro-finance: Evidence from Bangladesh", *Economic Development and Cultural Change, 54* (4): 791-831.

Sharma, C. (2008), "Can employment empower women more at the household level in India?" *The International Journal of Interdisciplinary Social Sciences, 3*(7): 43-51.

Appendix

Table A1: Description of the indicators with their respective scores

Components of EI	*Description of the Variables*	*Scores*
AMI	1. Has money for her own use 2. Have bank or savings account 3. Knowledge of loan 4. Given Loan	No = 1 Yes = 3
SPI	1. Spending money 2. Spending husband's earning 3. Large purchases	Other than respondent = 1 Jointly with husband = 2 Alone = 3
RHDI	1. Health care 2. Daily purchase 3. Visit to family, relatives and friends 4. Using contraception	Other than respondent = 1 Jointly with husband = 2 Alone = 3
MI	1. Allowed to go market 2. Allowed to outside village/community 3. Allowed to go health facility	No = 1 Yes = 3

Source: NFHS extracted data.

Table A2: Explanatory Variables/Casual Factors Used in the Study

Factors	*Items*	*Factors*	*Items*
Religion (RIL)	1. Hindu 2. Muslim 3 Others	Relationship to household head (RLHD)	1. Head 2. Wife 3. Others
Caste (CST)	1. Scheduled Caste 2. Scheduled Tribe 3. OBC 4. General	Respondent's type of earning (TYERN)	1. Not paid 2. Kind only 3. Cash and kind 4. Cash only
Age of respondent (in years) (RAGE)	1. 15-25 2. 26-40 3. 41-49	Wife's earning relative to her husband (ERNM)	1. Husband would not bring money 2. Almost half 3. More than husband
Age of Husband (in years) (HAGE)	1. 10-25 2. 26-45 3. 46+	Wealth Index indicating household's economic status (WI)	1. Low 2. Medium 3. High
Media (MED)	1. No exposure 2. Have exposure to either newspaper or radio or TV	Household Structure (HHST)	1. Nuclear 2. Non-nuclear
Marital Status	1. Others 2. Wife 3. Head	Empowerment (EI)	1. Low 2. Medium 3. High
Education of respondent and her partner (REDU and HEDU)	1. Illiterate 2. Primary 3. Secondary 4. Higher	Occupation of respondent and her partner (ROCU and HOCU)	1. No Job 2. Production labour 3. Sales and services 4. Clerical 5. Professional, technical and managerial

Source: Schedule Based on NFHS Scheme.

9

Cancer Care and Social Support: Challenges and Key Issues

Sourav Madhur Dey

INTRODUCTION

Cancer affects social relations in unique ways, depending, in part, on the type and the stage of disease. Cancer does not happen to just one person. Cancer happens to couples, families, and friends. The complex emotions and lifestyle changes that follow a cancer diagnosis can be almost as overwhelming for family members and friends as they are for the person with cancer. Cancer can change the way one relates to his family and friends the core making up the primary group and the way they relate to others or in Mead's rhetoric the 'generalized others'. It is entirely possible that everyone in the family and in circle of friends will be supportive throughout the recovery. But chances are that one may run into a few relationship obstacles. Friends and family love the person and are worried about him — but they may have strange ways of showing it. Some people withdraw and avoid talking to him. Others smother and treat him like a child. Many cancer survivors find that one barrier to a smooth transition out of cancer treatment is the reaction they get from friends and family.

The number of cancer patients in the world is increasing all the time. There were 14.1 million new cancer cases, 8.2 million cancer deaths and 32.6 million people living with cancer (within 5 years of diagnosis) in 2012 worldwide. 57 per cent (8 million) of new cancer cases, 65 per cent (5.3 million) of the cancer deaths and 48 per cent (15.6 million) of the 5-year prevalent cancer cases occurred in the less developed regions. (GLOBOCAN, 2012) Cure and supportive care of cancer patients apart from the treatment is a necessity. Care is a wide field and incorporates not only medicine and medical people, but also family members as its central force because family is the primary and basic institution in our lives and plays a pivotal role in shaping our social identity and psychological movements or propensities. For those diagnosed with cancer, psychosocial services should be available and should include the assessment of patients for the presence of anxiety and depression, support to help patients adhere to treatment plans, skill building for coping with cancer stress and basic emotional support. For those with clinical range anxiety or depression, care should be available to help ameliorate symptoms. Psychosocial support should also be available for families of cancer patients and staff members who treat cancer patients. Four generations of studies have focused on cancer and its effects on families and caregivers. The first generation of studies appeared as clinical papers and included recommendations on how to minimize disruption to the patient and spouse. However, these studies lacked data and were based on clinical impressions. The second generation of studies emerged in the 1970s and 1980s and primarily included cross-sectional, descriptive designs focusing mainly on the spouse or caregiver. The third generation of studies used complex statistical analyses to examine the processes by which family members were affected by cancer in the survivor. Such analyses enabled us to understand how the cancer "invaded" other family members' behaviour, how family members managed the illness, successfully or not, and why children were negatively affected. The fourth generation of studies has evolved quite recently and includes rigorous intervention studies for caregivers or family members. However, most of what we know about families, what affects them, and how well they do or do not manage the cancer are limited to short-term survivors and their families, not long-term survivors. Also, populations studied are primarily those affected by breast cancer.

There are four reasons based on data (as opposed to reasons based on speculation or clinical practice) to consider family-focused research in cancer survivorship: 1. Family members are considerably upset when a member has cancer. 2. Family members do not know, understand or respond supportively to the expressed thoughts, feelings, and behaviour of other family members about the cancer. 3. Families try to cope with both the impact of the cancer and with tension in the family caused or accentuated by the cancer. 4. Family members struggle to maintain their core functions when one of them is a long-term survivor. Family members are substantially distressed when a member has cancer. Even high-functioning families struggle and suffer when a member has cancer (Lewis, 2004). Both cross-sectional and longitudinal studies have demonstrated emotional distress and behavioural disruption in spouses of women with breast cancer.

CONJUGAL DYNAMICS

Significantly elevated levels of distress in spouses have been documented up to three years after diagnosis; according to some studies, distress in the spouse exceeds that in the diagnosed patient (Baider, De-Nour, 1984; Gotay 1984; Hoskins, 1995; Hoskins *et al.*, 1996; Northouse, Swain, 1987; Omne-Ponten *et al.*, 1993; Ptacek *et al.*, 1994; Toseland *et al.*, 1995). Couples experiencing the acute phase of breast cancer treatment are known to function in survival mode, during which time competing demands distract them from attending to each other's needs, thoughts, and feelings, as well as to specific needs for support about the cancer. Very little is known about the couples' interactions in long-term survivorship. We speculate two extremes: either benefit-finding behaviour (identifying positive aspects in the cancer experience), or heightened interpersonal tension in the couples' relationship. But scientists do not know what predicts a couple's ability to see the positive in long-term survivorship or what predicts heightened tension in the relationship. To date there has been scanty research in this area with long-term survivors. Sometimes, cancer treatments can interfere with interest in sexual activity. If one is female, she may experience pain with intercourse, vaginal dryness, or concerns regarding fertility. Perhaps treatment has put into sudden menopause. If male, one may be having difficulties in getting or maintaining an erection. It has been reported than men with urogential or colorectal cancer may experience erectile and ejaculatory dysfunction related to damage to the autonomic nervous system or a reduced circulation of blood to the penis. Hormonal impairment of sexual function is less common, but some men with cancer in the aforementioned organs, as well as cancer in the brain, leukaemia and lymphoma, experience a general decrease in libido (Nazareth, Lewin and King, 2001). Among women, sudden premature ovarian failure and direct effects of radiation fibrosis or surgical scar tissue may cause pain with sexual activity (Bergmark, Lundqvist, Dickman, Henningsohn, and Steineck, 1999). Counselling may help one develop strategies for dealing with these problems. Sometimes, counselling can help prevent the development of sexual problems in the future. One of the limitations of research in this area is the focus on experiences of sexuality after cancer that affects the reproductive organs (Wellisch, *et al.* 1978; Maughan, Heyman, Matthews, 2002; Harden, Schafenacker, Northouse, *et al.* 2002; Sanders, Pedro, Bantum, Galbraith, 2006). Chronic illnesses in general and certain cancer forms in particular may influence physical intimacy and sexuality, and thereby divorce rates. In addition, altered physical appearance due to e.g. a stoma, limb amputation or removal of a breast may affect sexuality both for men and women, and fatigue and chronic weakness may decrease libido (Schover, 2005).

Another issue is that a person's gender identity and 'sense of self' may be disturbed because of cancer in reproductive organs, with implications for the sexual desires (Fobair, Stewart, Chang, D'Onofrio, Banks and Bloom, 2006). Some have argued that this is particularly true for men (Monga, Alexandrescu, Katz, Stein and Ganiats, 2004; Joly, Heron, Kalusinski, Bottet, Brune, Allouache, Mace-Lesec'h, Couette, Peny and Henry-Amar, 2002). All these effects depend on both the extent of disease and on type of treatment received (Dorval, Guay, Mondor, Masse, Falardeau, Robidoux, Deschenes and Maunsell, 2005). Many treatment regimens have become less aggressive over the last few decades, both as a result of technological innovations and an increased awareness and recognition of cancer survivors' sexual functioning. For many localized cancers today, treatment may actually be presumed to be physically nearly non-afflicting. For more advanced cancers, however, treatments that harm sexual organs and/or hormonal production are still employed to cure the disease, as alternatives do not exist.

However, the dynamics of the care giving relationship and social constructions surrounding what constitutes appropriate sexual conduct after cancer may also interfere with a couples, sexual relationship. For example, partners who provide a great deal of intimate physical care to the person with cancer (such as helping with toileting or feeding) can experience difficulties in continuing to see them as a sexual person and reposition them as a "patient" or as asexual. Broader cultural constructions of normative sexuality may also be influential in determining the ability of couples to renegotiate sexuality and intimacy after cancer, particularly when sexual intercourse is no longer possible. As Judith Butler (1993) has argued, our understanding of sexual subjectivity is confined within a "heterosexual matrix", within which masculinity and femininity are performed through engagement in normative sexual practices described as the "coital imperative," (with failure to perform coitus positioned as "dysfunction", and other practices referred to as not "real sex". This provides a theoretical framework for understanding why many heterosexual couples who cannot physiologically engage in sexual intercourse after diagnosis and treatment of cancer cease all expression of sexual intimacy. It also suggests that the dynamics and pressures of the caring role, as well as constructions and beliefs about what is acceptable or appropriate sexually after cancer, are worthy of investigation.

CHILDREN EXPERIENCES

Most of our knowledge of children's experiences of a parent who has cancer is limited to two years after diagnosis (Armsden & Lewis, 1994). This distress relates directly to the child's illness-related concerns, as well as to the real and symbolic threats to the child's sense of security (Armsden & Lewis, 1993; Lewis *et al.*, 2000; Lewis, 1999). In a recent study of school-age children, 81 per cent of children whose mothers had early-stage breast cancer feared that she was going to die from the disease (Zahlis, 2001). There is substantial evidence showing that the quality of parenting is affected when a parent has cancer (Shands *et al.*, 2000 and Zahlis and Lewis, 1998). Most evidences for this claim come from studies of children whose parent have breast cancer (Lewis and Darby, 2004 and Compas *et al.*, 1994). Children of mothers with cancer sometimes think of themselves in negative terms compared with children of parents who are not ill. In a seminal study looking both at children whose mothers had breast cancer or diabetes and at children whose mothers were healthy, children of mothers with either cancer or diabetes tended to have lower self-esteem than that children of healthy mothers (Armsden & Lewis, 1994). Multiple studies provide evidence that family members do not know, do not understand, do not focus on, and report not having the skills or confidence to support other family members reacting to cancer in the family. This has been extensively documented in child-rearing families affected by breast cancer (Zahlis, 2001; Shands, *et al.*,

2000; Zahlis & Lewis, 1998) as well as in recent studies involving the spouse–patient dyad. Even when parents with cancer see that the disease distresses a child, parents say they do not know what to say or do. They report feeling excessively consumed by their own feelings of tiredness or sickness and by the struggle with their own illness experience (Zahlis & Lewis, 1998). Approximately 25 per cent of younger children and 15 per cent of adolescents whose mothers had cancer reported that no one, not even family members, helped them cope with the impact of the diagnosis (Issel *et al.*, 1990). No studies have looked at these factors beyond the acute phase.

The demands of cancer and treatment can make it difficult to take care of young children. Adult children may be available to act as a caregiver for a parent with cancer, but this role reversal can be difficult for both parents and children. Even for adult children, the fear of a parent dying can be enormous. Younger children may become overly clingy, impulsive, or want to stay home all the time. Older children or teenagers may be angry or distant and withdraw from family activities. Changes to their schedule or changes to the parent's appearance, such as hair or weight loss, might be more frightening if they are unexpected. To deal with these, assessing child's age and providing truthful, accurate and understandable information without overwhelming them with facts, is of great help as miscommunication will not only turn them hostile but also alienates them and invites unnecessary misunderstandings particularly among young ones who are best listeners, but worst interpreters. Verbal reassurance of parent's love and security to them even after getting ill avert such misinterpretations.

COMMON RELATIONSHIP ISSUES

Navigating relationships is a challenge for cancer survivors transitioning to life after treatment. Recognition of some of these common scenarios is important both as a reference to survivors as well as understandings for commoners. Anxiety (a feeling of worry or unease), fear, uncertainty, anger, and sadness are common feelings that patients and families sometimes have when coping with cancer. There are normal responses to the stress of cancer, especially when the cancer is first diagnosed. Changes in the ability to keep up family duties, loss of control over events in life, changes in the way one looks, or simply the shock of a cancer diagnosis might lead to feelings of fear or anxiety. A person could feel uncertain about the future and concerned about suffering, pain, and the unknown. Some people mourn the changes in their bodies, and the loss of the healthy future they may have expected. Fears concerning loss of independence, changes in relationships with loved ones, and becoming a burden to others may overwhelm the patient and complicate family life. Family members may have these feelings because they, too, are uncertain about the future or maybe even angry that their loved one has cancer. Some friends and family members may avoid talking with the patient because they just do not know what to say. Others may avoid talking about cancer for fear of upsetting the person. If the patient feels like talking about cancer, it is good to bring the subject up with his friends and family and let them know that it is okay for them to talk about it. Reassurance that he just wants someone who will listen to him and understand his feelings is healthy indeed. It is also okay to tell people when one just do not want to talk about cancer—sometimes he might just want to have a conversation about another topic or laugh with his friends. These approaches help in opening up an oral forum, spontaneous and sensible enough to help the person at hand.

"Coping" is a popular concept in nursing and behavioural medicine (Manne, 1994 & Wenzel *et al.*, 2002). Although the concept has salience in studies of an individual's adaptation to delimited stressors, its validity in depicting a family's response to long-term survivorship is less clear (Lazarus, 1984; McCubbin & McCubbin,1993). In two studies of families affected by maternal breast cancer, illness-related demands reported by both the patient and spouse–caregiver never significantly predicted family member coping behaviour (Lewis & Hammond, 1996; Lewis *et al.*, 1993). In another study involving 111 families of women with breast cancer, data obtained at three different occasions at four month intervals revealed that family members did not change their coping behaviour, even when the number of illness-related demands changed (Lewis & Hammond, 1992). Furthermore, in analyses over time involving these same households, family members' coping behaviour did not diminish the illness-related pressures over time (Manne, 1994). If family members are not coping with the illness-related demands, with what are they coping, if anything? There is evidence that family members attempt to manage tension in the family system, especially heightened tension in the patient-spouse dyad, accentuated or caused by the cancer (Lewis & Hammond, 1996; Lewis *et al.*, 1993; Lewis &

Hammond, 1992). However, there are no known studies of coping behaviour in families with long-term survivors. It keeps away isolation, negative waves and put in an informal platform that facilitates bipolar communication and reinforces one's identity as a strong sociable personality, which in turn helps in discovering lost autonomy and self-control. Letting people know about physical limitations is also vital as one might burnout from overwhelming and all encompassing expectations.

NUTRITION ISSUES AMONG CHILDREN WITH CANCER

Nutritional status affects the prognosis for children and young people with cancer (Andreyev *et al.*, 1998; Cunningham and Bell, 2000). Those who are well nourished are also better able to resist infection and tolerate treatment (Den Broeder *et al.*, 2000). Adequate nutrition must be sufficient to allow children and young people to maintain their body functions, engage in play and other activities, recover from trauma and illness and continue to grow and develop (Bryant, 2003; RCN, 2006).

It is important that decisions regarding nutrition should involve the child or young person who has cancer and their family, and should take into consideration the child's particular needs. Patients and their families should be given full information about the foods and supplements the patient is receiving and their own role in providing the right nutrition. They should have the opportunity to discuss any issues and be given contact details for further advice (NICE, 2006).

Children in hospital having treatment for cancer have particular dietary needs, and may have issues with eating. The combination of extended duration of treatment, high frequency of admission and prolonged length of stay may impact more severely on this group of children than most others. It is important that as a health professional, you are aware of the predisposing issues which can lead to inadequate nutrition. Understanding these can help you alleviate some of the predisposing factors, and prompt recognition and treatment may help prevent nutrition becoming a problem for some patients.

Children may present with poor nutritional status at diagnosis, but their nutrition may also be impaired as a consequence of treatment. Patients often experience a lack of appetite which can be exacerbated by nausea and vomiting, mucositis, stomatitis, taste changes, constipation, diarrhoea, pain, fatigue and metabolic abnormalities

(Hockenberry, 2004; Skolin *et al.*, 2006). The emotional impact of diagnosis and treatment may also result in psychological factors such as depression, fatigue or anxiety which can interfere with dietary intake (Capra *et al.*, 2001).

Early recognition of children with cachexia is essential, as prompt assessment and aggressive management is thought to improve nutrition and subsequent prognosis. Cachexia is a syndrome of progressive wasting associated with anorexia and metabolic alterations (Capra *et al.*, 2001). It is thought to result from an imbalance between the energy needed by the body *versus* the energy available due to reduced intake, alongside biochemical alterations (Nitenberg and Raynard, 2000).

Children with cancer face many difficulties with nutrition. It is crucial for hospital environments to respond to these particular needs—not only because they are obliged to, but because of the huge negative impact on the child and family that poor food provision can have. It is vital that hospitals and other health care environments provide education in nutrition to all health care professionals involved in patient care. Education should be relevant to a professional's post, and should be regularly reviewed and updated. Nutrition education should cover: the importance of providing adequate nutrition, including benefits of good nutrition and risk of malnutrition; nutritional needs and indications for support options available for nutritional support; how professionals can obtain further help (NICE, 2006). In addition, it is important that accurate weighing and measuring of children and young people should be covered.

The most common method of food provision in hospital wards is through a trolley service, providing a range of cooked food or cook-chill food delivered to the ward at set times, and served by housekeepers/nursing staff within a short meal time period. This system has a number of inherent problems: limited time for children to eat; food is not freshly cooked; food choice may be limited and repetitive; smells from the food trolley can be off-putting; food can look unappetising.

Children with cancer can experience greater problems, because their treatments and investigations are often ongoing at meal times; chemotherapy can induce frequent bouts of nausea; the times when a child feels able to eat do not always coincide with the arrival of the food trolley; those on chemotherapy sometimes report taste changes and request strongly-flavoured food; those taking steroids have an increased appetite or cravings for particular foods at unusual times; they are often in hospital for extended periods—children who are admitted for long periods frequently develop an aversion to the food trolley and refuse to eat from it. Parents, carers and guardians who are desperate for their child to eat cope with these problems by bringing in food from home or spending money at hospital food outlets.

Nutritional screening is essential to identify patients who are already malnourished or at risk of becoming so (NICE, 2006). It should be the responsibility of all professionals involved in the care of children and young people. Dissemination of nutrition information should include: the importance of maintaining the child's nutritional status during treatment; potential side effects of treatment that may interfere with an adequate oral intake; practical advice on nutritional problems associated with cancer and its treatment/referral to dietician; advice on the use of high calorie/energy dense foods if patient has poor appetite and/or poor weight gain; the variety of nutritional support methods available and when they would be recommended; general food safety guidelines.

There is no nutrition screening tool for children and young people that has been specifically assessed for use in oncology. A useful tool that is quick and easy to complete is more likely to be used by all professionals and benefit the patient. The feasibility of one such tool has recently been successfully investigated in the Netherlands (Hulst *et al.*, 2009). The preferred method of administering parenteral nutrition is *via* a central venous access device. This allows the use of more concentrated solutions to maximise a patient's nutritional intake, particularly when fluid for parenteral nutrition is limited due to large drug volumes, or blood and platelet transfusions (Han-Markey, 2000). There are risks associated with parenteral nutrition, including fluid overload and metabolic, vascular and septic episodes, so monitoring is important (Glynn, 2001; Koletzko *et al.*, 2005).

There is controversy about whether or not patients should be given vitamin supplements. Some authors suggest supplements are needed to compensate for the reduction in antioxidant status as a result of a tumour or treatment, and that supplements help to reduce the side effects of treatment. However, giving antioxidants during chemotherapy may interfere with the normal action of the chemotherapy drugs on the tumour, reducing their efficacy, or may interfere with the rate at which the drugs are able to work (Labriola and Livingstone, 1999; Lawenda *et al.*, 2008).

There are few studies looking at vitamin status and the use of vitamin supplements in children undergoing treatment for cancer and some of these studies only involved a small number of patients (Kokkonen *et al.*, 2002; Kennedy *et al.*, 2004, Dagdemir *et al.*, 2004; Kennedy *et al.*, 2005; Mazor *et al.*, 2008). More research is required.

THE EXTENT OF ISOLATION AMONG CANCER PATIENTS

One in four of the 3,25,000 people diagnosed with cancer in the UK each year (Facing the Fight Alone, 2013) could lack the support of family or friends during their treatment and recovery, according to a MacMillan Cancer Support Survey of people living with cancer. One in 14 people (7%) diagnosed with cancer—representing around 20,000 people in the UK each year—receive no help whatsoever, facing cancer completely alone. A further one in six (16%) only have support some of the time or occasionally. Over 90 per cent of healthcare professionals have treated cancer patients who do not have any support at all from family or friends. More than half (60%) have seen patients in this situation in the past month. For some cancer survivors, the isolation goes beyond their initial treatment and recovery. One in six people (17%) who were diagnosed with cancer more than 10 years ago have not been visited at home by a friend or family member for at least six months.

The majority of people who lacked support during their treatment and recovery told all or most of their family and friends about their diagnosis. Just 6 per cent did not tell any friends or family. Three in five say the reason they lacked support is because their family and friends were too busy to help or lived too far away. One in four says they did not want any support from family or friends in the first place. Some people may prefer to deal with their cancer in isolation—two in five of those who did not ask anyone else for help say they wanted to handle things on their own. However, just as many did not know where to turn, thought that there was no-one who could help them or felt too tired or ill to do anything.

A third of healthcare professionals do not always ask if a patient has support from family or friends; this increases to almost half of GPs. Around one in six people who lack support say they lost contact with family and friends as a result of their diagnosis. The same number has been unable to look after their children or grandchildren because of a lack of support. Worryingly, the financial cost of cancer makes isolation worse—four in five cancer patients who lack support say they can no afford to see their family or friends as much as they did before they were diagnosed.

Overall, women are more likely to be isolated than men. Almost three quarters of men with cancer say they are fully supported during their treatment and recovery, compared with only just over half of women. Women are twice as likely as men to say that a lack of support has left them feeling isolated, lonely or abandoned. However, slightly more men than women are completely isolated. Men are also more likely than women to be told they have cancer without having any family or friends with them—only one in five men have a loved one present when they hear their diagnosis, compared with almost two in five women. Almost half of women who received their diagnosis alone would have preferred to have someone with them, compared with just 15 per cent of men. Of people who lack support, women are more likely than men to say they would have found more support helpful—77 per cent of women would have preferred more support from family, compared with 60 per cent of men, and 79 per cent would have preferred more support from friends, compared with 55 per cent of men.

People with cancer aged between 35 and 55 are least likely to have support at all times—fewer than half (48%) say they are fully supported during their treatment and recovery, compared with two-thirds (66%) of those aged 55 or over. Compared with those in higher socioe-conomic groups, people in lower socio-economic groups have slightly lower overall levels of support, are more likely to feel stressed or anxious because of a lack of support and are more likely to have not been in touch with their family and friends before their diagnosis.

More than half of isolated cancer patients have skipped meals or not eaten properly because of a lack of support at home, with one in three often or sometimes not getting enough to eat. Among women, this rises to almost one in two. Four per cent are concerned they are malnourished because of a lack of support, and three-quarters have cut back on what they spend on food. One in four of those experiencing isolation are not always able to wash themselves properly, and three in five have been unable to do household jobs such as cleaning.

One in four say they have not been able to exercise because of a lack of support; among women, this rises to one in three. A third

(33%) say a lack of support has caused them stress or anxiety, and more than one in four (28%) say they have experienced depression. Isolation also makes it harder for people to self-manage their medical care. One in ten (11%) isolated people living with cancer have missed a hospital or GP appointment because of a lack of support, with women affected more than men. More than one in six (18%) have been unable to collect a prescription for their medication; among women this rises to one in four (24%).

Almost half (49%) of healthcare professionals say isolated cancer patients really struggle to get to and from hospital—more than four times as many that think non-isolated patients really struggle with this (12%). In addition, more than half of healthcare professionals: have seen patients who decided to skip treatment altogether because they have no support from family or friends; say isolated patients make poorer treatment decisions. Over 90 per cent of healthcare professionals have patients who they think struggle with the emotional impact of cancer because of a lack of support, with almost a third (30%) saying this is often the case. Some cancer patients are even forced to take risks with their personal safety because of a lack of support.

Thus, isolation is having a real, negative impact on people's health: patients are skipping meals, missing medical appointments and even deciding to reject treatment altogether and let their cancer run its course—all because of a lack of support. We know that many people go the extra mile to support a family member or friend who has cancer.

To improve the outlook for people diagnosed with cancer who lack support, following recommendations can be put into examination:

- *For people affected by cancer who lack support*: Recognition that isolation can have a real, negative impact on health and well-being; Awareness that there are alternative sources of support available, such as other registered cancer charities and social services; Speaking to the healthcare professionals involved with care to make sure they acknowledge lack of support and direct them to alternative sources of support; If not offered an alternative source of support, asking healthcare team what's available.
- *For family and friends of those affected by cancer*: Awareness that talking to someone about cancer or treatment is unlikely

to increase their distress; Making use of resources that can help one talk to loved ones affected by cancer; If one still find it too hard to talk to someone about their cancer, consideration of starting with practical ways that one could help them instead.

- *For healthcare professionals treating people with cancer*: Recognizing the fact that isolation can have a real, negative impact on patients' health and well-being and how they engage with their treatment; Always asking patients if they have support from family or friends; Making allowances for patients who lack support wherever possible; Being aware of all the alternative support available for isolated patients and make full use of these services wherever possible.

FAMILY CAREGIVERS

Family caregivers are those family members who are directly involved in the patient's cancer care. Family members are involved in a variety of care activities and often take responsibility for symptom management, equipment management, transportation, and the provision of emotional and social support. Family caregivers assume this role while simultaneously maintaining their own work, family, and other responsibilities. Cancer and cancer-related treatment may alter family functioning, family communication patterns, family member occupational roles, and social roles. Family members often assume the patient's previously held roles while coping with their own emotional responses to the patient's diagnosis and the uncertainty of the future. Decades of research have clearly demonstrated that assuming the role of caregiver can lead to feelings of overload, distress, and disagreement about goals of care, particularly when there is a lack of support from the health care team. Caregivers require support, coordination, and communication with health care providers if they are to be successful in carrying out the tasks of care.

Core functions of the family include maintaining an emotionally and physically safe environment, interpreting and reducing the threat of stressful events (including the cancer) for family members, and nurturing and fostering the development of individual family members. These functions include an attentive parenting environment for children and the provision of information and support to children when their sense of security or well-being is threatened (Harden, Schafenacker, Northouse *et al.*, 2002). Studies involving families experiencing both recently diagnosed and long-term breast cancer diagnoses provide evidence that these core functions are threatened when a member has cancer (Dorval, Guay, Mondor, Masse, Falardeau, Robidoux, Deschenes and Maunsell, 2005). Mothers of school-age or adolescent children report that they are unable, especially during the treatment phase of cancer, to be the parent that they want to be and that they know they should be (Schover, 2005). Spouses report that they do not know what to do to support their wives, and they struggle with what to say and how to help. Children report not wanting to talk about their cancer related worries, questions, or concerns for fear they will further burden the ill parent (Zahlis, 2001).

Family members are seldom prepared to be caregivers, and there is often little time for preplanning. They become caregivers immediately at the point of diagnosis and continue in this role over the disease, treatment, and survivorship trajectory. When a patient is diagnosed with cancer, family members often assume responsibility for providing care. They are typically involved not only with the diagnostic and treatment phases of care, but also across the care trajectory and into survivorship. These caregivers are a primary source of support to individuals with cancer.

Family caregivers over the course of the cancer treatment trajectory may reflect on what support the professionals can provide. Caregivers require support, coordination, and communication with health care providers if they are to be successful in carrying out tasks of care. Concern for caregivers as partners in patient care and caregiver outcomes deserves attention from health care professionals. Considering the caregivers' value to the health care team, this role should not be underestimated. From the point of diagnosis, caregivers have reported a lack of clear expectations and limited information from oncology professionals about what care is needed and expected. Direct care demands may include areas such as physical care, nutrition, spiritual support, symptom management, housekeeping, transportation, and financial support. Care can also include activities such as wound care, management of infusion pumps, and catheter care. Caregivers become vital cancer care team members in coordinating treatment and physician and laboratory appointments. Caregivers serve as a conduit for information from the patient to the provider and from the provider to the patient to keep the patient's plan of care intact. Among the variety of roles that caregivers assume, however, symptom and medication management are often the most commonly cited by caregivers. Patients experience multiple symptoms of varying severity, including pain, insomnia, nausea, vomiting, fatigue, diarrhea, constipation, shortness of breath, peripheral neuropathy, and anorexia. Symptom management, either from the cancer or from side effects of treatment, becomes an important caregiver activity. Medication management for pain and other symptom control may be particularly burdensome for family caregivers due to the complexity of symptom-management regimens, lack of information regarding "acceptable" symptom severity, and communication strategies with the health care team. For the caregivers, the severity of the patient's functional impairment and disability has been consistently shown to increase care demands and restrict other roles. Caregivers report work related challenges that require adaptation of their employment obligations to manage and meet care demands. This may result in missed days, work interruptions, leaves of absence, and reduced productivity.

The family caregiver assessment is the key component to identify caregivers' areas of needs so that they can obtain strategies and interventions that will aid the patient during and after active treatment. Professionals must consider their approach to the family based on the caregiver's level of knowledge and skills, and should tailor their interventions to those needs. Professionals need to be aware of family disagreements on care goals. Family members often use the Web as a source of information; thus, professionals should know which sites are credible and make recommendations of those preferred sites to the family members. Oncology professionals need to review Web sites regularly to ensure that accurate and up-to-date information is being presented. This augments the resources of the professional and is a ready resource for the caregiver. Web-based resources have the potential to promote problem solving, to provide advice and guidance, and to be an ongoing resource for care. Professionals need to use regular, thorough assessments as a way to determine need so that recommendations can include resources that caregivers would find beneficial. The duration, intensity, and depth of care provided by family members and the impact on patient outcomes are under recognized as important components of caring for a cancer patient. Caregivers as partners in patient care and caregiver outcomes deserve careful attention. Professionals are challenged to recognize the value of early and continued involvement of family members as care partners. Family plans of care, rather than a patient-only plan of care, also need to be considered. Caregivers are the first responders to cancer patients' problems—considering their value to the health care team, the role of the caregiver should not be underestimated.

Regarding decision on ongoing-treatment, in my doctoral work on 110 cancer patients from Cancer Centre Welfare Home and Research Institute, Thakurpukur, Kolkata, I have found, that majority of patients (56.36%) decisions are taken by family members with no involvement of patient whatsoever. Only 18.18 per cent patients responded decisions about treatment are taken jointly. In case of priority towards decision making in the family after the disease, 66.66 per cent of the males have been seen to be enjoying such decisions whereas a meager 19.71 per cent of females enjoy such decisions after their disease. Regarding neighbour's role I have seen that 13.63 per cent neighbour provided unexpected help whereas 0.9 per cent provided economic support and 19.10 per cent have caring attitude, but a majority of the 62.19 per cent neighbours either provided no support or have discontinued relation as they thought the disease as contagious. (*My thesis is entitled 'Health Hazards and Care of Cancer Patients: A Sociological Analysis' under the guidance of Prof. Ruby Sain, Department of Sociology, Jadavpur University, 2005.*)

Family caregivers play a crucial role in home care and commonly undertake complex care tasks, including assessment and management of symptoms, hygiene care, and administration of medications. (Barg, Pasacreta, Nuamah, Robinson, Angeletti, Yasko & McCorkle, R. 1998). Family caregivers not only assist in care alongside providers of palliative care services, but also provide the bulk of support within the home (Barg, Pasacreta, Nuamah, Robinson, Angeletti, Yasko & McCorkle, 1998). Without the input of family caregivers, the well-being of the majority of individuals with a life-threatening illness would be compromised.

HOW COUNSELLING HELPS PATIENTS

A lot of people have the view that psychologists and psychiatrists are not too far from being witch doctors. They do not understand what counsellors actually do. The job of the counsellor is not to solve patient problems. Instead, talking to counsellors may suggest directions that cancer patients can explore to find their own way through difficulties.

The greatest benefit of psycho-social care is that patients and families may experience a significant improvement in quality of life. The word "psycho-social" may seem intimidating, but it may help to break down what it means. The root of "psycho" means relating to the mind or the psyche, and the "social" part is about the relationships people have with family and with society. "Oncology" means the branch of medicine that deals with cancer. In other words, "psychosocial oncology" is a speciality in cancer care concerned with understanding and treating the social, psychological, emotional, spiritual, quality-of-life and functional aspects of cancer, from prevention through bereavement. It is a whole-person approach to cancer care that addresses a range of very human needs that can improve quality of life for people affected by cancer. Without emotional support, people can struggle unguided with issues of their own mortality, with complex questions about quality and quantity of life, and with the burden of coping with treatments and suffering, both physical and emotional. Through counselling, one may be better equipped to enjoy a fulfilling and productive life (Decker & Young, 1991).

The experience of cancer can have the effect of putting a magnifying glass over one's life: it tends to bring out the good, amplifying the strong supportive bonds with friends and family. However, the impact of the illness can also exaggerate the difficulties of everyday life, related, for instance, to marital problems or to family communication issues. These may add to the considerable anxiety of living with the cancer itself. Patients who receive emotional support are better equipped to cope with the relationship problems and the fear, depression and anxiety that are a normal part of dealing with cancer (Canadian Association of Psychosocial Oncology, 2012). Counselling can help to ease tensions within the family, and help with the complicated task of getting financial aid, making it easier for the person to get on with the important job of coping with the disease and its treatment. For many people, one of the greatest benefits of counselling is that it is an opportunity to have their problems given individual attention. Counsellors have a deep sensitivity to the fact that the life of every person with cancer is unique. Counselling work is about tailoring an individualized approach to each situation. Many family members consider one of counselling's biggest advantages the fact that they can express pent-up feelings and emotions which are often tightly under control when they are with the patient or other family members. Often, families and caregivers feel helpless when faced with the serious illness of a loved one. Counsellors recognize that care for the caregiver is integral to the care of the patient. Often caregivers need emotional support and counselling to be effective in their changing roles. Taking on the role of caregiver introduces a range of challenges, which have to do with self-management, sexuality, role changes, physical exhaustion, and emotional distress. Often the spouse or partner experiences higher levels of distress than the patient, yet may not feel entitled to these feelings. It is important to acknowledge that caregivers and family have very different stresses and needs than patients. While the person with cancer must focus on getting well and is the focus of attention, the caregiver must deal with everything and bear the burden of both the emotional and practical disruption.

Counsellors do much of their work one-on-one with patients, but they also work with families. Some departments offer group counselling, or peer support groups led by a trained professional. Dieticians who will customize a nutrition plan to your individual needs may also work as part of the counselling team. Advanced practice nurses with specialized knowledge and skill related to cancer also provide counselling. The counsellors in settings where cancer treatments are given are required to have specific psycho-social oncology training. Counsellors understand the physical and biological aspects of cancer treatment, and their specific impact on your overall well-being. Professional support helps to overcome these feelings of helplessness, to give strategies to cope with feelings, and a realistic idea about what can and cannot be done in any given situation. Often families and caregivers want to be very positive, caring and upbeat. This can place further strain on the family, as it allows no room for the sadness that is a very real part of everyone's experience of cancer. Family members and caregivers often react to their own distress by trying to be proactive; however, if their ideas do not mesh with wishes of the patient this can be a source of tension. The lack of meaningful communication can leave the patient feeling misunderstood and the family member feeling unappreciated and isolated. Counselling can be useful to work out some of these issues and ease family tensions, and play a very important role in aiding communication between patient, caregiver and family.

The fundamental aim of palliative care is to achieve the best quality of life possible for dying patients and their families (*Palliative Care Australia*, 2000b; WHO, 1990). Holistic support for the patient and family underpins the philosophy of palliative care (Willard, 1999). Both patient and family should be recognized as the "unit of care" (*Palliative Care Australia*, 1998). From a sociological perspective, life-threatening illness may affect family roles and relationships (Willard, 1999). Therefore, involving the family unit as well as the patient in delivery of care is recommended.

If we are to speed the translation of cancer research discoveries into new treatments, it is essential that all stakeholders work together to overcome the obstacles that discourage people from participating in clinical research studies. These obstacles may include a lack of information about the clinical research process, lack of awareness of studies for which patients are eligible, concerns about adverse side effects, the cost and quality of care, and a mistrust of the research establishment. Logistical challenges such as lack of transportation to and from distant trial sites may also make it difficult for otherwise willing volunteers to participate. To overcome these obstacles it will be important to improve outreach to patients, researchers, health care providers, policy-makers, and the general public with the goal of providing accurate information about the clinical research process and the value of public participation in research. These groups must also work together to identify and implement solutions to the barriers that hamper research participation. Promising research findings are relevant only when they reach the people they are designed to serve. Key scientific advances must be applied and evaluated, reflected in state and local health policies, and widely adopted as community practices across the country. We must:

- Support community-based prevention research to identify the causes of health inequities and the best ways to provide resources needed for health and access to high-quality preventive care and clinical services.
- Accelerate the translation of scientific findings into community and school practices to protect the health of people where they live, work, learn, and play.
- Apply scientific approaches to social marketing, health education, and consumer research in the design of effective communication strategies to inform and influence individual and community decisions on health.

Risk assessments of the caregiver's capacity and willingness to care, as well as of the patient care situation, are vital to provide information on resources needed for care. Congruence on the situation and care goals between the elements of the dyad is also important. The assessment should address major areas of functioning including work, social, and family functioning and should identify any practical problems stemming from patient care demands (e.g., symptoms, finances, household tasks, transportation, physical function, arranging appointments, and managing equipment) that increase caregivers' distress. Overall areas to be included in a comprehensive assessment include relationships between members of the dyad; necessary role changes; information about diagnosis and treatment; caregiver and care recipient expectations; care coordination; and projected hours of care.

Reassessment of the care situation should be conducted regularly and at all care transition points such as at the end of active treatment, when treatment fails, at recurrence, with disease progression, or when end-of-life care is needed. New approaches, new knowledge, new skills, and new or different demands will be needed at each transition point; reassessments of caregivers will produce benefits to patients and their caregivers, and have the potential to decrease unscheduled contacts with the oncology health team.

CONCLUSIONS AND SUGGESTIONS

Most family caregivers of dying cancer patients report that their role is physically and emotionally demanding and that they require additional support and information from health professionals. There is a consistent request for support-focused family caregiver interventions from caregivers and researchers, supported by appeals from health care organizations. However, few supportive palliative-stage family interventions have been conducted, not to mention rigorously evaluated. It appears that psycho-educational approaches directed toward, individual primary family caregivers, rather than groups, may be worth pursuing. New interventions should be evaluated over time and, ideally, by way of randomized controlled trials. Unless new evidence-based supportive strategies for families are realized, there is a real danger that health care professionals will not be meeting the core elements of family centred delivery of palliative care. Therefore, there is an urgent need for new strategies to be designed and tested; otherwise the principle of the family as the unit of care will not be upheld.

Expanding our understanding of quality of life and the factors that contribute to it should help subsequent investigations of who might benefit from which psychosocial support interventions. Knowledge about the determinants of psychosocial functioning and behavioural outcomes is needed as a basis for the development of appropriate supportive and potentially preventive interventions throughout a continuum of care, from diagnosis through treatment and over the long-term. We need a fuller, more comprehensive understanding of what contributes to long-term survivors' positive adaptation. Equipped with this understanding family members along with health care professionals, programme Planners and policy-makers can re-develop and create appropriate services and systems that facilitate and enhance quality of life.

Since much of the care-giving research remains descriptive, there are many gaps in the evidence-based research to promote patient safety and quality care for caregivers as secondary patients and caregivers as providers to vulnerable patients. To advance our knowledge in this field, we recommend several strategies for future research. Because care-giving is a day-in, day-out role that fluctuates as the needs of the care recipient change, it is not well understood through cross-sectional research designs. It is essential that descriptive and longitudinal designs be employed to follow the care requirements over the course of the illness trajectory. A special focus on safety, risk for negative outcomes, and adverse effects for both the caregiver and care recipient should be noted. Key variables to include in these studies are the type and stage of the disease and the treatments because they will be related to the types of continuing therapy. These various therapies will be related to the needs of the patient and assistance with self-care, as well as the patient's ability to perform other customary daily activities. We need to investigate the interplay between the formal and informal systems of care for the ongoing needs of patients as well as caregivers. More research needs to be conducted that focuses on how family influences care-related decisions and the impact to clinically significant processes of care and/or client outcomes. Interventions must recognize professional or formal caregivers and family caregivers as partners in health care—partners who offer unique and vital skills and resources—and engage them in the entire plan of care. Such interventions are critical as we increase the focus on outcomes of care and as providers are paid for outcomes performance. Family members as partners are critical.

Policy and environmental changes can affect large segments of the population simultaneously. Adopting healthy behaviours is much easier if we establish supportive community norms and adopt a philosophy that embraces health in all policies and settings. We must promote proven social, environmental, policy, and systems approaches that support healthy living for individuals, families, and communities.

REFERENCES

Andreyev, H.J.N., Norman, A.R. Oates J. and Cunningham, D. (1998), "Why do patients with weight loss have a worse outcome when undergoing chemotherapy for gastrointestinal malignancies?" *European Journal of Cancer*, 34 (4): 503-509.

Armsden, G.C., Lewis, F.M. (1993), "The child's adaptation to parental medical illness: theory and clinical implications." *Patient Educ Couns*, 22(3):153-65.

Armsden, G.C., Lewis, F.M. (1994), "Behavioural adjustment and self-esteem of school-age children of women with breast cancer." *Oncol. Nurs. Forum*; 21(1):39-45.

Baider, L., De-Nour, A.K. (1984), "Couples' reactions and adjustment to mastectomy: a preliminary report". *Int. J. Psychiatry Med.,* 14(3):265-76.

Barg, F., Pasacreta, J., Nuamah, I., Robinson, K., Angeletti, K., Yasko, J., & McCorkle, R. (1998), "A description of a psychoeducational intervention for family caregivers of cancer patients." *Journal of Family Nursing*, 44: 394-413.

Bergmark, K., Lundqvist, E., Dickman, P.W., Henningsohn, L., and Steineck, G. (1999), "Vaginal Changes and Sexuality in Women with a History of Cervical Cancer". *N. Engl. J. Med.*, 340(18):1383-89.

Bryant, R. (2003), "Managing side effects of childhood cancer treatment", *Journal of Pediatric Nursing*, 18 (2): 113-125.

Butler, J. (1993). *Bodies That Matter: On the Discursive Limits of Sex*. New York: Routledge.

Capra, S., Ferguson, M. and Ried, K. (2001), "Cancer: Impact of nutrition intervention outcome—nutrition issues for patients", *Nutrition*, 17 (9): 769-772.

Compas, B.E., *et al.*, (1994), "When mom or dad has cancer: markers of psychological distress in cancer patients, spouses, and children." *Health Psychol.*, 13(6):507-15.

Cunningham, R.S. and Bell, R. (2000), "Nutrition in cancer: an overview", *Seminars in Oncology Nursing,* 16 (2): 90-98.

Decker, S., and Young, E. (1991), "Self-perceived needs of primary caregivers of home-hospice clients." *Journal of Community Health Nursing*, *8*: 147-154.

Den Broeder, E., Lippins, R.J.J., van't Hof M., Tolboom, J.J., Sengers, R.C. and Staveren, W.A. (2000), "Association between the change in nutritional status in response to tube feeding and the occurrence of infections in children with solid tumour", *Pediatric Hematology Oncology*, 17(7): 567-575.

Dorval, M., Guay, S., Mondor, M., Masse, B., Falardeau, M., Robidoux, A., Deschenes, L., and Maunsell, E. (2005), "Couples Who Get Closer After Breast Cancer: Frequency and Predictors in a Prospective Investigation." *J. Clin.Oncol.*23(15):3588-96.

Fobair, P., Stewart, S.L., Chang, S., D'Onofrio, C., Banks, P.J., and Bloom, J.R. (2006), "Body Image and Sexual Problems in Young Women with Breast Cancer." *Psycho-Oncology*, 15(7):579-94.

GLOBOCAN (2012), "Estimated Cancer Incidence, Mortality and Prevalence Worldwide in 2012", Retrieved from: http://globocan.iarc.fr/Pages/fact_sheets_cancer.aspx, IARC-2014.

Glynn R. (2001), "Parenteral nutrition", in Shaw V. and Lawson M. *Clinical Paediatric Dietetics* (2nd edition), Oxford: Blackwell Science, pp. 43-52.

Gotay, C.C. (1984), "The experience of cancer during early and advanced stages: the views of patients and their mates". *Soc. Sci. Med.*, 18(7):605-13.

Han-Markey T. (2000). "Nutritional considerations in pediatric oncology", *Seminars in Oncology Nursing*, 16 (2): 146-151.

Harden J., Schafenacker A., Northouse L, *et al.* (2002), "Couples' experiences with prostate cancer: focus group research." *Oncol. Nurs. Forum.*, 29(4):701-709.

Hockenberry, M. (2004) "Symptom management research in children with cancer", *Journal of Pediatric Oncology Nursing*, 21 (3):132-136.

Hoskins, C.N., *et al.* (1996), "Adjustment among husbands of women with breast cancer". *Journal of Psychosocial Oncology*, 14(1):41-69.

Hoskins, C.N. (1995), "Adjustment to breast cancer in couples". *Psychol. Rep.*, 77(2):435-54.

Hulst, J.M., Zwart, H. and Joosten, K.F. (2009) "Dutch national survey to test the STRONG (kids) nutritional risk screening tool in hospitalized children", *Clinical Nutrition*, August 12.

Issel, L.M., *et al.* (1990), "How children cope with mother's breast cancer." *Oncol. Nurs. Forum,* 17(3 Suppl): 5-12.

Joly, F., Heron, J.F., Kalusinski, L., Bottet, P., Brune, D., Allouache, N., Mace-Lesec'h, J., Couette, J.E., Peny, J., and Henry-Amar, M. (2002), "Quality of Life in Long-Term Survivors of Testicular Cancer: a Population-Based Case-Control Study." *J. Clin.Oncol.*, 20(1):73-80.

Koletzko, B., Goulet, O., Hunt, J., Krohn, K., Shamir, R., "Parenteral Nutrition Guidelines Working Group, European Society for Clinical Nutrition and Metabolism, European Society of Paediatric Gastroenterology, Hepatology and Nutrition (ESPGHAN), European Society of Paediatric Research (ESPR) (2005), Guidelines on paediatric parenteral nutrition of the European Society of Paediatric Gastroenterology, Hepatology and Nutrition (ESPGHAN) and the European Society for Clinical Nutrition and

Metabolism (ESPEN), "supported by the European Society of Paediatric Research (ESPR), *Journal of Paediatric Gastroenterology and Nutrition*, 41 (supp. 2): S1-S87.

Labriola, D. and Livingstone, R. (1999), "Possible interactions between dietary antioxidants and chemotherapy", *Oncology*, 13 (7): 1003-1008.

Lawenda, B., Kelly, K., Ladas, E., Sagar, S.M., Vickers, A. and Blumberg, J.B. (2008), "Should supplemental antioxidant administration be avoided during chemotherapy and radiation therapy?" *Journal of the National Cancer Institute*, 100 (11): 773-783.

Lazarus, R.S., (1984), Folkman S. *Stress, Appraisal, and Coping.* " New York: Springer Publishing Co.

Lewis, F.M., Darby, E.L. (2004), "Adolescent adjustment and maternal breast cancer: a test of the 'faucet hypothesis.'" *Journal of Psychosocial Oncology*, 21(4):81-104.

Lewis, F.M., *et al.* (1993), "The family's functioning with newly diagnosed breast cancer in the mother: the development of an explanatory model." *J. Behav. Med.*, 16(4): 351-70.

Lewis, F.M., *et al.* (2000), "Blowing away the myths about the child's experience with the mother's breast cancer." In: Baider, L., *et al.*, editors. *Cancer and the Family*". 2nd ed., New York: Wiley; pp. 201-21.

Lewis, F.M., Hammond, M.A. (1992), "Psychosocial adjustment of the family to breast cancer: a longitudinal analysis." *J. Am. Med., Womens Assoc.*, 47(5):194-200.

Lewis, F.M., Hammond, M.A. (1996), "The father's, mother's, and adolescent's functioning with breast cancer." *Fam. Relat.*, 45 (4):456-65.

Lewis, F.M. (1999), "Family issues in cancer care." In: Miaskowski C., Buchsel P.C., editors. *Oncology Nursing: Assessment and Clinical Care*. St. Louis: Mosby, pp. 319-32.

Lewis, F.M. (2004), "Family-focused oncology nursing research: a healing paradigm for future studies". *Oncol. Nurs. Forum.*, 31(2):288-92.

Manne, S. (1994), "Couples coping with cancer: research issues and recent findings." *J. Clin. Psychol. Med., Settings*, 1(4):317-30.

Maughan, K., Heyman, B., Matthews, M. (2002), "In the shadow of risk. How men cope with a partner's gynaecological cancer." *Int. J. Cancer Stud.*; 39:27-34.

McCubbin, M.A., McCubbin, H.I. (1993), "Families coping with illness: the Resiliency Model of Family Stress, Adjustment, and Adaptation." In: Danielson C.B., *et al.*, editors. *Families, Health and Illness: Perspectives on Coping and Intervention*. St. Louis: Mosby, pp. 21-63.

Monga, M., Alexandrescu, B., Katz, S.E., Stein, M., and Ganiats, T. (2004), "Impact of Infertility on Quality of Life, Marital Adjustment, and Sexual Function." *Urology*, 63(1):126-30.

National Institute for Health and Clinical Excellence (NICE) (2006), *Nutrition Support in Adults*, London: Stationary Office (Clinical guidelines CG32).

Nazareth, I., Lewin, J., and King, M. (2001), "Sexual Dysfunction After Treatment for Testicular Cancer: a Systematic Review". *J. Psychosom. Res.*, 51(6):735-43.

Nitenberg, G. and Raynard, B. (2000) "Nutritional support of the cancer patient: Issues and dilemmas", *Critical Reviews in Oncology/Hematology*, 34 (3): 137-168.

Northouse, L.L., Swain, M.A. (1987), "Adjustment of patients and husbands to the initial impact of breast cancer". *Nurs. Res.*, 36(4):221-25.

Omne-Ponten, M., *et al.* (1993), "Psychosocial adjustment among husbands of women treated for breast cancer; mastectomy vs. breast-conserving surgery". *Eur. J. Cancer*, 29A (10):1393-97.

Ptacek, J.T., *et al.* (1994), "Coping with breast cancer from the perspectives of husbands and wives." *Journal of Psychosocial Oncology*, 12(3):47-72.

Royal College of Nursing (2006), *Malnutrition: What nurses working with children and young people need to know and do*, London: RCN.

Sanders, S., Pedro, L.W., Bantum, E.O., Galbraith, M.E. (2006), "Couples surviving prostate cancer: long-term intimacy needs and concerns following treatment." *Clin. J. Oncol. Nurs.*, 10(4): 503-508.

Schover, L.R. (2005), "Motivation for Parenthood after Cancer: A Review." *J. Natl.Cancer Inst.Monogr,* (34):2-5.

Shands, M.E., *et al.*, (2000). "Mother and child interactions about the mother's breast cancer: an interview study." *Oncol, Nurs., Forum*; 27(1):77-85.

Skolin, I., Wahlin, Y.B., Broman, D., Koivisto Hursti, U.K., Larsson, M.V. and Hernell, O. (2006), "Altered food intake and taste perception in children with cancer after start of chemotherapy: perspectives of children, parents and nurses", *Supportive Care in Cancer*, 14 (4): 369-378.

The Emotional facts of Life with Cancer, Canadian Association of Psychosocial Oncology, (2012), Retrieved from: *capo.ca/docs/bookletREVISED.pdf*

Toseland, R.W., *et al.* (1995), "A problem solving intervention for caregivers of cancer patients." *Soc. Sci. Med.*, 40(4):517-28.

Wellisch, D.K., *et al.* (1978), "Psychosocial aspects of mastectomy: II. the man's perspective." *Am. J. Psychiatry*, 135(5):543-46.

Wenzel. L., *et al.* (2002), "Stress, coping, and health behaviour." In: Glanz. K., *et al.*, editors. "*Health Behaviour and Health Education: Theory, Research, and Practice*". (3rd ed.) San Francisco: Jossey- Bass; pp. 210-39.

Zahlis, E.H., Lewis, F.M. (1998), "The mother's story of the school-age child's experience with the mother's breast cancer." *Journal of Psychosocial Oncology*, 16(2):25-43.

Zahlis (2001), "The child's worries about the mother's breast cancer: sources of distress in school-age children." *Oncol. Nurs. Forum*, 28(6):1019-25.

10

Education and Identity: A Case Study of A Santal Village of West Bengal

Sujata Chakraborty and *Bhola Nath Ghosh*

INTRODUCTION

The term education has got a multi-dimensional approach, whether, it is studied as an aspect for the development of the tribals or that of the non-tribals. Education in the sense of the term, always leads us to think in the context of formal education in the form of schools and educational institutions. But, though these institutions have a very important role to play in the process of socialization of an individual, we at the same time cannot deny the fact of the other informal educational means that are equally responsible for the above mentioned process. This becomes quite vivid when we make an attempt to study the tribal society.

Tribals till date more or less depend on the means of informal education through family, youth dormitories, rituals attached to, rites de passage, etc. An important part of their social education takes place in their youth dormitories. Also, nature and social environment plays an important role in socializing individuals to the society.

The pre-independence era was a period of negligence to their educational formal development. It was only after the independence that Government felt the need to promote the backward areas and for the first time tribal development got its prominence through the Constitutional provisions. But, though lots of plans and programmes have been taken up on the part of the Governmental as well as Non-Governmental Organizations, but ironically no progress or only a meager progress has taken place. Another reason for poor response of tribal children to formal education relate to the denial of schooling in their mother tongue. Economical condition and irrelevance of the modern system of education played an important role in the relative backwardness in the field of education.

Another major aspect of formal education is that the curriculum is such that the tribal children feel alienated and separated from the lot. Therefore, they are not happy to follow the formal educational system meant for the general population. They are thus, passing through a transitional phase whereby, their culture and tradition is in the verge of extinction on the one hand and so-called jobs and other avenues of life on the other. Their struggle for the identity gets expression through various movements, one of which is the 'Ol-Chiki' movement by the Santals.

The Santals of West Bengal are now living in a changed environment, where there is an increasing interaction with the neighbouring non-tribals. The interaction, whether due to economic pressures or an inherent urge for knowledge, the identity of a once self-sustained community, is now at the verge of extinction. Education leads to a complete intellectual growth of an individual in the context of the culture of the community to which he belongs. It further helps in forming a kind of self-realization among the tribals, which gives identification or a sense of belongingness to the group. Therefore, in this regard, my attempt would be to study the impact of education in this community and how far they have been succeeded in utilizing their intellectual development in the long drawn battle for re-establishing the identity.

Language has always played an important role in the identity formation of any community *per se,* as it is one of the most influential medium of communication. The Santal struggle for deciphering the lost script of their language 'Ol-Chiki', is symbolic to their efforts to go back to their roots, an attempt made on their part to revitalize their culture and to discover their lost identity, enriched in traditional customs and rituals. Education among the Santals is usually imparted through the family and the community. Family being the smallest and primary unit of the social organization, education is imparted by association and at some places through the initiation rites and subsequent discipline. The whole procedure of the rituals is such that a Santal is time and again, reminded of his Santal identity. Special care is taken to make the members of the community conscious of their affiliation with the community with the help of the village and inter-village level celebrations, festivals and recitation of their mythology in prose and in verse. But more than this, they are trying to galvanize their cultural moorings with the political requirements. The Ol-Chiki movement has become a symbol of their ethnic drive both in Jharkhand and in West Bengal.

THEORETICAL FRAMEWORK

This chapter has been given a theoretical dimension mainly with Mead (1943) and Tajfel's (1986) Social identity theory. It proposes that we as a member of any community desire to belong to social categories, which gives us a positive social identity; it articulates the conditions under which they are positively differentiated from relevant outgroup. This further helps us to understand why some groups maintain their own language, dialects and non-verbal styles while others lose them and assimilate with the communicative patterns of a more powerful group. Mead gives much emphasis on the group identity than the individual identity.

The broad **objectives** of the study are as follows:

1. To identify the socio-economic status, educational background and level of living of the tribals in the selected village of Jhargram in Midnapur district of West Bengal.
2. To identify the cultural aspects of the Santals of these regions with special emphasis on the tribal languages scripts mainly the 'Ol-Chiki' script, which plays an important role to identity.
3. To examine the role of education as a means of cultural transmission in order to preserve identity.

GAP IN THE RESEARCH

From the above analysis of the contents of various available literatures, it is found that mainly the subjects are related to the Santal lifestyles though they belong to different regions—Mayurbhanj, Santal Pargana or Midnapore. Few books such as that of Troisi (2001), Hembrom (1972) and others have dealt mainly with the religious aspect of the Santals. Some others like Somers have taken a particular entity of their society like headmanship and studied it in a holistic way. Whereas Suchibrata Sen (1984) studied the Santals of Jungle Mahal and the agrarian changes due to the introduction of the permanent settlement in 1793 and Chaturbhuj Sahu (1996) have studied the Santal women from several perspectives only. Only Sitakanta Mahapatra (1986) has studied about the Santal identity but in the context of modernization. N.K. Dasgupta (1963) though have studied about the Santal education, but have only given his opinion in favour of the dominant language as the medium of instruction in the schools mainly attended by the Santal students. In this way, it is evident that no literature has exactly dealt with the fact that literacy or education of an individual actually awakens the consciousness within him and the person realizes his potential value of existence and as such question of identity or search for the root comes to the forefront.

METHODOLOGY

This study is a synchronic study conducted in the Santal village of Kesia in Jhargram in the Midnapur district of West Bengal. Jhargram has been affected directly and indirectly by the identity upsurge of the tribal people. This district is close to Odisha and Bihar borders, where the intensity of the movement is very high. The Santals of these regions have some unique features, which can be determined by the peculiar socio-political conditions of the state such as an extensive urban and industrial life, a heritage of its active participation in the freedom movement, longer tradition of formal education and a prolonged exposure to the leftist politics. Though, there is difference in political ideologies among the Santals in these regions, there is an overall ethnic solidarity and they are trying to maintain its ethnic identity by demanding promotion of literature in Santali with the help of 'Ol-Chiki' script, which have been introduced in few village primary schools of this region. This is very high in West Bengal rather than in Bihar and Odisha.

This is an exploratory and in-depth case of the Santal Village of Kesia. A rapid survey has also been done in another Santal dominated village of Jhargram in order to have an intense understanding of their perception of identity and how they are fighting to re-establish it. The sources of data collection included both primary sources and secondary sources. Main primary sources were individual respondents, community members groups, Government officers (Education) and the secondary sources would be Census Reports, Reports of Government Departments, District Statistical Handbooks, Newspapers and Journals. Methods and tools adopted for data collection include direct observation, participant observation, and canvassing of schedules. Group discussions has also been done. Interview guides has been framed to assist the data collection. Unstructured interview was conducted as the study mainly involves about the opinion and perception of the population. Households were selected randomly covering 25 per cent of the households of the village. Non-probability Sampling method was used for the selection of the respondents.

REVIVALISM OF THE SANTAL SCRIPT

As the script is a device used to record a language, in recent years the identity of a language has been defined not only in terms of it being a mother tongue, but also in terms of whether it has a script. "A language is mother, a script is father" says a tribal leader. The introduction of the 'Ol-Chiki' script for Santali as well as other similar attempts, are part of the effort to define and assert one's identity (Singh, 1995). Santali script is known to be the 'Ol-Chiki' script. This language contains some phonetics, which generally is not used in English, and also neighbouring Indian languages. Santali has, to some extent, been influenced by the neighbouring Aryan languages like Bihari, Bengali in the east and Oriya in the South. Though however, the structure and the general character of the language has remained unchanged. The purest Santali is spoken in the north, especially in the Santal Parganas and in Manbhum.

The meaning of 'Ol-Chiki' is writing symbol or writing script. This script was founded by Pandit Raghunath Murmu. But there is also a lot of controversy amongst the Santals itself on the question of the 'Ol-Chiki' script. Quite a sizeable portion of the population particularly in Bihar and to some extent in West Bengal is in favour of the Roman script for the Santali language. According to Dr. B.B. Hembram, "The Santali language has its own original existence, its own entity. As Bengali language cannot be written in English script and *vice versa*, so is Santali. If it is written then within a short period the Santali language will be phonetically deformed" (Hembram, 1972).

Mahapatra, S. (1986) here argues that the supporters of the script however, do not seem to take into account two other important points. One is that a script for a language needs a communication setting, an environment in which it can be commonly used in social, inter-personal and other situations. Some of the educated Santals of the village opined that the career and jobs require the knowledge of the dominant languages and scripts apart from English. Social communication outside their village also demands the knowledge of the dominant language. These are posing problems in actually spreading of the language amongst the concerned masses. As such many even forget how to write the script. The second factor that the popularity of a script is largely dependent on the popularity and strength of the language and the quantity of available literature in it.

As one of the villagers and also an active participant in the movement Kesab Soren said that textbooks are not printed in the Ol-Chiki script and there is the absence of properly trained teachers who can impart education in the script. Though, books written by Raghunath Murmu in the Ol-Chiki script are published by the influential Santal men and ASECA (Adivasi Socio-Educational and Cultural Association) of Rairangpur in Odisha, Chakulia in Bihar and Bhawanipur (Calcutta) in West Bengal but spreading of the language at the grassroot level is still limited. Kundu, M. points out that the present detribalizing tendency among tribals and the little spread of education among them is mainly due to the fact that no provision has been made to teach them through their mother tongues (M. Kundu,1994). Therefore, one of the demands made by the Jharkhand Movement is recognition of 'Ol-Chiki' by the Central and State Governments. Though, after much effort the Santali language and literature has been recognized by the Central Government and State Government of Bihar, Jharkhand, West Bengal and Odisha. For example, the Government of West Bengal is publishing a Santali magazine "*Puchhim Bangla*" regularly and recognized Ol-Chiki script for Santali in 1979.

These cultural outfits of the Santals have also been vehemently demanding inclusion of Santali language in the Eighth Schedule of the Constitution and its recognition. However, all their demands were not given much importance and the Ol-Chiki movement fell. The question here is that how far this revitalization of script movement helps the concerned community in their long struggle for reassertion of their identity. An important goal of education is to impart the universally recognized moral values to the individual and integrate these with the ethnic-specific eco-centric values, cultural norms, and worldview (Thirumalai, M.S., 2001). When this is not done, a gap between the education system and the society results. This gap is often a result of using a language other than the language of the society as the medium of instruction. The curriculum, syllabus, teaching methodology and content of the lessons contribute to this gap and leads to an increase in the school dropout rate among the minority linguistic and less-privileged communities in India (*Ibid.*, 2001).

In Kolkata, on 2nd June, 1979, West Bengal Government recognized the Ol-Chiki script as an appropriate script for the Santali language. Though such promises were made but we find no initiative is taken by the Government either to implement or to execute such an order and it is only confined to the papers. Though in last few years some of the primary schools in the tribal areas have started to teach through the medium of Santali language and script, but the progress is very slow and sluggish.

Apparently, there is no other way than to organize a huge mass movement against this exploitation. As such the ASECA (Adivasi Socio-Educational and Cultural Association) along with other small and big organizations joined together and formed a strong language movement called Santali Language Morcha. This movement mainly stressed on the education by Santali language and the Ol-Chiki script from the primary to the higher education in West Bengal. Apart from this, it also fought for the inclusion of Santali language in the 8th Schedule of the Constitution and to stop the exploitation and attacks on the Santals.

Therefore, it is quite evident from the above analysis that even after more than 30 years of the recognition of the Ol-Chiki script, the Government has not taken any step to introduce it in any of the primary schools in West Bengal. This issue was even taken to the Lok Sabha and even in State Assembly and a strong demand was made for the inclusion of Santali language in the Eighth Schedule of the Constitution. The recognition by the Constitution is necessary in the interest of national integrity and advancement. Some languages spoken by people who are much less in number than the Santali speaking people, have been included in the Eighth Schedule of the Constitution. Here the question arises, then why not Santali language when it is spoken by such a large number of people. Not only Santali, but no other tribal language has been recognized by the Constitution of India. They hope that if it is recognized by the Constitution then the Government might take steps seriously in introducing the language in schools and colleges.

The reality is that many things remain in paper and does not ever get in touch with the concerned people. Gradually with the course of time, their inherent struggle for the recognition of their script has been given importance by the Government and we find that the 100th Constitutional Amendment Bill included Santali language in the Eighth Schedule of Constitution of India which was passed both by Lok Sabha on 22nd December, 2003 and Rajya Sabha on 23rd December, 2003.

But it is found that this script movement is confined to the educated Santals only. It has yet to take a definite shape. It can be considered here that majority of the Santal people are poor and are much more concerned to have two meals a day. Though they understand the problem, but active participation on their behalf is negligible. As far as the illiterate masses were concerned, the parents realize this problem when they send their children to schools. They opine that knowledge gained in mother tongue makes easier for the children to understand what is taught. They feel interested to study and hence go to the school. So, we find that though these illiterate parents are not actively involved in this movement, but are conscious and support Santali language as a medium of instruction. Also we can rationalize this fact on the basis that the educated people have confidence and can make their voice heard and lay their opinion strongly before the opponent party. Therefore, leadership or initiative on their part to start a movement is natural.

The medium of instruction for the education of the Santal children has been a controversial issue for a long time. Though, the Santal children of West Bengal are bilingual, but they are found comfortable when the instruction is given in their mother tongue in the class. When some of the children of the primary school of the village were asked about their preference regarding the medium of instruction, they said that as they speak in Santali at home they are much more acquainted with the language and understand whatever is taught in the class. The age groups of these children are between 6-10 years. It can be concluded that the children of this age are mainly confined to the village within their family and does not have any contact outside the village. As such they are not well-versed in the dominant language, i.e., Bengali. Therefore, the parents prefer primary schools where education is imparted through the Santali language. But, this medium of instructions has become a matter of controversy amongst the eminent personalities at the Government level and the society as well. Usually, the medium of instruction in many of the primary schools in Santal villages are in the dominant languages such as Oriya, Bengali, Assamese, etc. Therefore, the Santal students find a difficulty in understanding the things in an alien language. Instruction in their mother tongue would have made the study much simpler to them. In the village Kesia though Santali as a separate language is taught, but the textbooks are in Bengali and the instructions are also in Bengali. The movement for the Santal script is going on, but it is yet to take any concrete shape. As a result, the students lose interest in the studies and as such drop-out rates increase amongst them.

In spite of all harshness and austerity of life, the light of education is gradually spreading in this village. It has started one Anganwadi and one Shishu Shiksha for their future generation. It was started from the year 1991. The initiative of starting an Anganwadi was taken by ICDS (Integrated Child Development Scheme) office under the education department, Government of West Bengal.

The parent's opinion regarding the medium of instruction was found to be of mixed preferences. Manohar Hembrom of the village opined that Santali as a medium of instruction should be started especially in the primary schools because it will be easier for them to understand whatever is taught in the class. Their conception on different subject matters would be clear if taught in their mother tongue. Later, after primary education they might be given education in other language.

But, at initial stage alien language might create disinterestedness amongst them. On the other hand, some parents were of the opinion that learning system through the dominant Bengali language might give them a better access to jobs which, they think they can get only knowing Bengali language. Their idea is that as they are poor they want their children to get a good job for a better living therefore, by whatever means they can get it is no problem for them. They are conscious of their identity as a Santal, and as a result some of them tend to protest against the curriculum and imparting of education through the dominant Bengali medium.

Table 10.1 shows the State-wise literacy rate of Scheduled Tribes in India.

But, poor economic condition and an urge for two meals a day has made them rooted to the ground reality. Both the parents in almost all the houses work. Most of the parents do not have any formal

Table 10.1: Literacy Rate for Scheduled Tribe (ST) in India

State/Sex-wise Literacy Rate of Scheduled Tribes in India (Census 2001)

State/UTs	*Rural*	*Urban*			*Total*				
	Person	*Male*	*Female*	*Person*	*Male*	*Female*	*Person*	*Male*	*Female*
Arunachal Pradesh	45.04	54.33	35.83	77.39	85.92	69.05	49.62	58.77	40.56
Assam	61.29	71.29	51.04	86.75	92.43	80.62	62.52	72.34	52.44
Bihar	25.91	37.57	13.30	65.67	74.18	55.28	28.17	39.76	15.54
Chhattisgarh	50.95	63.96	38.21	71.71	82.87	59.77	52.09	65.04	39.35
Jharkhand	38.08	51.67	24.38	67.80	77.83	57.38	40.67	53.98	27.21
Maharashtra	52.31	64.52	39.88	74.18	82.98	64.70	55.21	67.02	43.08
Manipur	65.09	72.44	57.58	80.94	87.94	74.28	65.85	73.16	58.42
Meghalaya	56.36	58.72	53.97	86.67	88.95	84.58	61.34	63.49	59.20
Mizoram	82.00	86.11	77.71	96.77	87.55	96.01	89.34	91.71	86.95
Nagaland	62.55	67.09	57.72	88.70	91.63	85.60	65.95	70.26	61.35
Odisha	36.13	50.35	22.07	58.12	69.80	45.77	37.37	51.48	23.37
Sikkim	65.37	72.32	58.03	84.89	89.32	80.59	67.14	73.81	60.16
Tripura	55.46	67.19	43.35	91.97	94.45	89.26	56.48	67.97	44.60
West Bengal	42.35	56.60	27.88	58.67	68.57	48.20	43.40	57.38	29.15
India	**45.02**	**57.39**	**32.44**	**69.09**	**77.77**	**59.87**	**47.10**	**59.17**	**34.76**

Source: Department of Secondary and Higher Education, Ministry of Human Resource Development, Government of India.

education. Therefore, in most of the cases they cannot guide their children in the home regarding their studies. If the students want to go to school, they go or not. They are not compelled.

Most of the students were in favour of education and want to study as far as possible. They think that education will open up job opportunities to them. Though, they had to fight with the poor economic condition and were found to have either dropped out from schools or have not joined the school. The students those who go to the schools said that the medium of instruction was Bengali. Initially, they had to face problems as they talk in Santali in their home. It was like learning a new language. But they are now used to it. According to them, as the non-tribal students go to the English medium schools for their education and whatever problems they face there is like the same for us. They prefer to be educated in their own mother tongue, at least in the initial stages, because they think learning an alien language at so early an age is difficult. It weakens the base of their understanding of the subjects. Also, when gaining knowledge is the main aim then it should be done in a way that makes easier for us to know it rather than in a complicated and ambiguous way. And language is such a mean by which knowledge can be acquired. Therefore, if it is in our own language then it will be easier for us to gain it. Contrary to this, another student said that the meaning of education is to gain knowledge and it has nothing to do with the language. Their culture and tradition are also not taught in these schools. Some of the students were found to go to residential schools which are exclusively meant for the Santal students. There they said the medium of instruction is Santali and also co-curricular activities included programmes like Santali dances and songs. Some of the students opined that as the parents are illiterate they do not get any help in their studies from them. Though, they are interested in giving education to them and some have even went to the extent of sending their children to the residential schools. But during the harvesting seasons or during monetary crises they are compelled to leave the schools even if they wanted to go. The students were found to understand that their identity as a Santal is being affected by such a system of education. But circumstances are so that they are more or less helpless. For better jobs and good living they are accepting the ways they are given to. They are fighting it back with rallies, meetings in the Government offices etc., and have nothing to do but to wait for the time to come.

CONCLUSION

In a broad sense, education and identity have close linkage, as education helps in the making of the conscious, which acts on reflection. Thus, when one regains consciousness, the question of identity comes to the forefront. Identity, like personality is a construct by which individuality presents its distinctiveness and characteristics that mark one individual from another and one community from another (Chakraborty, 1996). Education plays an important factor informing the construct rather refining it and to make one realize the potential value of existence.

Education amongst the tribal people brings about two aspects of identity consciousness in them. Firstly, it might lead to an identity struggle to retain their almost disappearing culture and loss of control over natural resources. Secondly, it tends them in merging with the dominant way of living leading to a high disregard for their own traditions and culture. But, we find the former aspect more prominent in recent times.

Now, the point here to be noted is that, then what kind of education is needed to be imparted to the tribal children. Whether, it would be same as the non-tribals or different? As far as the Santals are concerned, they cannot be considered an inferior race than the non-tribals. Therefore, from this point of view, separate curriculum for the Santals is rather a baseless argument. But, definitely certain differences are there in the social heredity between the Santals and culturally dominant group. That is to say, from the cultural, social, educational and economic standpoints there are marked differences. (Mahapatra, S. 1986). Though apart from this we find that the Santals of this region are now almost at par with the non-tribal rural population of the plain, as far as the economic pursuits are concerned. In this regard (Mahapatra, S. 1986) suggests a vocational bias in the curriculum with a consideration with the need of the people suitability for the occupation. As, Santal economy is predominantly agricultural, therefore, some subjects such as agriculture, including gardening, weaving and spinning, leather work, clay-work and pottery etc., needs to have a special place in the curriculum of the Santal children as well as the adults. But, in reality we find there are no such provisions as far as the formal school education is concerned. In the primary school they are given education of a very different kind such as social sciences including history and geography, natural sciences and arithmetic, which is very alien to their culture. For example, in the history textbook, they are taught about the freedom movement, India's Independence, Swadeshi movement, etc. though these information helps in enhancing the knowledge of the individual, but in case of a Santal child it does not have any significance. Therefore, it becomes difficult for them to relate to their life and as a result they lose interest in their studies and drop out of the school. As, basically the Santals are deeped in poverty and their basic existence is based on two square miles a day, therefore, such kind of education does not holds any value for them.

The Government of India took the decision of converting the ordinary primary schools into basic primary schools. This step on behalf of the Government proved very advantageous as this mixed type of institutions helped to remove isolation of the tribal people to a great extent and thus lead to their integration with the non-tribal population.

What we find that the developmental process has only led to the tribes to suffer in a dilemma. If they go back to isolation this would only leave them "practically condemned to total extinction" (Fuchs, S., 1992) and adjusting to developmental changes to lead to a compromise with their own identity. Heredia (2001) opines that "in India educational policy seems to be more articulate and eloquent about goals but grossly lacking in the political will and administrative ability to establish appropriate means to these objectives". Therefore, he concludes, what we have evolved along the way is a dual system of education, repeatedly bemoaned yet eventually accommodated, i.e., limited access to quality education for middle class elite, and less than universal availability of massive mis-education for the underprivileged masses (Heredia, 1992).

Thus, from the above analysis it is evident that education and identity has a positive relation in which education leads to self-realization and ultimately to the recognition of one's self. In the tribal world, the identity of an individual is much related to its community and the group. The members of the community in the form of family or peer group helps in transmitting the values and norms prescribed for their men. Here, we find the society plays a dominant role in forming one's identity. This is the difference we find between the education provided by the school and that provided by the family. The school might provide an environment in which the self-identity is enhanced, but the family transmits the culture of the community which gives a feeling of belongingness to one's culture. Though this is applicable to all the communities of the world and not only tribes, but we find the group feeling is much more intense amongst the tribes only. Therefore, Mead's theory of social identity is much more applicable to the tribal world. Mead (1943) points out that an individual's experiences, thoughts and feelings are much influenced by the group to which the individual belongs. Even within the Santals we find this authority of the elders upon their children. They impart knowledge about their people, myths and stories in an informal way when they chat in the evenings in the courtyard or when men and women participate together in a community dance or any other festivals. Their society lives within this togetherness and an individual cannot separate himself from this. The bond of this unity and collectivity is so strong amongst them that the cultural transmission or the influence of the more experienced and elderly person is natural. Their existence depends on the cooperativeness between its kinsmen and as such they tend to maintain aloofness to the outside world. Tajfel's (1986) social identity theory emphasizes on this point that the cultural bond emphasizing on their own values and norms between the members of the community distinguishes it from the outsiders. They prefer to maintain their own language, script and dialects so that they can be easily differentiated from others. These feelings of maintaining one's culture gives distinctiveness as a particular community member to them.

ACKNOWLEDGEMENTS

I would like to begin with expressing my deep sense of gratitude to the almighty God. My special indebtedness is given to my guide Dr. J.J. Roy Burman, from Tata Institute of Social Sciences (TISS), for his careful and insightful help and also to the Director of the Institute, Dr. R.R. Singh (TISS) for the facilities provided to me in doing the research. Thanks are also extended to my family members, respondents specially Amit Kishku and friends who assisted throughout the process of my data collection.

REFERENCES

Chakravarty, K.K. (1996), *Tribal Identity in India: Extinction and Adaptation*, Bhopal: Indira Gandhi Rashtriya Manav Sangrahalaya.

Dasgupta, N.K. (1963), *Problems of Tribal Education and the Santals*, New Delhi: Bharatiya Adimjati Sevak Sangh.

Fuchs, S. (1992), "The Religion of Indian Tribals", in Chaudhuri, B. (ed.), *Tribal Transformation in India*, Inter-India, New Delhi, Vol. V, p. 50.

Hembrom, P.C. (1972), *Sari-Sarna (Santal Religion)*, Mittal Publications, New Delhi.

Heredia, R.C. (1992), *Tribal Education for Community Development*, Concept Publishing Company, New Delhi.

Kundu, M. (1994), *Tribal Education: New Perspective*, Gyan Books, New Delhi.

Mahapatra, S. (1986), *Modernization and Ritual: Identity and Change in Santal Society*, Oxford University Press, Kolkata.

Mead, M. (1943), *Coming of Age in Samoa*, Penguin Books, London.

Sahu, C. (1996), *The Santal Women: A Social Profile,* Sarup & Sons, New Delhi.

Sen, S. (1984) *The Santals of Jungle Mahal: An Agrarian History (1793-1861)*, Ratna Prakashan, Kolkata.

Singh, A.K. (1995), "The Cultural Construction of Home and School Knowledge in Tribal India", *Prospects*, 25 (4): 735-747.

Somer, G.E. (1977), *"The Dynamics of Santal Tradition in a Peasant Society"*, Abhinav Publications, New Delhi.

Tajfel, H., & Turner, J.C. (1986), "The Social Identity Theory of Intergroup Behaviour". In S. Worchel and W.G. Austin (eds.), *Psychology of Intergroup Relations* (pp. 7-24) Chicago, IL: Nelson Hall.

Troisi, J. (1976), *Santals*, New Delhi: Manohar Publications.

Troisi, J. (2000), *Tribal Religion: Religious Beliefs and Practices Among the Santals*, Manohar Publications, New Delhi.

11

Development or Counter-development? Response of the Jharkhand Movement

Jyotiprasad Chatterjee

INTRODUCTION

Societies all-over the world are now encountering the conflict emanating out of the issues of ethnic distinction. This is not to say that group tension emanating from ethnic exclusiveness is a typical phenomenon of the twenty-first century. In fact, covering the entire span of the twentieth century and particularly since the Second World War we have witnessed the outbreak of ethnic conflict that often turned violent in all the corners of the globe. But in the beginning of the twenty-first century, it is assuming immense significance due to the formulation of new policies of 'globalization' through which the present century is uttering its commitment to create a united and homogeneous global social order that is expected to cut across any national, ethnic and/or any other 'parochial' social ties. Keeping aside the scholarly disagreement regarding the impact of the process of globalization in the accentuation of ethnic discontent, it may be said that the present society is witnessing an interesting co existence of two avowedly opposed tendencies; the universalistic trend of globalization and the particularistic drive towards ethnic autonomy and distinctiveness.

The construction of group identity in contrast and contradiction to 'others' constitutes the essence of the ethnic process. As long as these groups occupy the same socio-economic and political status, there is no crisis in the realm of society. But this is rarely so. Most often these groups enjoy unequal social treatment, inequitable access to economic and political resources. In such situations, the social structure turns out to be differentiated in terms of ethnicity and becomes ethnicized. Such a social structure is marked by the presence of dominant (majority) and subjugated (minority) ethnic group(s) that results into conflictual inter-group relationship between them.

Historically, the Indian society is a society of diversities. People of all the major racial, religious and linguistic groups meet here. The immense variation in geographical and climatological traits has been instrumental here in developing different regions with distinct cultural patterns. Consequently, Indian society is composed of a great multiplicity of social groups with tremendous variation in their composition and characteristics. Religion, language, region so on and so forth, often build up a complex system, which makes the perception of the process of group formation in Indian society problematic. Moreover, the caste based stratification system in India makes the social arrangement far more complicated.

The colonial idea of political integration of the country, marked by such a tremendous range of diversities, destroyed the structural balance of Indian society. This political integration of the country should be viewed as a mechanism to satisfy the imperialistic need of British colonialism. As in many other countries, in India too, imperialism proved to be anti-people. Coupled with the severe economic exploitation, the imperialist colonial state in India also acted as an instrument of cultural oppression. By designating the vividly diversified Indian population as common 'subjects', it suppressed their long nourished cultural heritage and practices. The colonial developmental project, assuming the "white man's burden" and driven by the "modern" Western value structure and ideas resulted into the systematic annihilation of the cultural diversity of India. The group of Indian intelligentsia, developed by the colonisers for the smooth administration of the country, became the carriers and advocates of such values. Being English educated this group tried to import the Western liberal principles in India ignoring the social reality and the minimum socio-cultural infrastructure required to suit those in the Indian context. The conception of Indian nationalism, a brainchild of this group, was also an imitation of the Western principle of nationalism and was imposed on Indian society without considering its substantive cultural ethos composed of the diversities. The divergent cultural groups of India felt threatened under such a circumstance and resisted the advent of Indian nationalism. This should be regarded as the root of ethnic discontents in India. It is the result of British colonialism (Ahmed 1996: 2-3). The: independence of the country, which marked the transfer of power from the colonial authority to its Indian counterpart, however, failed to provide any solution to the growing ethnic conflicts. The nation-building project of Indian society, after the colonial withdrawal, has encountered serious threat from the ever-expanding spectrum of ethnic conflict and is yet to overcome the challenge.

After independence, the ethnic discontent and conflict readily transformed themselves in ethnic movements. The goals and objectives of ethnic mobilization in India, however, are not uniform. Partha S. Ghosh (1998) identifies three broad categories of ethic demands in India. In the first category fall those demands, which at times have shown strong *secessionist* urges. The ethnic upsurges in the north-east India, Kashmir, Punjab (the demand for independent Khalistan), Bihar (the demand for an independent Kolhan state) and Tamil Nadu are the examples of such mobilization. In the second category are included those which are not secessionist in nature but seek *more autonomy* by creating more states within the political boundary of the federal republic of India. The demands for the new States of Uttarakhand, Jharkhand, Gorkhaland, Vidarbha and Bodoland carving out from the existing states of Uttar Pradesh, Bihar, West Bengal, Maharashtra and Assam respectively, within the Indian union serve as instances here. Although some new states were created in the mid-1950s on the basis of linguistic and/or ethnic criteria, these were not enough to resist the multiplicity of such demands. In the year 2000, however, three new states were created again. Whether these can withstand the growing ethnic mobilization in India is a point to be noticed in future. In the third category there are demands, which try to attain more autonomy preferably through new state creation, but considering the dynamics of the situation can settle at an *intermediate level of autonomy* for the time being. The Gorkhaland agitation in West Bengal is a classic example of such type of mobilization. The Bodos of Assam and the Jharkhandis also at times exhibited this tendency.

In spite of this, in actual situation depending upon the responses of the Central and State Governments, there has been certain overlapping. In these the roles of international agencies are also very important (Carment, 1994). In the context of the problem of insurgency in North-East India, K.V. Madhok (1996) tries to explore the possible intentions of China, Pakistan, Bangladesh, Myanmar and Bhutan to create tensions in this part to achieve their respective goals. Whatever be the reasons, ethnic movements in north-eastern India have exhibited this assortment of objectives quite often. In the context of Bodoland movement, it can be noticed that while the All Bodo Students' Union (A.B.S.U.), Bodo Liberation Tiger Force (B.L.T.F.) have been demanding a separate state for the Bodos, for the Bodo Security Force (Bo.S.F.) in contrast, the urge for sovereignty *via* secession from India becomes important. Quite naturally, there has been considerable bloodshed in Assam due to the clash of interest of these organizations (*The Statesman*, April 11,1997). The same is true for the ethnic movement in Nagaland also. The General Secretary of the Naga Hoho, Mr. Vihuto Yepthomi describes the trend of the movement in Nagaland as well as in Naga-inhabited areas in adjoining states as, "sovereignty *versus* statehood" (*The Statesman*, September 23, 1999).

Analysis of the nature of ethnonationalism in the Indian context, is currently receiving greater importance from the social scientists. Such an understanding is extremely significant, as far as the stiff challenges thrown by the competing group identities to the much fancied notion of national integration of the country is concerned. By unveiling the nature and mechanism of ethnic group formation such an analysis can throw sufficient light on the changing issues and concerns involved in the process and the conflict emanating out of this. To achieve this goal, the present chapter strives to analyse the nature of ethnic mobilization in Jharkhand Movement as it is continuing in Chotanagpur plateau covering a large part of the Central Indian plateau region. The genesis of the movement was in the early days of British penetration in India. Since, those days of the second half of the eighteenth century it is continuing till date in one form or another. Due to its long history the movement occupies a distinct place in the galaxy of ethnic movements in India. Moreover, as the movement never assumed secessionist character, hence, this has a recognisable role in the body politic of Indian society, particularly in its efforts at nation building. At the regional level too the movement proves to be successful in ensuring the participation of the Jharkhandis in the democratic political processes.

The Central Indian plateau region, popularly known as Jharkhand, is the home of a large number of Austric communities. Having migrated from north-western India, these people, probably due to

Aryan invasion, entered this hilly and forest tracts of central India. Converting this difficult terrain liveable, both economically and socially, with their extensive labour, they claimed their natural right over it. This early story of their forced migration is a definite evidence of their non-Hindu origin. As it happens to the conquered people anywhere, the dominant Hindu society of India accorded these communities a very low social status even lower than the lowest stratum of the fourfold *Varna* scheme of the Hindu society. The 'manufactured' concept of social backwardness became instrumental to the dominant Indian mainstream to have a complete grip over the natural resources of this region rich with minerals and forest products. To defend this onslaught, the indigenous communities attempt to redefine their identity that sufficiently carries their aspiration and claimed rights as the original inhabitants of the region. Hence, by the term '*adivasi*' ('*adi*'= original and '*vasi*'= inhabitants), as opposed to the colonial 'tribe' and the Hinduised '*vanavasi*' (forest dwellers), which contain a derogatory and primitive image of them, the indigenous people assert themselves and try to symbolise their distinctive socio-cultural existence *vis-à-vis* the Indian mainstream.

In the present study, the ongoing Jharkhand movement has been viewed from this broad perspective. Jharkhand's history is actually the history of appropriation of its natural and human resources by the dominant Indian majority. Not only Jharkhand movement but also all the ethnic movements in India, perhaps, are the responses to the same legacy of oppression and exploitation. What makes Jharkhand situation distinct is the process of continuous augmentation of such deprivation consequent to large-scale developmental activities, witnessed by the region since early twentieth century, leading to a parallel expansion and consolidation of the movement. The ethnic upsurge, which the movement has exhibited, has been located theoretically in this general framework of exploitation and deprivation of the indigenous people on economic as well as cultural grounds. The study in its attempt to analyse the patterns of ethnic mobilization in the course of the movement has paid sufficient attention to this historically evolved realities of appropriation and discrimination.

THE HISTORICAL TREND

The long history of the Jharkhand Movement allows the sociologists to scrutinise it in order to have generalizations regarding the nature of ethnic movements. The movement since its inception in the early days of British encroachment in India has passed through different phases to reach its present state. The analysis of these phases helps in unveiling the underlying trend of the movement. Through this we come to know about the major concerns of the movement in its different phases. The analysis of the factors and the manner in which they influence the movement are of great utility in the sociological interpretation of not only Jharkhand Movement but also any social movement. In the course of the Jharkhand Movement this attempt clearly brings into light the role of economic and cultural forces in shaping it up. Jharkhand movement has a strong legacy in the *adivasi* uprisings of the eighteenth and nineteenth century. Starting from the early days of British penetration in India in the second half of the eighteenth century as *adivasi* protest movements against the exploitative colonial policy, it has passed a long way to reach its present form. To analyse this vast course of historical development of the movement, the present study has divided it into four discernible phases.

The first phase (1765-1845) was characterized by the *adivasi* protests against the British agrarian policy, which resulted in the economic ruination and cultural oppression of the *adivasis* either through conscious effort or in a twisted manner. The resistance to colonial rule by indigenous people of Jharkhand involved two pronged onslaughts, one directly against the new land revenue structure epitomized in anti-zamindar and anti-landlord rebel [First Chuar Rebellion (1767) Dhalbhum Rebellion (1769 -1774), Tilka Majhi's War (1780-1785) etc.] while the other predominantly for cultural autonomy [Second Chuar Rebellion (1798-1799), Kol Insurrection (1831-1832), Ganga Narayan's Movement (1832-1833) etc.].

With Christianity, during the second phase (1845-1920), came in the modern liberal values of self-identity and self-assertion, which had a clandestine effect on the development of ethnicity and ethnic mobilization. The prevailing ethnic consciousness, reflected by the agrarian movements during the first phase, had become more consolidated through the liberal values preached by the Christian missionaries. In this phase, it grew and matured to such an extent that almost all the uprisings of this phase demanded a '*raj*'[1] of their own which meant self-rule or self-determination. The conception of this '*raj*' either was imaginary or a representation of revival of an earlier golden political order, free of any sort of exploitation.

The third phase (1920-1970) was marked by the inauguration of formal politics in Chotanagpur. Unlike the first and second phase, hardly any spontaneous or unpremeditated uprising with indigenous and class specific demands had taken place in this period. Moreover, this phase also witnessed the rolling on of the processes of industrialization and urbanization leading to the emergence of an urban, educated middle class in the region. As a result of these twin processes, the area was also flooded by the entry of outsiders from the neighbouring states. Entry of the outsiders from a completely different linguistic and antagonistic cultural set-up became a consistent threat to the cultural distinctiveness of the people of this region. A number of social reform organizations, the Christian Association, the Roman Catholic Cooperative Society, the Christian College Union, the Munda-Oraon Education Conference (Shiksha Sabha), Chotanagpur Charitable Association, "Chotanagpur Unnati Samaj" (Chotanagpur Improvement Society) came up to maintain and protect the *adivasi* cultural uniqueness. Primarily under the influence of the Christian Missionaries, these organizations tried to develop some of the decadent aspects of *adivasi* culture like language, folk tradition etc. To safeguard these, the 'Samaj' for the first time demanded a separate 'sub-state' (Singh, 1977 : 320) of Chotanagpur independent of Bihar and submitted a memorandum to that effect to the Simon Commission in 1928. This was the necessary groundwork on the basis of which the Adivasi Mahasabha and the Jharkhand Party raised the demands for a separate Jharkhand state. In this phase, the process of development of Jharkhandi ethnicity, however, suffered a lot due to certain inherent contradictions. First, although it is true that this region is the birthplace of a number of *adivasi* communities, it is also inhabited by some non-*adivasi* communities too who occupy a very low stratum in the traditional caste hierarchy of the Hindu social order. These groups, known to be Sadans in Jharkhand, developed a symbiotic relationship with the *adivasis*. Culturally, they are not very far away from the *adivasis*. In fact, in many of the *adivasi* uprisings of the earlier two phases, they participated and moved shoulder to shoulder with the *adivasis*. But too much emphasis on *adivasi* distinctiveness by the Adivasi Mahasabha and the Jharkhand Party had isolated them. Second, the urban as well as educated and middle class orientation of the organizations alienated a sizeable section of the marginal rural population. Third, as the urban and industrial centres became the locus of the movement the issues pertaining to villages and agriculture got neglected. Fourth, mostly the Mundas and Oraons, the two important *adivasi* communities of Chotanagpur, maintained an overwhelming control and supervision over the organizations. This frustrated a number of other *adivasi* communities, most importantly the Santals, who had a distinguished tradition of struggle for autonomy. Undoubtedly, the alienation and dissociation of the Santals restricted the process of ethnic mobilization. Finally, and most importantly, the Christian *versus* the non-Christian divide among the *adivasis* weakened the movement from within. This resulted in the growth of fissiparous tendencies among the movement participants. The Hindutwa forces, afterwards, have utilized this hiatus quite efficiently and intensified it in a significant manner. Consequently, a confusion and disintegration had surfaced the entire third phase.

The emergence of the J.M.M., in the fourth phase (1970-1999), under the command of a firebrand leader Shibu Soren and his associates, has regenerated the movement with a particular appeal to the grassroot-excluded people and upholding their causes. Influenced by the ideology of radical Marxism, Soren successfully has resolved the contradictions that ruined the movement in the third phase. Realizing that the ethnic oppression of the Jharkhandis was inextricably linked with their class exploitation, he has tried to assimilate class and ethnicity. Redefining the concept of 'Jharkhandi' in class terms and the portrayal of Jharkhand to be the first 'Lalkhand' (Red State) of India, the Morcha under his leadership has successfully resolved the *adivasi versus* non-*adivasi*, Christian *versus* non-Christian *adivasi* contradiction. Incorporating the Mahatos (an agriculturalist caste in Jharkhand) and the Sadans within it, through a well-designed plan of rural development, the Morcha enforced its political strength considerably. This reflects a shift in the ideology of the movement from the third phase. What has distinguished the J.M.M. from its predecessors of the third phase is its assertive stand for the political autonomy to end the age-old ethnic and class exploitation. The Morcha, however, has failed to adhere to this 'class-ethnic' ideology in the long run. What has been started as a radical movement to bring an end to any sort of exploitation in the early 1970s got institutionalized very soon. This was primarily due to the alliance of Shibu Soren with the Congress (I) in the beginning of the 1980s. The process of co-option of Shibu Soren in parliamentary politics has been manoeuvred to dilute the class antagonistic approach of the J.M.M. The leader, who occupied the position of a legendary hero in the hearts of the exploited people of Jharkhand, engaged himself in the dirty game of opportunistic parliamentary politics. In these days deviating far away from the Marxist ideology, he gradually has become dissociated from his oppressed brethren and got trapped into corrupt political practices. The J.M.M. also, as a result of all these, got fragmented. Shedding off the integrated class-ethnic approach and embracing a host of opportunistic moves to attain political gains has led to estrangement of a large many oppressed Jharkhandis who were the original support base of the J.M.M.

The development and the articulation of ethnic consciousness in the context of the movement are well documented by its relatively long history. The seeds of ethnic self-perception of the indigenous people of Jharkhand, initially, had been sowed by the British agrarian policy. The economically exploitative and culturally oppressive colonial policy brought the people in the arena of agrarian movement. In their struggle against the new class of landlords and moneylenders, the by-products of the new revenue structure, the people of the region for the first time came to defend their cultural heritage. Be it the question of law of inheritance, local police administration or payment of land revenue, everywhere the alien colonial policy was challenged with a mission to protect the traditional cultural practices of the *adivasis*. This self-assertive ethnic feeling got a fillip in the hands of Christian missionaries. By imparting among the *adivasis* a sense of pride and glory for their cultural heritage, Christianity nurtured and gave a concrete shape to their ethnic sentiment. This unidimensional ethnic self-realization received a boost with the incorporation of new developmental parameters brought in by industrialization and urbanization in the beginning of the twentieth century. Advancement of education, a necessary offshoot of this, produced an ambitious group of *adivasis* who used to take pride of the *adivasi* cultural uniqueness. The enlightened segment undertook concerted effort to safeguard *adivasi* cultural distinctiveness. It was at this height of ethnic awareness that the demand of a separate Jharkhand state was put forward to fulfil the ethnic aspiration of the *adivasis*. The course of ethnic mobilization in this region has been steadily incorporating multifarious issues reflecting inherent and conscious contradictions emanating from religious, linguistic and regional dimensions. This is, however, a common feature of the process of ethnic identity formation everywhere. When people are going to be mobilized centring on either or some of these dimensions a considerable confusion may be a natural outcome which make them perplexed. Such ambiguity often influences the ideology, goals and strategies of any social movement. Jharkhand movement in its course of development in the twentieth century experienced this as the contradictions concerning the parameters of ethnicity somehow destabilised it. Moreover, the movement also suffered due to the interplay of the factor of class in it. The factors of ethnicity and class, often crossed by each other, make the social reality in Jharkhand a complicated one. Ethnic oppression of the people of this region has been reinforced by their class exploitation and the *vice versa*. Only in the closing decades of the twentieth century, the movement could get hold of it. By integrating these two dimensions in its ideology, the movement possibly resolved some of the contradictions responsible for its downfall in the earlier periods.

Integration of class and ethnic contradictions in Jharkhand has been symbolized in a sarcastic manner by the term '*diku*'. In *adivasi* parlance the term has been used to designate the outsider non-*adivasis*. The outsiders (mostly non-*adivasis*) in Jharkhand, since the beginning of the colonial intrusion, involved themselves in the unjust appropriation of the natural and human resources of the area, hence the term also contains a definite sense of hatred towards them. The mechanism of ethnic group formation here has revolved round the *dikus*' which came to signify the 'other' of the indigenous population of Jharkhand. In fact, Santal and other Mundari *adivasis* of this region refer to the members of their own community as "Hor" which means: 'our men', and to other as *Diku*, which means the 'alien' (Murmu, 2002). The essential core of the identity and solidarity of the Jharkhandis, thus, has been counterpoised against the *dikus* (Corbridge, 1993). In an embedded ethnic situation both of these groups impose certain negative stereotypes on each other. While for the *adivasis* the '*dikus*' are, "... looters, trouble-makers, deceivers, exploiters, cheats, unreliable..." for the non-*adivasi* outsiders, the *adivasis* are, "*Jangli, Jangal jhar ke log, Jangli hat, Vanyajati, Banjati...*"[2] (Sinha, Sen, and Panchbhai, 1969: 127). The terms, apart from their objective meaning, quite definitely imply a sense of primitiveness, savagery etc. On the basis of these, the non-*adivasis* tend to characterise the *adivasis* as hostile, cruel, violent, and irrational. This duality in the characterization of the 'other' has resulted into conflictual inter-group relationship and serves as the core of the process of ethnic identity formation in Jharkhand. The movement in its long history has consistently maintained an enmity with these *dikus*. But it also had to counter certain problems emanating from the interpretation of the term in different periods. The term '*diku*' contains not only ethnic differences between the *adivasis* and the non-*adivasis*; it also indicates the phenomenon of class difference. But on the basis of a heightened ethnic awareness, especially in the mid-twentieth century, the Jharkhandi organizations tended to emphasis too much on its ethnic connotation. This led to certain misunderstanding, and the resultant confusion made the mobilization of a wide section of the exploited Jharkhandis bit difficult. In the fourth phase, the movement, perhaps, on the basis of an understanding of the historical significance of the term, could extend its scope of mobilization considerably. In the initial period of the fourth phase, the movement quite clearly considered that segment of the population, whether *adivasi* or non-*adivasi*, exploiting the working people of Jharkhand as the '*dikus*.' But in the later period of this phase, possibly due to co-option of its militant leadership by the mainstream political parties for their electoral benefit, a shift in the movement from this fundamental contradiction has become apparent.

THEORETICAL FRAMEWORK

There is a great deal of ambivalence in sociological discourse regarding the nature and relevance of ethnic mobilization in modern society. Particularly, it centres on the issue of contextualization of ethnicity. Is ethnicity relevant in modern society? This is the question that has divided the sociological domain into two camps. In one side of the debate there is the sociological paradigm, which hardly attach any significance to ethnicity in modern society. It argues that sanctity of blood ties, kinship networks, language, community, custom, common ancestry, common territory and the other dimensions of ethnic identity formation are mostly primordial in nature and are no more important for the creation of social bond among the people of modern society. The modern society strives for rationality in all the aspects of social life and in it the various markers of ethnicity just simply do not fit. Analysing in this manner it consider ethnicity and ethnic mobilization to be the phenomena of the gone-by, pre-modern societies. Along with others, this viewpoint is subscribed by some of the prominent classical sociological thinkers too. For the purpose of present analysis this orientation has been designated as primordialist.

On the other side is the sociological paradigm, which considers ethnicity to be an important feature of the modern society. In this the phenomena of ethnicity and ethnic conflict have been positively correlated with the processes of development and modernization. According to this viewpoint, the modern social structure provides enough space for the emergence of the ethnic groups. The principle of democracy and its corollary values of liberty, autonomy, sovereignty propagated by the institutions of the modern society, coupled with the dramatic advancement of technology and the information revolution of late, create a congenial environment for the development of ethnicized social bond and the consequent conflict. This orientation has been termed here as 'modernist', which stands out in sharp opposition to the primordial view of ethnicity. As a matter of fact, the expectation of the latter that the universal forces of modernization will sweep away anything 'pre-modern', has not only been unfulfilled but also, at present, we are witnessing that ethnicity is gradually gaining more and more momentum as far as the process of group formation and inter-group relationships are concerned (Glazer and Moynihan, 1963; Friedman, 1990). Along with other societies, the same is perhaps true about Indian society also. The nature of developmental endeavours undertaken in India since the beginning of the twentieth century, particularly since independence, and the principle of democracy, providing the necessary impetus for self-determination, have successfully fuelled the growing ethnic conflicts that ultimately resulted in a considerable augmentation of social tensions in India. It is precisely due to this, the modernist paradigm has been adopted here to analysis the nature of ethnic mobilization in the context of Jharkhand movement.

In the modernist paradigm the phenomena of ethnicity and ethnic mobilization have been approached from two apparently contradictory and fundamentally complementary theoretical angles, namely, (1) the ethnic separation theory, and (2) ethnic competition theory. A host of sociologists (Clark, 1998; Belangar and Pinard, 1991; Hechter, 1975, 1978; Nielsen, 1985; Hannan, 1979; Bergesen and Herman, 1998) have dealt with either of these.

Ethnic separation theory argues that ethnic conflict emerges in that type of societies where people are divided or segmentally placed along such dimensions that coincide with racial or ethnic boundaries. Naturally, the more divided the people are, the chance is also more for the conflict to emanate. Among the separation theorists Michael

Hechter (1975) deserves a special mention who through the model of reactive ethnicity tries to study the persistence of ethnicity in modern societies. In this model, ethnicity and the resultant solidarity are viewed primarily as a reaction of the culturally distinct and deprived periphery against the exploitation by the privileged centre. Michael Hechter (1978: 312) examines this issue through the "cultural division of labour" approach. According to him, "whenever individuals having different cultural markers are distributed through an occupational structure, a cultural division of labour is thereby formed." In the hierarchically arranged occupational structures of the modern societies, the assignment of individuals in different positions according to their respective ethnic statuses gives birth to cultural division of labour. The dominant ethnic groups, naturally, under such conditions, monopolize the high paid and respectable jobs by frustrating the efforts of the subjugated ones. This is precisely the assumption of the "internal colonialism" theses as discussed by John Stone (1979).

The *competition* model, on the contrary, believes that the process of modernization influences distinct ethnic groups in a more homogeneous manner by virtue of its orientation towards status to be achieved through rational pursuits. This, however, cannot do away with ethnic distinctions. On the contrary, due to the standardizing impact of the process of modernization, different groups, find themselves in a similar position to compete for the same scarce resources and try to organize, or strengthen their group solidarity along the very ethnic dimensions that at times may lead to ethnic conflict (Chaklader, 1985; Gill, 2000). Clark (1998: 1269) is also of the same opinion as he argues, "The more people come into contact with or are similar to one another, the more they will have to compete for the same resources and the more likely it is that conflict will occur."

The treatment of ethnic solidarity of these two models flows from two different and opposite standpoints. While ethnic separation theory highlights the development of ethnic solidarity through the concept of cultural division of labour, the competition model traces it in the more uniform processes of modernization that takes as its precondition the breakdown of the cultural division of labour. But Francois Nielsen (1985: 147) feels that these two standpoints are not incompatible. In his words, "These two theories differ by the emphasis they attach to various trends associated with the development process...one would expect to find instances in which each model is appropriate, in the sense that the social correlates of ethnic solidarity differ from one social system to another and over time." Thus, following Nielsen it can be stated that these two theories can be applied to the societies, which are in different levels of modernization at a given point of time or to the same modernizing society in different points of time. In the initial phase, the developmental process may result into the creation of ethnic cleavages by discriminating the privileged 'core' from the underprivileged 'periphery.' But further development can eradicate these differences and bring them all in the competition for the same resources. This competition in its turn can generate ethnic conflict by increasing group solidarity along ethnic dimensions.

DEVELOPMENT, DEPRIVATION AND DEMOCRACY: THE INTERFACE IN JHARKHAND

Developmental endeavours resulting in severe economic disparities among different segments and sections of the newly developing societies can be considered as the most classic instances exhibiting the intersection between the principles and processes of development, deprivation and democracy. Besides augmenting the magnitude of economic inequality, this has also pushed a number of communities in the periphery of their respective societies by undermining their cultural uniqueness. Such a development-induced deprivation of the people, in economic as well as cultural terms, has its root in the colonial rule. In most of the underdeveloped countries such developmental efforts were initiated by the colonisers, so any attempt to realize the nature of emerging ethnic conflicts in these societies must have a reference to the impact of colonialism. From this perspective, a number of scholars (Patel, 1996; Ahmed, 1992, 1996; Sharma, 1995; Segal, 2000; Adhikary, 1998) have argued the impact of colonialism in enhancing social segregation and ethnic inequalities in the countries of Asia, Africa and Latin America. Colonialism in these countries proves to be instrumental in intensifying the consciousness of differences and weakening of the comprehension of inter-ethnic relationships and commonalties among the indigenous population. Moreover, it successfully stratifies these societies into several dimensions of inequality; most prominent among these are class and ethnicity. The underprivileged, subjugated and marginalized people belonging to different class and ethnic groups, in such a condition of inequality, fail to fulfil their aspirations and become frustrated for which intolerance increases and most often than not ethnic violence is manifested.

The systematic division of societies into the dominant and the subjugated, although a colonial construction, does not confine itself only in the colonial situation. It is effective in the post-colonial context too. The structural inequality prevailing in the post-colonial societies debars the fruits of developmental projects to reach every corner and segment of their population in an even manner. Here, the dominant, core ethnic groups, enjoying all the benefits of economic development, exploit the subjugated, peripheral ethnic groups and, hence, create a situation, of "internal colonialism." In this background, the protests of the exploited excluded groups often follow the ethnic course and produce ethnic conflict.

The imbalance in economic development leading to a situation of internal colonialism has been considered to be the root cause of ethnic conflict by a large number of researchers. Premdas, while writing on Fiji, holds responsible its "ethnically-specialized economy" for the outbreaks of ethnic conflict. In his words:

> "In Fiji, many indigenous Fijians regard their lot as unfair since on an average the Fijian, as compared with the Indian, European or Chinese was poorer. Fijians who have been socialized into a subsistence pattern of economic life do not display the same level of acquisitiveness, individualism, and competitiveness as the other ethnic groups. Consequently, over time, in a growing market economy, Fijian economic well-being has become conspicuously inferior to other groups" (1995: 165-66).

This type of economic discrimination having an ethnic bias has also been reported by Buddhadeb Chaudhuri (1991) in his study of the Chittagong Hill Tribes of Bangladesh. *Adivasi* communities in the Chittagong hills are essentially different from the majority of Muslim Bengalis of Bangladesh in social, religious and cultural terms. Due to huge scarcity of land in Bangladesh the poor people from the plains are forced to migrate to the Hill Tracts, which has been legally endorsed. Such encroachment in the *adivasi* 'homeland' poses a serious threat to the distinct identity and independent existence of the *adivasis*. This naturally results into ethnic conflict. Sengupta (1982), Das (1992), Munda (1992), Devalle (1992), in their writings on the Jharkhand Movement in India mention the simultaneous exploitation of the indigenous people of Jharkhand, in ethnic and economic fronts, by the mainstream Indian population as one of the key factors of the movement. Since, the early twentieth century and particularly, since independence, the Jharkhand region, rich in mineral and natural resources, has witnessed wave of developmental programmes. These have, however, failed to improve the socio-economic conditions of the people of Jharkhand at large. Sengupta (1982: 11) quite aptly describes the paradoxical nature of the developmental process when he resolves, "Jharkhand is developing fast; but not the Jharkhandis." Victor Das (1992) also observes it quite deeply.

> "With the lands and forests being acquired by the industrial and mining companies, the tribals not only became almost bonded labourers in their own land on wages so meagre that it could not buy them a frugal meal in a day, but they also lost their cultural, traditional and spiritual identities" (p. 403).

Regarding the magnitude of migration of the outsiders in the Jharkhand region, Ram Dayal Munda (1992) writes:

> "The industrial cities and the vicinities of Ranchi, Jamshedpur and Dhanbad have simply exploded with population to the extent of going out of control. Even in civil jobs like primary and secondary school teaching outsiders dominate due to red-tapism and favouritism on caste lines. The influx of an outside population has led the 60/40 tribal non-tribal population ratio in 1951 to become 40/60 in 1981, just the reverse in 30 years" (p. 384).

The relative ascendancy of the outsiders is prominent not only in those professions, which requires a lot of skills but also it is there for the jobs where the factor of skill is not that much significant (Ghosh, 1998).

The drastic reversal of the ratio is due to both the immigration of the outsiders in the Jharkhand region and the emigration of the *adivasis* of Jharkhand in neighbouring states primarily for the search of jobs there.[3] The development of industries and mines since the closing decade of the nineteenth century, both under the public and private sectors, has resulted in large-scale displacement and land alienation of the *adivasis* in Jharkhand. Added with the problem of land alienation of the *adivasis* created by the landlords and other vested interest groups, this posed a real threat to the economic existence of the predominantly agriculturist *adivasis* of the region. Moreover, the creation of reserved forests by the colonial rulers following the Resolution on Forest Policy in India (Resolution No. 22-F) 1894, as mentioned by Corbridge (1993), restricted the *adivasis'* access to the forests severely. Forests and land are the major sources of livelihood to the *adivasis*. Moreover, these are also the core elements in the process of their identity formation. The large-scale alienation of the *adivasis* from their land and forests has dealt with the most severe blow to the economic existence and cultural distinctiveness. In such a situation no other options were left to them, but to revolt or migrate to places where a living, however poor, can be earned. The *adivasis* followed both. On the one hand, under the leadership of Birsa Munda, in the closing period of the nineteenth century, they tried to resist the colonial forest policy, while migration to Assam, where at that time there was the need for plantation workers in the tea gardens, also occurred in large scale on the other. The *adivasis* of Chotanagpur and Santhal Pargana in this manner became a pool of cheap labour. It is not that the *adivasis* who had migrated to Assam experienced a good fortune there. Kaushik Ghosh (1999) in his analysis of the colonial discourses of aboriginality and primitivism argues that the *adivasis* of Chotanagpur for the 'attribute' of their 'aboriginality' were regarded to be the 'first-class' coolies. In this manner being relegated to the status of coolie proletariat in the tea gardens of Assam they faced the ferocity of capital in a severe manner. The plight of the migrants is quite succinctly expressed by the following Jhumur folk song, which is very popular in the Jharkhand area:

Chal Mini Assam jabo
Deshe baro dukh re
Assam deshe re Mini chabagan hariyal.

....

Sardar bole kam kam
Baboo bole dhori aan
Saheb bole libo pither cham
re jaduram, fanki diya
pathaili Assam.

["Eh Mini, lets go to Assam where the tea gardens are green, there's so much suffering in our place. (But there) the sardar (*the labour leader*) says catch hold of him (*the labour*), Saheb (the proprietor) threats to skin the back. Oh Jaduram (*the middleman*), you have sent us to Assam by deceiving"[4]] (Basu, 1994: 46).

The song narrates the pathetic situation of the migrated tea plantation worker. He left his native place with immense pain and water in the eyes to have a living in the tea gardens of Assam. But in exchange what he got? He had to face intense exploitation and torture of the owners of the gardens and his/her associates. The unfortunate *adivasis* of Chotanagpur, being uprooted from their place of origin and expropriated from their means of production had practically no resource to develop even a minimal resistance to such exploitation. Thus, they developed a docile character, which is quite uncharacteristic of the people who were basically freedom lovers and prepared to pay any price for its protection. In fact, for this passive character they were the most desired coolies to the planters *vis-à-vis* the local Assamese labourers. The colonial discourse of 'aboriginality' hence, capitalising on this 'split-labour market' (Bonacich,1972) went on to accumulate capital in an even large scale. In so doing it also sowed the seed of ethnic discord among the autochthons and the immigrants. The migrated *adivasis*, mostly the Santals, are not regarded here as Scheduled Tribes and consequently do not enjoy the Constitutional privileges of reservation too. Mr. Salkhan Murmu, the M.P. from Mayurbhanj, Odisha and the Santhali Bhasa Morcha (an organization to promote the cause of Santhali language) Chief alleged that the Assam government was intentionally denying this right to the Santals (*The Statesman,* May 10, 1998). Moreover, the rules promulgated by the Central Board of Forests in 1950 (Chaudhuri, 1997), which restricted traditional rights of the *adivasis* over the forests, in their place of origin, blocked any possibility of returning back as there was little economic opportunity left to them to have a subsistence without the forests. Thus, they were caught and perhaps trapped in a catch 22 situation. Unwillingly although, they settled down in Kokrajhar district of Assam, a heartland of the Bodos, but not without problems. Besides economic crisis, an unprecedented ethnocide in Indian society occurred when the Bodo militant outfits picked up these *adivasis* in the mid-1990s as a source of their deprivation. Hundreds of people (both the Santals and Bodos) were killed; thousands of houses were set ablaze and lakhs of people were displaced as a result of the ethnic riots. The ethnic clash here is still continuing. The latest one being on December 23, 2014, when Bodo militants belonging to the I.K. Songbijit faction of the National Democratic Front of Bodoland (NDFB-IKS), gunned downed 69 *Adivasis* in Chirang, Sonitpur and Kokrajhar Districts of Assam. In retaliation, on 24th December, 2014 eight Bodos were killed by Santhal mobs (Gill, 2014). Under pressure from an ever dwindling productivity of the *jhum* or *slash* and burn method of cultivation the Bodos, out of sheer desperation regarded the Santals' encroachment in their lands responsible for their economic crisis. Another explanation of this ethnic unrest speaks of the pro-Congress attitude of the Santals, which irked the Bodos considerably because in their perception the Congress (I) governments in the Centre as well as the State of Assam were the main opposition to their autonomy demands (*EPW*, 2008).

It is really an irony that while Jharkhand is opening up so much job opportunities, its autochthones are finding it extremely difficult, if not impossible, to find any room in it. The following word of Shibu Soren, which may sound bit rhetoric, nevertheless, captures the nature of discriminatory developmental pattern of the region most succinctly:

> "Out of the total electricity generated in Bihar, more than 90 per cent is produced in the Jharkhand region. While 20 per cent villages of rest of Bihar apart from Jharkhand region has electricity, the rate of rural electrification in Jharkhand, such a big producer of electricity, is only a meager 5 per cent...A number of water reservoir has been constructed here to supply drinking water to the city people but not a single pipe is there for those villagers whose land has been taken away to build this. There are a large number of cement factories in Jharkhand, but still most of the houses here are built of mud and wood...In spite of having a fertiliser factory in Sindhri, the rural agricultural folk surrounding it do not ever have the good fortune of using fertiliser. There is an aluminium industry in Muri, but the villagers in its close vicinity still use the earthen pots for the purpose of cooking. It is often stated that steel is the prime mover of civilization. But it is perhaps not true for those unfortunate *adivasis* who relinquished their lands to construct the steel plants of Tata, Rourkela and Bokaro...For these enterprises a large number

> of villages of the region has been devastated, a large number of villagers were displaced, their traditional social system has been destroyed, their culture has been smashed under the feet and thousands of people were driven out of their homes. But what the Jharkhandis acquired in return of all these? They received insult, rebuke, extreme deprivation, liquor shops, *bhang, ganja,* brothel, illness, poverty, hunger, corrupted government machinery, thieves, *goondas* and plunderers" (Soren, 1992: 24).

Despite the possible failure of this translation to reflect the real spirit of Soren, it perhaps successfully takes note of his concerns regarding the inhuman nature of the developmental process, which has transformed Jharkhand, a region rich in mineral and natural resources in a land of destitute people.

The Jharkhand case thus appears to be a classic situation where the hue and cry of development has resulted in the inhuman economic exploitation and cultural oppression of the indigenous communities. Not only in Jharkhand, 'development' since Second World War, has been allegedly either accentuating the magnitude of already prevailing social inequalities or giving birth to newer ones in many of the so-called underdeveloped societies. Sachs (2010) describes it quite succinctly:

> "As governments and businesses, urban citizens and rural elites mobilize to forge ahead with development, more often than not the land, the living spaces and the cultural traditions of indigenous peoples, small farmers or the urban poor are put under pressure. Freeways cut through neighbourhoods, high-rise buildings displace traditional housing, dams drive tribal groups from their homelands, trawlers marginalize local fisherfolk, supermarkets undercut small shopkeepers ... The shiny side of development is often accompanied by a dark side of displacement and dispossession..." (p. ix).

Devalle (1992: 78) terms this process as "development of underdevelopment." To substantiate this she continues (1992: 90), "Social degradation, racial discrimination, deculturation and cultural distortion have acted as effective mechanisms in the process of economic control and exploitation of the *adivasis*, pervading all aspects of their lives." The dominant discourse of 'primitive', 'aborigine' etc. as embodied in the concept of 'tribe' precisely helps in reproducing this oppressive developmental process. Rajkishor Meher (2001: 291) terms this process as "hegemonic development", which is basically inegalitarian in nature as it "...favours the privileged few and marginalises the backward tribals, the poor and downtrodden." Hence, development to the indigenous people of Jharkhand has actually come to mean a process of counter-development. The developmental process of the Jharkhand region leading to mass destitution of its people fits quite illustratively with the internal colonialism theses as discussed by Stone (1979), and the cultural division of labour approach of Michael Hechter (1978).

Collective mobilization of the oppressed segment of the Jharkhandi populace in response, since, the beginning of the twentieth century, has largely followed the democratic path. The developmental activities undertaken in the region, besides resulting in severe exploitation of the indigenous communities, also produced an enlightened section among them who were indeed very eager to shoulder the responsibility of emancipating their oppressed brethren. The leadership of the movement, except in some period of the fourth phase, has largely remained in the hands of this liberal section. The first demand of separation of Chotanagpur from Bihar raised by the Chotanagpur Unnati Samaj in 1928, and the similar attempts made by the subsequent Jharkhandi organizations later were the brainchild of this section. Their adherence to the democratic spirit has been exemplified by the demands, which always has a reference to the Constitution of India. It is also revealed by the strategy of mass mobilization in the movement with the slogan of "Jai Jharkhand Jai Bharat." The participation of the major Jharkhandi political organizations in the electoral process in India since independence undoubtedly remains a significant contribution in the consolidation of the democratic foundation of Indian polity.

This, however, is a common outcome of the development process everywhere. It requires the participation of the people at large for its successful expansion. In the contemporary period, according to the post-development theorists, participation has turned out to be a politically attractive slogan and economically appealing proposition (Rahnema, 2010). Needless to mention that free market and the free flow of human and natural resources are the necessary preconditions for its farther consolidation. Only a modern state based on the concept of popular sovereignty, can guarantee all these. But in the context of extreme social structural inequality, the process of development turns out to be uneven favouring a tiny minority at the cost of the vast majority. Participation in this condition serves as "...a manipulative trick to involve people in struggles for getting what the powerful want to impose on them..." (Esteva, 2010: 3). Following the principle of social stratification it can also be argued that this relatively disadvantaged majority also do not compose a socially homogeneous group. The relatively well off and the enlightened cross-section of this disadvantaged majority, to satisfy their rising aspirations, use the values of political sovereignty and its derivatives like, equality, social justice, self-determination, rule of the law etc. of the modern state to mobilize the people. In such an attempt ethnicity often serves as the most tangible dimension.

CONCLUSION

Jharkhand movement has largely been the expression of a democratic mobilization of the victim's of the lopsided, uneven and 'hegemonic' development process. It is a classic exposition of the relation between the so-called 'development' endeavours of the modern democratic state and ethnic mobilization. If development is defined in purely economic terms divorced from its social implications pertaining to the freedom of the members of any given society, it is bound to become narrow in scope and leave enough room for the organization of dissent against it. The Jharkhand experience is a perfect proof of this. The paradoxical nature of the developmental process here has not only pauperised a large section of the Jharkhandis economically, but also posed a serious threat to their distinct cultural ethos. Deprivation on these accounts, in an interrelated manner, constitutes the conflict core of the movement. At present the movement is passing through a very weak phase, perhaps because of the leaderships' failure to realize this important nexus. The middle class elitism, which has engulfed the movement since the 1980s might have been successful in the formation of the Jharkhand state, but it is yet to solve the problem of exploitation faced by the wretched section of the Jharkhandis. To cover up this failure the ruling elites of the new state has resorted to the policy of creating ethnic hostilities and tensions within the Jharkhandi communities to survive politically in the region. The proposed domicile policy of the Jharkhand state, probably, has been devised to attain this goal. Today instead of the united struggle to achieve the unfulfilled ethnic aspirations of the different communities, Jharkhand is gradually turning into a hotbed of intra ethnic clashes. Conflict of this type, leading to ethnic cleansing, however, is not a very healthy sign for the cause of Indian democracy. It is high time for the Jharkhandi leadership to realize the fundamental conditions of the conflict in Jharkhand and mobilize people around these. Moving forward in this direction the movement can emancipate the underprivileged Jharkhandis from the clutches of exploitation, which should be the basic aim of any developmental activities.

NOTES

1. The rebellious Santhals demanded a 'Santhal Raj' during the *Santhal Hool* of 1855, while the Mundas insisted to form a 'Munda Raj' under the leadership of Birsa Munda during the *Munda Uprising* (1895-1900).
2. These terms literally mean the forest dwellers.
3. For the statistical details of this migration pattern, see Corbridge (1993).
4. Italics are added.

REFERENCES

Adhikary, A.K. (1998), "Ethnic Pluralities and Nation-State in India: A Study of Contemporary Social Formations", *Journal of Indian Anthropological Society,* Vol. 33, No. 1, March, 9-16.

Ahmed, I. (1992), "Politics of Ethnicity, and the Rise of Separatist Movements in South Asia" in Lars Rudebeck (ed.) *When Democracy Makes Sense: Studies in the Democratic Potential of Third World Popular Movements,* AKUT. Sweden: Uppsala University: 31-68.

—— (1996), *State, Nation and Ethnicity in Contemporary South Asia.* London, New York: Pinter Publishers.

Basu, S. (1994), *Jharkhand Movement: Ethnicity and Culture of Silence,* Shimla: Indian Institute of Advanced Study.

Belanger, S. and Pinard, M. (1991), "Ethnic Movements and the Competition Model: Some Missing Links", *American Sociological Review,* Vol. 56: 446-57.

Bergesen, A. and Herman, M. (1998), "Immigration, Race, and Riot: the Los Angeles Uprising", *American Sociological Review,* Vol. 63: 39-54.

Bonacich, E. (1972), "A Theory of Ethnic Antagonism: The Split Labour Market", *American Sociological Review,* Vol. 37: 547-59.

Carment D. (1994), "The Ethnic Dimension in World Politics: Theory, Policy and Early Warning." *Third World Quarterly*, Vol. 15, No. 4: 551-82.

Chaklader, S. (1985), "Majority-Minority Relationships and State Politics in Eastern Region of India", *ICSSR Research Abstracts Quarterly*, Vol. XIV, Nos. 3 & 4.

Chaudhuri, B. (1991), "Ethnic Conflict in the Chittagong Hill Tracts of Bangladesh" in Reed Coughlan and S.W.R. Samarasinghe (eds.) *Economic Dimensions of Ethnic Conflict: International Perspective,* London: Pinter Publishers.

Chaudhuri, K. (1997), "Bodo Autonomy: Regrouping of New Radical Forces", *The Statesman*, February 12.

Clark, S. (1998), "International Competition and the Treatment of Minorities: Seventeenth Century Cases and General Propositions." *American Journal of Sociology*, Vol. 103, No.5: 1267-1308.

Corbridge, S. (1993), "Ousting Singbonga: The Struggle For India's Jharkhand" in Peter Robb (ed.) *Dalit Movements and the Meaning of Labour in India,* Delhi: Oxford University Press, 153-82.

Das, V. (1992), *Jharkhand: Castle Over the Graves.* New Delhi: Inter-India Publications.

Devalle, S.B.C. (1992), *Discourses of Ethnicity: Culture and Protest in Jharkhand.* New Delhi, Newbury Park, London: Sage Publications.

Eriksen, T.H. (1993), *Ethnicity and Nationalism: Anthropological Perspectives,* London: Boulder, Colorado: Pluto Press.

EPW (2008), "Violence in Bodoland", *Economic and Political Weekly*, Vol. XLIII, No. 41: 6.

Esteva, G. (2010), "Development", in W. Sachs (ed.) *The Development Dictionary: A Guide to Knowledge as Power*. London: Zed Books: 1-23.

Friedman, J. (1990), "Being in the World: Globalization and Localization". In Mike Featherstone (ed.) *Global Culture*. London: Sage Publications: 311-28.

Ghosh, A. (1998), *Jharkhand Movement—A Study in the Politics of Regionalism.* Calcutta: Minerva Associates (Publications) Pvt. Ltd.

Ghosh, K. (1999), "A Market for Aboriginality: Primitivism and Race Classification in the Indentured Labour Market of Colonial India" in Gautam Bhadra, Gyan Prakash and Susie Tharu (ed.) *Subaltern Studies X*, New Delhi: Oxford University Press: 8-48.

Ghosh, P.S. (1998), "Ethnic Conflict and Conflict Management: The Indian Case", in Iftekharuzzaman (ed.) *Ethnicity and Constitutional Reform in South Asia*. New Delhi: Manohar: 49-83.

Gill, R. (2000), "Cities and Ethnicity: A Case of De-ethnicization or Re-ethnicization?" *Sociological Bulletin*, Vol. 49, No. 2: 211-28.

Gill, K.P.S. (2014), "Assam: Cyclical Butchery", *South Asia Intelligence Review.* Volume 13, No. 26, December 29. Available at: http://www.satp.org/satporgtp/sair/Archives/sair13/13_26.htm accessed on 27.06.2015.

Glazer, N. and Moynihan, D.P. (1975), *Ethnicity: Theory and Experience,* Cambridge, Massachusetts, and London: Harvard University Press.

Hannan, M.T. (1979), "The Dynamics of Ethnic Boundaries in Modern States", in John, W. Meyer and M.T. Hannan (Eds.) *National Development and the World System.* Chicago: University of Chicago Press: 253-75.

Hechter, M. (1975), *Internal Colonialism: The Celtic Fringe in British National Development.* Berkeley: University of California Press.

Hechter, M. (1978), "Group Formation and the Cultural Division of Labour", *American Journal of Sociology*, Vol. 84, No. 2: 293-318.

Madhok, V.K. (1996) "India's North-East: A Time-Bomb Ticking Away", *The Statesman,* April 15.

Meher, R. (2001), "Degeneration of the Periphery under Hegemonic Development: The Case of Marginalization of the Aboriginal in a Tribal Region", *Indian Social Science Review*, Vol. 3, No. 2: 289-385.

Munda, R.D. (1992), "In search of a Tribal Homeland", in Buddhadeb Chaudhuri (ed.) *Tribal Transformation in India,* Vol.III, New Delhi. Inter-India Publications: 377-86.

Murmu, G. (2002), "Development of Santali Language and Literature and its Recognition. (Language/Script movement)" Paper Presented at *First National Seminar on Linguistic, Landscaping in India with particular reference to the new States* (21-22 February, 2002) Central Institute of Indian Languages, Mysore. For details see: http://wesanthals.tripod.com/santals/index.html.

Nielsen, F. (1985), "Toward a Theory of Ethnic Solidarity in Modern Societies", *American Sociological Review,* Vol. 50, April, 133-149.

Patel, P.J. (1996), "The Problem of Ethnicity and Social Cohesiveness: A Critique of Modernism and Postmodernism." In A.R. Momin (ed.) *The Legacy of G.S. Ghurye: A Centennial Fetschrift.* Bombay: Popular Prakashan: 115-29.

Premdas, R.R. (1995), *Ethnic Conflict and Development: The Case of Fiji,* Aldershot: Ashgate Publishing Limited.

Rahnema, M. (2010), "Participation", in W. Sachs (ed.) *The Development Dictionary: A Guide to Knowledge as Power*, London: Zed Books: 127-44.

Sachs, W. (2010), "Preface to the New Edition." In W. Sachs (ed.) *The Development Dictionary: A Guide to Knowledge as Power.* London: Zed Books: vi-xiv.

Segal, E.S. (2000), "Intersections Among Tribalism, Ethnicity and Gender in the Light of African Data", *Sociological Bulletin.* Vol. 49, No. 1: 1-17.

Sengupta, N. (1982), "Background of the Jharkhand Question", in Nirmal Sengupta (ed.) *Fourth World Dynamics: Jharkhand.* Delhi: Authors Guild Publications: 1-39.

Sharma, S.K. (1995), "Multiculturalism and Minorities in Canada: Some Reflections on Ethnic Conflicts", *Social Action,* Vol. 45, No. 1: 11-23.

Singh, K.S. (1977), "From ethnicity to Regionalism: A Study in Tribal Politics and Movements in Chotanagpur from 1900 to 1975", in S.C. Malik (ed.) *Dissent, Protest and Reform in Indian Civilization,* Shimla: Indian Institute of Advanced Study: 317-45.

Sinha, S.C., Sen, J. and Panchbhai, S. (1969), "The Concept of Diku among the Tribes of Chotanagpur." *Man in India.* Vol. 49, No. 2: 121-138.

Soren, S. (1992), "Jharkhand Rajya Ki Sawal" (in Hindi) in S. Narayan (ed.) *Jharkhand Movement: Origin and Evolution,* New Delhi: Inter-India Publications: 19-27.

Stone, J. (1979), "Internal Colonialism", *Ethnic and Racial Studies,* Vol. 2, No. 2: 255-259.

The Statesman (1997), "No Peace still Bodo state is created", April 11.

The Statesman (1998), "Santhals of Kokrajhar may hit back", May 10.

The Statesman (1999), "Sovereignty *vs.* Statehood divides Nagas: Hoho", September 23.

12

Bullying: A Social Issue

Rumki Gupta and *Jayeta Dhara*

INTRODUCTION

Social issues are matters that can be explained only by factors outside an individual's control and immediate social environment which affect many individuals in a society. There are many social issues that need to be addressed, but bullying in one way or another has affected everybody. Bullying behaviour is a social problem most commonly associated with schools and workplaces, but can take place in any environment where people live, work and play together. Bullying is a serious problem for schools, parents, and public-policy-makers. It also creates risks of health, both physical and mental and social problems in childhood. It needs to be mentioned here the definition of bullying.

Violence and aggression in schools are a problem in many countries around the world (Rigby and Slee, 1991; Pepler *et al.*, 1994; Smith and Sharpe, 1994; Genta *et al.*, 1996; Okabayashi, 1996; Olweus, 1991). One form of aggression that takes place at school is bullying. Bullying is an interaction in which a dominant individual (the bully) repeatedly exhibits aggressive behaviour intended to cause distress to a less dominant individual (the victim) (Olweus, 1991; Smith and Thompson, 1991). Aggression in childhood tends to become a lifestyle, i.e., aggressive patterns developed during the elementary years tend to continue into adolescence and adulthood (Berthold and Hoover, 2000). Farrington (1993) defined bullying as repeated oppression, physical or psychological, of a less powerful person by a more powerful person or group. It may not the same thing as conflict, violence or disagreement—although it may involve all these. Illustrative other views are:

(a) It is deliberate, harmful, verbal, physical and psychological behaviours (Tattum and Tattum, 1992).
(b) It is the context of an imbalance of power between the bully or bullies and the victim (Rigby, 2000).

Bullying among school children is a very old phenomenon. The fact that some children are frequently and systematically harassed and attacked by other children has been described in the literary works, and many adults have personal experience of it from their own school days. For a number of years, these efforts were largely confined to Scandinavia. Norwegian Researcher Dan Olweus is pioneer in this area who started after 1970. In the 1980s and early 1990s, however, bullying among school children also has attracted attention in other countries such as Japan, Great Britain, the Netherlands, Australia, Canada, and the USA. Olweus (1987) described bullies as having an aggressive personality pattern that predisposes them to respond aggressively. By bullying, these children employ their aggression to assert power and dominance. In contrast, victim's are characterized as being passive, anxious, weak, lacking self-confidence, unpopular and as having low self-esteem. Olweus (1978) described bullies as physically strong, aggressive, impulsive, demonstrating the need to dominate, and expressing a positive attitude towards violence. Bullying appears to fit the overall pattern of anti-social and risk behaviour. Most studies agree that overall, boy/girl bullying was rated as more distressing than girl/boy bullying (Soutter and McKenzie, 2000). Along with the immediate effects of bullying and victimization, this behaviour has long-term negative consequences for all those involved. Aggressive behaviour identified in the school years can also persist in adulthood as higher rates of criminality, marital violence, child abuse and sexual harassment. Researchers have also found that there are developmental patterns in the type of aggression (Bjorkqvist *et al.,* 1992). Evidence from longitudinal studies indicates that the tendency to bully others at school significantly predicts subsequent antisocial and violent behaviour (Rigby, K., 2003).

EFFECT OF BULLYING

There are different forms of bullying which may result into irritability, sense of panic, social ostracism, feeling of loneliness, anxiety and depression, aggressive behaviour, formation of subgroups, introvertness and shyness and impaired concentration and hampering of educational progress etc. It is one of the root causes in the development of cognitive process, personality, academic achievement and future behaviour profile.

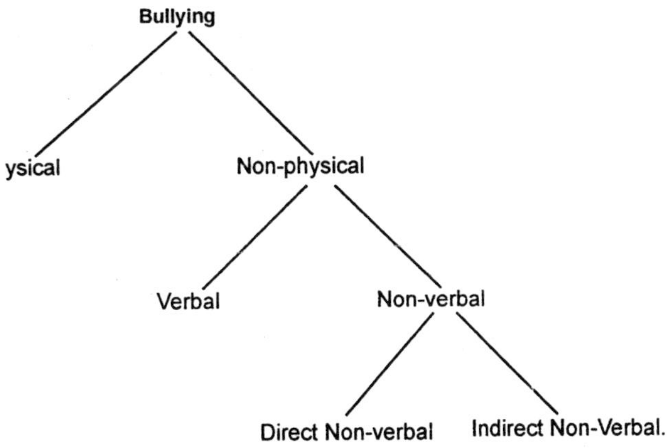

Fig. 12.1: Forms of bullying.

Examples of all the forms of bullying are presented below:
Physical bullying—Hit, kicked
Non-physical bullying is of two types–

(i) *Verbal*—Abusive telephone calls, name calling, threatening etc.
(ii) *Non-Verbal*—It is not directly physical. It is also of two types—
    (a) Direct non-verbal: Rude gestures
    (b) Indirect non-verbal: Ignoring, excluding, isolating.

During the last decade, bullying of and by children of all ages has become a prominent social, educational, legal and media issue. Many recent studies have sought to quantify students' experience of bullying in schools (Glover, Cartwight and Gleeson, 1998; Rigby, 1999). Bullying is an issue of concern to educators because it has the potential to affect student's academic and social development (Banks, 1997; Griffiths, 1996). There is no common consensus in defining bullying (Besag, 1989).

Numerous research reports document the relationship between bullying and a variety of academic, social and mental health issues. Eisenberg and Neumark-Sztainer (2003) found that peer harassment, i.e., bullying is negatively related to connection to school and academic achievement. Dewey Cornell (Website reference 1) studied school safety and declared that schools with high levels of reported bullying had lower passing rates by an average of 3 to 6 per cent across tests—when compared with schools with less reported bullying. The gap was reflected on state exams in algebra, world history and earth science. Konoshi and others (2010) examined the link between school bullying and academic achievement for 15 year old students in Canadian schools and showed that Mathematics and Reading achievement was negatively related to school bullying. Smokowski and Kopsaz (2005) reviewed bullying characteristics and explained how bullying is directly related to school achievement. This review of research on bullying indicates substantial evidence for the negative impact of bullying on student achievement. Bullying (Olweus and Alsaker, 1991) and other types of antisocial behaviour put students at risk for failure in school. Regarding the relation between school achievement and victimization, it has been shown that bullies and aggressive victim's have low achievement (Austin and Joseph, 1996).

Males tend to bully more overtly and more physically. They are more likely to be caught bullying, and their behaviour is more likely to be categorized as bullying because it fits in the more traditional definition of what bullying is. Female bullying tends to occur behind the scenes and in more subtle ways. Their particular brand of bullying does not always get included in the bullying definition. For over 50 years, researchers have been studying how boys and girls interact. Statistics show that boys are almost twice as likely to bully as girls. Olweus studied in seven elementary education schools in Portugal. The sample consisted of 387 students between 7 and 14 years old. Data are presented in terms of descriptive statistics and differences between proportions were analyzed using chi-square tests. The gender analysis of victimization and aggression shows that boys and girls are both victim's and aggressors, and there are significant differences in involvement in bullying between genders and the roles played.

From the review of the literature, it has been observed that various types of studies have been done in Western countries. Moreover, in many studies girls' consistently reported being less bullied than boys. Evidence of enough research does not appear to be there to gain a clear picture of bullying especially in India and in West-Bengal also. Considering the paucity of data from India and taking into account the potential of this phenomenon which causes damage to the well being of children, this research problem is felt needed.

The objective of the study is to assess the effect of bullying in school and its relation to Subject-wise as well as total academic achievement of the school students. Gender is also taken into consideration to explore whether there is any variation of effect of bullying and nature of relationship on the school going students as well.

METHOD

Sampling

Only Government or Government Aided Schools of Kolkata and 17 districts of West Bengal excluding Darjeeling, but including Siliguri Sub-Division of Darjeeling District were covered.

From Kolkata, an SRSWOR (Simple random sampling without replacement) of 20 such schools have been chosen. From each chosen school 5 students of Class VII have been chosen by SRSWOR and also 5 such of Class VIII have been chosen by SRSWOR giving a sample of $(5+5) \times 20 = 200$ students. SRSWOR of 2 teachers teaching in Class VII and 2 teachers teaching in Class VIII have been chosen. Each of the teacher was asked to give a list of students those can be identified as bully in his or her opinion.

Similarly, out of all the cities and towns of Hooghly 2 have been chosen by SRSWOR. Out of all the villages in Hooghly District an SRSWOR of 10 villages have be chosen. Out of every such chosen cities/towns/villages 2 schools have been chosen by SRSWOR method. Thus, in all 24 schools have been chosen altogether. From each chosen school an SRSWOR of 5 students of Class VII and 5 of Class VIII have been chosen giving altogether a sample of 240 students of Hooghly district. In addition, from each chosen school 4 teachers teaching in classes VII and VIII have been chosen by SRSWOR method. They provided the list of marked bully from respective classes. Thus, final sample comprised of 1147 students including randomly selected students and students identified by teachers.

MEASURES USED

The following measures have been used depending upon the purpose of the study. As the medium of instruction in all the selected schools is Bengali, the Bengali Version of the Questionnaires was administered on the students and psychometric property of the questionnaire has been calculated:

(a) Schedule for identification of bullying behaviour by teachers' opinion.
(b) Personality Questionnaire—It contains 50 items, separated into 5 dimensions viz., (i) Intellectual curiosity (IC), (ii) Self-disciplined and dutiful (SD & DU), (iii) Assertiveness (AS), (iv) Cooperativeness (CO) and (v) Emotional Stability (ES). The value of Cronbach's α is 0.81 for this questionnaire.
(c) Peer relation Questionnaire by Ken Rigby and Phillip Slee. It contains 20 items and 3 sub-scales, i.e. Bully Scale, Victim Scale and Pro-Social Scale. The value of Cronbach's α is 0.75 for this questionnaire.
(d) Academic Achievement—Annual Examination marks of Bengali, English, Mathematics, Science and Average Academic Achievement scores of the students.
(e) One Biographical Questionnaire.

PROCEDURE

The measures have been administered on the selected students of the sampled schools. At the same time annual examination marks of the students have been collected from the school records. After collecting the data, these were scrutinized carefully and scoring was done following the scheduled scoring procedure.

RESULTS AND DISCUSSIONS

Table 12.1 reveals Mean, SD and t-value between Bully and Non-bully group. It is seen from the results that subject-wise performances

Table 12.1: Mean, SD and t-value of Bully and Non-bully

Variables	*Bully (262)*		*Non-bully (885)*		*t-values*
	Mean	*SD*	*Mean*	*SD*	
Bully Score	9.56	1.793	5.20	1.162	46.521**
Pro-social Score	13.71	2.347	14.27	2.051	3.750**
Bengali Score	41.01	18.068	45.84	18.676	3.587**
English Score	36.46	18.950	41.01	19.823	3.191**
Mathematics Score	26.92	19.675	31.53	22.496	2.891**
Science Score	35.41	18.745	40.20	20.215	3.310**
Total Score	321.59	151.629	363.11	147.749	3.859**

Source: Field Survery. **Significant at the 0.01 level.

of the non-bully students are better in comparison to the bully group and the t-values are also significantly different. In case of bully score significant differences exist between the Bully and Non-bully students. Average Pro-social score of Non-bully students is greater than Bully students and the difference is significant at 1 per cent level.

Product moment correlation for the Bully group was computed and the results are presented in Table 12.2. It has been seen that all the subjects are negatively related with bully score though the relations are not significant. Only in case of science subject the relation is negatively significant. There is positively significant relationship among all the subjects and pro-social score in this group.

Table 12.2: Correlation Table for Bully

	Bully	*Pro-social*	*Bengali*	*English*	*Mathematics*	*Science*	*Total*
Bully	1	–.081	–.112	–.126	–.079	–.169**	–.084
Pro-social		1	.259**	.267**	.190**	.260**	.273**
Bengali			1	.699**	.672**	.745**	.698**
English				1	.725**	.741**	.714**
Mathematics					1	.776**	.725**
Science						1	.767**
Total							**1**

Source: Field Survey.

Product moment correlation for the Non-bully group was computed and the results are presented in Table 12.3. It has been seen that all the subjects are negatively related with bully score and all the relations are significant. There is positively significant relationship among all the subjects and pro-social score in this group.

Table 12.3: Correlation Table for Non-bully

	Bully	*Pro-social*	*Bengali*	*English*	*Mathematics*	*Science*	*Total*
Bully	1	–.071*	–.135**	–.145**	–.116**	–.105**	–.104**
Pro-social		1	.161**	.170**	.172**	.200**	.198**
Bengali			1	.723**	.687**	.742**	.775**
English				1	.739**	.746**	.733**
Mathematics					1	.736**	.751**
Science						1	.791**
Total							**1**

**.Correlation is significant at the 0.01 level (2-tailed).
*. Correlation is significant at the 0.05 level (2-tailed).
Source: Field Survey.

Table 12.4: Mean, SD and t-value of Bully Boys and Non-bully Boys

Variables	*Bully (222)*		*Non-bully (748)*		*t-values*
	Mean	*SD*	*Mean*	*SD*	
Bully Score	9.61	1.826	5.22	1.157	42.848**
Pro-social Score	13.85	2.160	14.32	1.994	3.060**
Bengali Score	41.61	18.276	46.29	18.138	3.251**
English Score	37.65	19.391	42.34	19.524	3.028**
Mathematics Score	28.04	20.287	32.46	22.297	2.544**
Science Score	35.86	18.918	40.55	19.964	3.001**
Total Score	**331.22**	**157.098**	**370.65**	**141.800**	**3.439****

**Significant at the 0.01 level.
Source: Field Survey.

Table 12.4 shows the mean, SD and t-value of the Bully score, Pro-social score and different subjects between Bully Boys and Non-bully Boys. It is revealed from the results that the average of all the scores of Non-bully students is higher than the Bully students and the difference is significant at 1 per cent level.

Table 12.5: Correlation Table for Bully Boys

	Bully	*Pro-social*	*Bengali*	*English*	*Mathematics*	*Science*	*Total*
Bully	1	–.070	–.128	–.149*	–.082	–.176*	–.097
Pro-social		1	.221**	.274**	.154*	.255**	.255**
Bengali			1	.694**	.671**	.742**	.710**
English				1	.719**	.733**	.713**
Mathematics					1	.777**	.729**
Science						1	.778**
Total							**1**

*Correlation is significant at the 0.05 level (2-tailed).
**Correlation is significant at the 0.01 level (2-tailed).
Source: Field Survey.

A perusal of inter-correlations reveals significant correlation among all the subjects and Pro-social score. In this group bully score is negatively related with Pro-social score and all the subjects, but the relationship is significant at 5 per cent level for English and Science.

Table 12.6: Correlation Table for Non-Bully Boys

	Bully	*Pro-social*	*Bengali*	*English*	*Mathematics*	*Science*	*Total*
Bully	1	–.081*	–.130**	–.160**	–.112**	–.111**	–.109**
Pro-social		1	.147**	.143**	.145**	.177**	.186**
Bengali			1	.714**	.682**	.743**	.766**
English				1	.713**	.747**	.716**
Mathematics					1	.727**	.753**
Science						1	.784**
Total							1

**Correlation is significant at the 0.01 level (2-tailed).
*Correlation is significant at the 0.05 level (2-tailed).
Source: Field Survey.

An examination of the inter-correlations reveals negatively significant relationship between bully score and all the subjects. Like bully boys, Pro-social score reveals significant correlation with all the subjects.

Table 12.7: Mean, SD and t-value of Bully Girls and Non-bully Girls

Variables	*Bully (40)*		*Non-bully (137)*		*t-values*
	Mean	*SD*	*Mean*	*SD*	
Bully Score	9.28	1.585	5.08	1.182	18.191**
Pro-social Score	12.98	3.125	14.01	2.328	2.273
Bengali Score	37.85	16.798	43.40	21.275	1.498
English Score	30.21	15.180	33.83	19.973	1.048
Mathematics Score	21.08	14.997	26.51	22.988	1.389
Science Score	33.06	17.863	38.27	21.506	1.378
Total Score	**270.51**	**106.118**	**322.08**	**171.550**	**1.777**

**Significant at the 0.01 level
Source: Field Survey.

It may be stated from the results presented in Table 12.7 that the average pro-social score and average scores of all the subjects of non-bully girls are higher than that of bully girls though the differences are not significant. It may be said that perhaps bullying has no effect in case of this particular group. The results also reveal that the difference in average bully score between bully and non-bully girls is significant (t-value—18.191) at 1 per cent level.

Table 12.8: Correlation Table for Bully Girls

	Bully	*Pro-social*	*Bengali*	*English*	*Mathematics*	*Science*	*Total*
Bully	1	–.195	–.051	–.050	–.139	–.156	–.088
Pro-social		1	.396*	.193	.318*	.279	.343*
Bengali			1	.730**	.673**	.760**	.613**
English				1	.725**	.815**	.660**
Mathematics					1	.789**	.615**
Science						1	.726**
Total							**1**

* Correlation is significant at the 0.05 level (2-tailed).
** Correlation is significant at the 0.01 level (2-tailed).
Source: Field Survey.

A perusal of inter-correlations reveals significant correlation among Pro-social score and Bengali, Mathematics and Total achievement score. In this group bully score is negatively related with Pro-social score and all the subjects but the relationship is not significant.

Table 12.9: Correlation Table for Non-bully Girls

	Bully	*Pro-social*	*Bengali*	*English*	*Mathematics*	*Science*	*Total*
Bully	1	–.040	–.175*	–.115	–.166	–.085	–.115
Pro-social		1	.206*	.256**	.267**	.286**	.220*
Bengali			1	.777**	.706**	.739**	.810**
English				1	.858**	.763**	.792**
Mathematics					1	.783**	.735**
Science						1	.832**
Total							**1**

**. Correlation is significant at the 0.01 level (2-tailed).
*. Correlation is significant at the 0.05 level (2-tailed).
Source: Field Survey.

An examination of the inter-correlations reveals negative relationship between bully score and all the subjects though the relationships are not significant except Bengali score. Here, Pro-social score reveals significant correlation with all the subjects.

OBSERVATION

Mean, SD and 't'-value of Bully—Non-bully and Bully Boys—Bully Girls students on Bully questionnaire and subject-wise and total Academic Achievement for Classes VII and VIII are presented from Tables 12.1 to 12.9. Bully and non-bully students differ significantly on Bully questionnaire and subject-wise and total Academic Achievement score. The same results have been found out for bully boys and non-bully boys. But in case of bully girls and non-bully girls no such difference was found out. The results are in expected direction as bully score is negatively related with the subjects' scores and total Academic Achievement score.

REFERENCES

Austin, S. and Joseph, S. (1996), "Assessment of Bully/Victim Problems in 8 to 11 Year-Olds", *British Journal of Educational Psychology,* 66: 447-56.

Banks, R. (1997), "Bullying in Schools. *Eric Digest, EDO-PS*-97-17.

Berthold, K. and Hoover, J. (2000), "Correlates of bullying and victimization among intermediate students in Midwestern USA". *School Psychology International*, 21: 65-79.

Besag, V.E. (1989), *Bullies and Victims in Schools: A Guide to Understanding and Management.* Philadelphia: Open University Press.

Bjorkqvist, K., Osterman, K. and Kaukiainen, A. (1992), "The Development of Direct and Indirect Aggressive Strategies in Males and Females", in K. Bjorkgvist and P. Niemela (eds.) *Of Mice and Women: Aspects of Female Aggression*, San Diego: Academic.

Eisenberg, M.E., Neumark-Sztainer, D. and Perry, C.L. (2003), "Peer harassment, school connectedness and academic achievement". *Journal of School Health,* 73, (8): 311-316.

Farrington, D.P. (1993), "Understanding and Preventing Bullying", in M. Tonry and N. Morris (eds.) *Crime and Justice*, p. 17. Chicago: University of Chicago Press.

Genta, M.L., Menesini, E. Fonzi, A., Costabile, A. and Smith, P.K. (1996), "Bullies and Victims in Schools in Central and Southern Italy", *European Journal of Psychology of Education,* 11: 97-110.

Glover, D., Cartwight, N. and Gleeson, D. (1998), *Towards Bully-Free Schools: Intervention in Action*. Open University Press, UK.

Griffiths, C. (1996), *Dealing with Bullying*. Kids Help Line, Milton: Brisbane.

Konishi, C. (2010), "Do school bullying and student-teacher relationships matter for academic achievement? A multilevel analysis", *Canadian Journal of School Psychology*, 25, 1, Thousand Oaks: Sage Publications.

O Kabayashi, H. (1996), "Intervention for school Bullying: Observing American Schools", *Psychologia,* 39: 163-178.

Olweus, D. (1991), "Bully/Victim Problems among School children: Basic Facts and Effects of a School-based Intervention Program", in D. Kepler and K. Rubin (eds.) *The Development and Treatment of Childhood Aggression*, 411-48. Hillsdale, NJ: Erlbaum.

Olweus, D. and Alsaker, F. (1991), "Assessing Change in a Cohort-Longitudinal Study with Hierarchical Data", in D. Magnusson, L. Burgman, G. Rudinger and B. Torestad (eds.) *Problems and Methods in Longitudinal Research: Stability and Change*, 107-32. London: Cambridge University Press.

Olweus, D. (1978), "School-yard Bullying—Grounds for Intervention", *School Safety,* 6: 4-11.

Olweus, D. (1978), *Aggression in the Schools: Bullies and Whipping Boys*. Washington, DC: Hemisphere.

Pepler, D.J., Craig, W.M., Ziegler, S. and Charach, A. (1994), "An Evaluation of an Anti-bullying Intervention in Toronto Schools", *Canadian Journal of Community Mental Health,* 13: 95-110.

Rigby, K. (2003), Consequences of Bullying in Schools. *Canadian Journal of Psychiatry,* 48 (9): 583-590.

Rigby, K. (2000), "Sharks of many shapes and colours". *Prime Focus*, 22: 3-5.

Rigby, K. (1999), "Peer victimization at school and the health of secondary school students". *British Journal of Educational Psychology*, 69: 95-104.

Rigby, K. and Slee, P.T. (1991), "Bullying among Australian School Children: Reported Behaviour and Attitudes towards Victims", *The Journal of Social Psychology,* 131: 615-627.

Smith, P.K., and Thompson, D. (1991), *Practical Approaches to Bullying*. London: David Fulton.

Smith, P.K. and Sharpe, S. (1994), *School Bullying: Insights and Perspectives*. London: Routledge.

Smokowski, P.R., and Kopasz, K. (2005), Bullying in school: An overview of types, effects, family characteristics and intervention strategies, *Children and Schools*, 27(2): 101-110.

Tattum, D. and Tattum, E. (1992), *Social Education and Personal Development*. David Fulton, London.

Website reference: 1. www.washingtonpos.com/local/education/bullying-linked-to-lower-school-achievement/2011/09/01/gIQ Arm Qw4_sl

13

Right to Equality: Indian Women

Himansu S. Ghosh

INTRODUCTION

We live in 'democracy'. The success or failure of a democracy depends largely on the extent to which equality is enjoyed by the people. Equality is a precondition of a democracy. But, social inequality has been a historical fact. According to Tom Bottomore, "During the greater part of human history this inequality among men has been generally accepted as an unalterable fact."[1] With the development of democracy, the idea of equality was formulated to remove social injustice. Fundamentally, thus equality implies a certain levelling process, but that does not mean identity of treatment and identity of reward for efforts and according to H.J. Laski equality implies three things — (i) absence of special privilege; (ii) provision for adequate opportunities to all; and (iii) most largely a matter of proportion, i.e. "urgent claims of all must be met before we can meet the particular claims of some".[2]

HISTORY OF EQUALITY

Historically, equality is a matter of enquiry in West and East since the dawn of civilization. Great Greek thinker Pericles, for instance, in famous 'Funeral Speech' mentioned about equality with reference to momentary indifference to worldly life in 430 B.C. Similarly, Plato to uphold equality propounded the theory of communism of wives, children and property with reference to his great theory of justice (Republic 427—347 B.C.). On the other hand, Aristotle

(384—322 B.C.) discovered that inequality was a cause of rebellion in many a state. According to him "treating equals equally and unequals unequally" is justice and thus man and woman or slave cannot be equal.

Anyway, the equality in modern sense was first developed during the French Revolution of 1789. The battle cry of the said revolution was "Liberty, Equality and Fraternity" and in "Declaration of the Rights of Man and of the Citizen" it was said "Men are born free and remain free and equal in rights .... (Art. 1)". The aim of all political organizations is the conservation of the natural and imprescriptible rights of man (Art. 2). The foundation of sovereignty rests essentially in the Nation; no agency or individual can exercise authority except such as comes expressly from the Nation.[3] In fact, this is the first institutional demand for abolition of inequality. And finally based on U.N. Charter the "Universal Declaration of Human Rights" was adopted in 1948, where in Article 1 it was said that "All human beings are born free and equal in dignity and rights. They are endowed with reason and conscience and should act towards one another in a spirit of brotherhood."[4]

INDIAN HISTORY OF RIGHT TO EQUALITY

In India ancient Sanskrit Literature and proverbs clearly show that people of India were also concerned with the question of equality and inequality. For instance, the *Rig Veda* which was composed around 4000 BC, mentioned that worship process must be followed jointly, i.e. both husband and wife should act together as they are equal. Swami Abhedananda pointed out: "Therefore, in India, what is claimed for the women, there should be no partiality shown for either man or woman according to the ethical, moral and religious standards of the Hindus .... The Old Testament, the Quran and the Zend Avesta have made women the scapegoats for all the crimes committed by man. It is the special injunction of the *Vedas* that no married man shall perform any religious rite, ceremony or sacrifice without being joined in it by his wife."[5] But gradually the position of Indian women had been lowered down by thinkers like Manu and others. Besides, the urge for male child and growth of non-Aryan wives were the major causes for such degradation of women in India which continued until India became free from British Raj and adopted her constitution in November 26, 1949.

INDIAN CONSTITUTION AND RIGHT TO EQUALITY

In 1948, the United Nations General Assembly unanimously adopted the resolution of Universal Declaration of Human Rights which proclaimed the idea that all humans are free and equal by birth. Naturally, the Founding Fathers of the Constitution of India laid immense emphasis on the principle of equality and, thus, the Constitution of India in Articles 14 to 18 presented the Right to Equality as the first and foremost of the Fundamental Rights.

According to Article 14 of the Constitution of India, "The State shall not deny to any person equality before the law or equal protection of the laws within the territory of India."[6] This implies that all Indians are equal before the law. The first part of this chapter, i.e., "equality before the law" is drawn from the British concept of "Rule of law" which implies that whatever highly placed one might be, one does not have any special status before the law. The second part of the chapter "Equal protection of law" is taken from the American Principle of "Due Process of Law". The implication of this part is that the law will protect all equally. According to M.V. Pylee, "equality before the law is a somewhat negative concept implying the absence of any special privilege in favour of any individual and the equal subjugation of all classes to the ordinary law, equal protection of laws is a more positive concept employing equality of treatment under equal circumstances."[7]

Article 15 states that "The State shall not discriminate against any citizen on grounds only of religion, race, caste, sex, place of births or any of them"[8] in regard to access to shops, public restaurants, hotels and places of public entertainment. The same conditions apply in connection with the right to use wells, tanks, bathing *ghats*, roads and places of public resort maintained wholly or partly by the state funds. In fact this Article is more assertive against sex discrimination.

Article 16 guarantees that "There shall be equality of opportunity, for all citizens in matter relating to employment or appointment to any office under the State"[9] and that no citizen shall on grounds of religion, race, caste, sex, place of birth or any of them, be ineligible for any office under the state.

According to Article 17, "untouchability is abolished and its practice in any form is forbidden. The enforcement of any disability arising out of "untouchability" shall be an offence punishable in accordance with law".[10] The Parliament has enacted the

Untouchability Offences Act, 1955 (later amended and renamed in 1976 as Protection of Civil Rights Act) which details the penalties and punitive measure, to be adopted if untouchability is practiced.

Lastly, according to Article 18, "No title not being a military or academic distinction, shall be conferred by the state." Even an Indian citizen cannot accept any title from abroad. In fact, this creates a division in society. The Janata Government from 1977 to 1980 stopped the practice of awarding titles unlike the British Government to create division among the members of society. However, this system was reinforced since 1980 onwards.

Besides, in various judgements of Supreme Court of India, e.g. Smt. Champakam Dorairanjan case[12], Chiranjitlal Chawdhuri case[13] etc. it was clearly stated "that among equals the law should be equal and should be equally administered, that like should be treated alike."

Thus, constitutionally speaking equality prevails in India. Both male and female theoretically enjoy equal rights.

WOMEN IN INDIA *VIS-À-VIS* THE WORLD

In the above context the question arises in our mind, does the Indian women enjoy equal right with male counterpart? In short, the answer would be negative and to justify this contention we can examine the Census Reports, regarding ratio of male and female (Table 13.1) which clearly show the female-male ratio is appallingly low.

Table 13.1: Gender Ratio of Census Report in 1901—2011

Census Year	*Ratio*	
	Male	*Female*
1901	1000	972
1911	1000	964
1921	1000	955
1931	1000	950
1941	1000	945
1951	1000	946
1961	1000	941
1971	1000	930
1981	1000	935
1991	1000	927
2001	1000	933
2011	1000	943

Source: Registrar General of India, Provisional Population Tables (New Delhi, 2011).

Table 13.1 shows that since 1901 first 90 years of period sex-ratio (FMR) registered a significant decline from 0.972 to 0.927 in 1991. However, during 1990s there has been some improvement and declining trend in sex-ratio is checked to some extent in next decades. Preference for male-child has been widespread in India, particularly in the North. This is probably the most important factor that explains the existing sex composition of population and so far there is no change in respect of their preference for sons. It is evident from the Census Reports that the child sex-ratio (0-6 Age group) is declining since 1991 (0.945 in 1991, 0.927 in 2001 and 0.914 in 2011). Thus, there is little possibility of sustained rise in the FMR in India.

This adverse sex-ratio has a tremendous effect on the position of women in general and inequality of women in particular. In the words of Leela Visaria, "Many studies have shown that behavioural factors, including care seeking practices operate against young female children. Girls are less likely to receive medical attention than boys and if they do get treatment then it tends to be at a later state of illness and to be provided by less qualified personnel. Many of the discriminatory practices involved are subtle and lie deep within intimate family behaviour."[14]

Inequality between men and women prevails in India though about 67 years ago we adopted our beloved Constitution and pledged for right to equality. But India is not alone; other countries do have such inequality between man and woman. Amartya Sen and Jean Dreze emphatically said about this female deprivation and missing women in India. In their words "Inequality between men and women is one of the most crucial disparities in many societies, and this is particularly so in India."[15]

To have a brief understanding regarding the position of Indian women in the context of world scenario we may see various indexes developed by various organizations and we think the way the Report of the Global Gender Gap is prepared may be helpful for our easy understanding. World Economic Forum was established in 1971 in Geneva, Switzerland and it prepares the Global Gender Gap Report annually to capture the magnitude and scope of gender based disparities and track their progress at regular interval since 2002. Basically, they use 4 benchmarks to locate the inequality between man and woman. These are: (i) Economic participation, (ii) Educational attainment, (iii) Political empowerment, and (iv) Health and survival. After detailed survey in these four variables they provide country-ranking of the world. In their report, i.e. the Global Gender Gap Report 2013, they have studied 136 countries and examining the disparities they put the countries serially.[16] The Gender Gap Ranking is shown in Table 13.2.

Table 13.2: Women in World—2013 Gender Gap Ranking

Country	*Rank*
Iceland	1
Cuba	15
U.K.	18
U.S.A.	23
Sri Lanka	55
China	69
Bangladesh	75
India	101
Nepal	121
Pakistan	135
Yemen	136

Source: The Global Gender Gap Report, 2013, World Economic Forum.

The gender gap ranking of India has further deteriorated in 2014 (114 out of 142 countries).[17] Now, let us examine the case of Indian women in details only on the basis of the above mentioned 4 parameters.

A. Economic Participation and Opportunities

Economic deprivation of women in the world is so vast and so universal that we cannot explain it in one article. To have a glimpse on this subject Table 13.3 is presented.

Table 13.3: Global Position of Women

- 2/3rd of the work of the world performed by the women
- 1/10th world income enjoyed by women
- 1/100th ownership of the world belong to women
- 2/10th of the world women are deprived from education
- 70 per cent of 130 crore world poor are women
- 80 per cent of 2 crore 7 lakh world refugee are women
- 10.5 per cent seats of Parliament belong to women
- Among HIV patients 42 per cent are women

Source: UN Statistics 1980.

To assess the gender gap in economic activities one pioneer thinker Ester Boserup mentioned that they took part in production but their role in production is not recognized, e.g. women are simply called housewife.[18]

Similarly in India, the women's contribution in economic activities is not considered as productive. Thus, the women are engaged in subsistence farming, their labour is never felt as productive and considered as household work. Even if we look at our own family we see such discrimination also. Thus, in a family the working hours of a male and female are unequal particularly in rural areas. Table 13.4 may help us to get a true picture of such discrimination in India.

Table 13.4: Average Daily Activity of Female and Male (Rural)

Activity	*Female*	*Male*
Kitchen	3.5 hrs	Nil
Water Collection	1 hr	Nil
Fuel Collection	1 hr	Nil
Look After of Cattles	1.5 hrs	0.5 hr
Child Rearing	2 hrs	Nil
Other Household Work	2 hrs	Nil
Cultivation and Related Works	5 hrs	8 hrs
Recreation	0.5 hr	2 hrs
Ritual/Religious function	0.5 hr	Nil
Joint/Group function	0.5 hr	Nil
Total	**17.5 hrs**	**10.5 hrs**

Source: Time Use Survey, India 2000.

Out of 24 hours of a day women are engaged in economic and other activities for 17.5 hours while men are only 10.5 hours, yet women are not recognized as economically or socially productive. Thus, herein lies inequality between male and female.

B. Educational Attainment

Education is vital in our life. It is a process through which we develop our 'self'. There is an oft quoted phrase "Education brings consciousness and consciousness brings revolution." If we look at the world, we will find in the Western countries equilibrium between male and female is achieved as there is 100 per cent literacy. In Third World countries, especially in India the standard of education of women is miserable. They are lagging far if we compare with male counterpart (Table 13.5).

Table 13.5: Literacy Rate in India—1951-2011

Census year	*Male (%)*	*Female (%)*	*Total (%)*
1951	27.16	8.86	18.33
1961	40.40	15.35	28.31
1971	45.96	21.97	34.45
1981	56.37	29.75	43.56
1991	64.13	49.29	52.21
2001	75.26	53.67	64.84
2011	80.89	64.64	72.99

Sources: Census of India.

In fact, according to the Census 2011 out of total population 1,21,05,69,573 only 76,34,98,517 are literate of which 43,46,83,779 male and 32,88,14,738 female. Even in Kerala where the highest literacy rate is recorded, there also women are not at par with the males (*vide* Table 13.6).[20] According to Dreze and Sen "Literacy is a basic tool of self-defense in a society where social interaction often involves the written media. An illiterate person is that much less equipped to defend her in court, to obtain a bank loan, to enforce her inheritance rights, to take advantage of new technology, to compete for secure employment, to get on the right bus, to take part in political activities, in short, to participate successfully in the modern economy and society."[21] Thus, women in India are quite unequal with men in educational attainment.

C. Political Empowerment

Right to vote and right to be elected are two means of political empowerment. But everywhere the political space has been monopolized by men. Representation of women among members of parliament and other statutory bodies has never exceeded men. History and experiences prove this contention.

The U.K. as the first politically conscious country led Glorious Revolution in 1688 and introduced Representative Government in 1832 but the women had nothing to do with that 'democracy' until 1918 only when 30 yrs old women were first allowed to vote. Similarly in France during French Revolution in 1789 there was a declaration

Table 13.6: Comparison of Literacy Rates by Gender (National Sample Survey 2007-2008)

Sl. No.	*India/State/Union Territory#*	*Literacy Rate*		
		Persons	*Males*	*Females*
1.	Jammu & Kashmir	68.74	78.26	58.01
2.	Himachal Pradesh	83.78	90.83	76.60
3.	Punjab	76.68	81.48	71.34
4.	Chandigarh#	86.43	90.54	81.38
5.	Uttarakhand	79.63	88.33	70.70
6.	Haryana	76.64	85.38	66.77
7.	NCT of Delhi#	86.34	91.03	80.93
8.	Rajasthan	67.06	80.51	52.66
9.	Uttar Pradesh	69.72	79.24	59.26
10.	Bihar	63.82	73.39	53.33
11.	Sikkim	82.20	87.29	76.43
12.	Arunachal Pradesh	66.95	73.69	59.57
13.	Nagaland	80.11	83.29	76.69
14.	Manipur	79.85	86.49	73.17
15.	Mizoram	91.58	93.72	89.40
16.	Tripura	87.75	92.18	83.15
17.	Meghalaya	75.48	77.17	73.78
18.	Assam	73.18	78.81	67.27
19.	West Bengal	**77.08**	**82.67**	**71.16**
20.	Jharkhand	67.63	78.45	56.21
21.	Orissa	73.45	82.40	64.36
22.	Chhattisgarh	71.04	81.45	60.59
23.	Madhya Pradesh	70.63	80.53	60.02
24.	Gujarat	79.31	87.23	70.73
25.	Daman and Diu#	87.07	91.48	79.59
26.	Dadra & Nagar Haveli#	77.65	86.46	65.93
27.	Maharashtra	82.91	89.82	75.48
28.	Andhra Pradesh	67.66	75.56	59.74
29.	Karnataka	75.60	82.85	68.13
30.	Goa	87.40	92.81	81.84
31.	Lakshadweep#	92.28	96.11	88.25
32.	Kerala	**93.91**	**96.02**	**91.98**
33.	Tamil Nadu	80.33	86.81	73.86
34.	Puducherry#	86.55	92.12	81.22
35.	Andaman & Nicobar Islands#	86.27	90.11	81.84
	INDIA	**74.04**	**82.14**	**65.46**

Source: Census of India, 2011 (Provisional).

of rights but that was for man only. It is named as "Declaration of Rights of Man and of Citizens" and Article 1 runs accordingly. In U.S.A. also Declaration of Rights expressly demanded equality for men only, equal right to vote for both U.S. men and women were guaranteed only in 1919 barring the Black People. Even Switzerland which is popularly known as land of 'direct democracy' allowed women equal right to vote only in 1971.

India, however, played a revolutionary role in granting equal right to vote to all its citizens including women. In 1949 when the Constitution of free India was adopted it was declared in Article 326 that "The election to the House of the People and to the Legislative Assembly of every State shall be on the basis of adult suffrage, that is to say, every person who is a citizen of India and who is not less than twenty one years of age .... shall be entitled to be registered as voter at any such election."[22] Subsequently, the age of voting was lowered down to 18 years by 61st Amendment to the Constitution of India, 1989.

Now, let us see the actual picture of women representation (Table 13.7) in the Lower house of Parliament, i.e. in Lok Sabha.

Table 13.7: Women Representation in Lok Sabha

Year	*Total Members*	*Women*	*Percentage*
1952	499	22	4.4%
1957	500	27	5.4%
1962	503	34	6.7%
1967	523	31	5.9%
1971	521	22	4.2%
1977	544	19	3.4%
1980	544	28	5.1%
1984	544	44	8.1%
1989	517	27	5.2%
1991	544	39	7.4%
1996	544	36	6.7%
1998	544	43	7.9%
1999	544	46	8.4%
2004	543	49	9.02%
2009	543	59	10.86%
2014	543	62	11.41%
Total	**8500**	**588**	**6.91%**

Source: Indian Parliamentary Reports.

Thus, at the national level political empowerment of women is negligible. It has never crossed 11 per cent benchmark if we compare with male counterpart. But at the same time it should be recalled that at the grassroot level, i.e., at Panchayat level there is a sea-change. Thus, from the 4th Panchayat Election (1993) 33 per cent seats and from the 8th Panchayat Election (2013) 50 per cent seats are reserved for women and they are accordingly elected at the grassroot level. In spite of this trend we can safely conclude that there is a clear difference between male and female in the arena of power.

D. Health and Survival

It is an age old proverb that "Health is wealth" or in the words of Bickerstaff "Health is the greatest of all possessions, a pale cobbler is better than a sick king." In West we see much greater health consciousness everywhere if we compare with Third World countries. In 1978, World Health Organization also demanded: "Health for all".

But in India, poor health is a normal feature for majority of people and also we find a gender asymmetry in the utilization of health survives — during illness, fewer women than men seek and receive treatment. Attendance and admission figures at hospitals are significantly lower for women than for men. According to a study it is found that for every three men who avail of hospital facilities, there is only one woman who does so and in some areas the skewness is as high as five men for every one woman.[23]

In fact, India had no health policy before 1944 and only in this year Nutrition Advisory Committee of India was framed, but its recommendations are yet to be implemented. Table 13.8 shows the age-wise nutrient intake pattern in India.[24]

Table 13.8: Age-wise Nutrient Intake Pattern (Recommended Daily Allowances/RDA)

Age/Type	*Protein (grm)*		*Fat (grm)*		*Energy (K cal)*	
	RDA	*Intake*	*RDA*	*Intake*	*RDA*	*Intake*
1-3 yrs	22	18.3	25	9.2	1240	693
4-6 yrs	30	25.7	25	10.9	1690	1009
7-9 yrs	41	29.6	25	12.8	1950	1220
Over 18 yrs (M)	60	50.1	20	21.4	2425	2067
Sedimentary worker (F)	50	43.0	20	17.4	1875	1839
Over 18 yrs (M)	60	54.1	20	17.6	2875	2409
Moderate Worker (F)	50	45.6	20	15.2	2225	1988
Pregnant	65	45.3	30	16.6	2175	1664
Lactating	75	44.2	45	17.3	2425	2007

Source: Chakravorty 2003 using NNMB: 2002.

From Table 13.8, it is clear that in terms of food intake, women suffer greater deprivation. Besides, as a part of culture of self-effacement and service to others women eat at last and if there is insufficient food, the men and children get fed first and women go without.[25] Because of gender bias in the allocation of food, malnutrition is a significant factor in many of the female death (Mother's mortality 212 in one Lakh—Sample Registration System 2011).

Moreover, the cultural construct of son-preference (abortion of female fetus), dowry-death (17 women are killed every day)[26], violence against women, poverty, crime against women (National Crime Record Bureau's Reports) etc. are the reasons of adverse position of women in India. That is why from 0.972 at the beginning of the twentieth century, the sex-ratio has been dropped to 0.943 in 2011. (Census Figures).

Hence, we are to go a long way to achieve equality for women in India.

NOTES

1. Bottomore, T.B., (1965), *Classes in Modern Society*: London, George Allen & Unwin, p. 11.
2. Laski, H.J., (1973), *A Grammar of Politics*, London: George Allen & Unwin, pp. 153-158.
3. Frank, M. Anderson (ed.) (1908), *The Constitution and Other Select Documents Illustrative of the History of France, 1789-1907*, New York: Russel & Russel, p. 9.
4. Human Development Report 2000, UNDP (2000), New York: Oxford University Press, p. 14.
5. Ghosh, Santinath, (1999), Qtd. in '*Stri Sikshar Sekal*', Bethune School: Hundred Fifty Year Commemorative Collection.
6. *The Constitution of India* (1981). Government of India, New Delhi, Ministry of Law, Justice and Company Affairs, New Delhi, p. 6.
7. Pylee, M.V. (2001), *India's Constitution*, New Delhi, S. Chand & Company Ltd., p. 78.
8. *The Constitution of India*, *op. cit.*, p. 6.
9. *Ibid.*, *op. cit.*, p. 7.
10. *Ibid.*, *op. cit.*, p. 7.
11. *Ibid.*, *op. cit.*, p. 7.
12. Smt. Champakam Dorairajan *vs.* State of Madras, AIR S.C. 226.
13. Chiranjit Lal Choudhuri *vs.* The Union of India, AIR 1951 SC 1.
14. Robert Classes and Visaria Leela, (eds.), (2004). *Twenty First Century India*, Delhi: Oxford University Press, p. 41.

15. Dreze Jean and Amartya Sen (1995), *India Economic Development and Social Opportunities*, Delhi: Oxford University Press, p. 140.
16. *The Global Gender Gap Report 2013*, World Economic Forum, Geneva, p. 7.
17. *The Global Gender Gap Report 2014*, World Economic Forum, Geneva, p. 222.
18. Boserup, Estar (1970) *Women's Role in Economic Development*, New York: St. Martin Press.
19. *Grover India, Time Use Survey: Picture of 24 Hours.*
20. *Registrar Figures at a Glance* (2014), New Delhi: Registrar General of Census, p. 120.
21. Dreze Jean and Amartya Sen, *op. cit.*, p. 109.
22. The Government of India: *The Constitution of India*, *op. cit.*, p. 131.
23. Pan Ira and Tara Gopal Das (1994) "Availability and Utilisation of Health Services in India—A Delivery System", Romi Baruah etc. (eds.) *Capturing Complexity*, New Delhi: Sage Publications, p. 253.
24. Chakravorty, S. NNMB, 2002 (2003).
25. Narasimhan Sukuntala, (2001), *Empowering Women, An Alternative Strategy From Rural India*, New Delhi, Sage Publications, p. 25.
26. *India: The Road to Human Development*, UNDP (1997), New Delhi, p. 7.

14

Woman on Trial in Mainstream Hindi Films: An Analysis with Special Reference to 'Aradhana' (1969), 'Andaz' (1971) and 'Daag' (1973)

Pallav Mukhopadhyay

INTRODUCTION

There were characters symbolizing a favoured theme that dominated Hindi films in the 1950s and the 1960s, women playing the central characters. They could adorn every frame in a film with their grace and beauty, precisely in those classics that also is a treasure of melody. The soft melancholy look in the dark eyes of actresses released an ocean of suppressed emotions among men and unveiled a mirror reflection of what women wanted to be. The warmth of her smile and the protective embrace of her companionship conjured up the ideal portrait of an educated woman as partner-*cum*-wife. The uninhibited openness of her laugh, the teasing abandon of her smile, the sensuous toss of the locks of hair around her high cheekbones, her slim hourglass figure, all made her into a sublime sexy human being. The films of 1950s, 1960s and 1970s gave a generation of actresses the perfect platform from which to cast a spell over the audience's heart. Her look tugged at the heartstrings of the audience. Many exhibited the talent behind their beautiful face. She charmed the audience with her pensive look. Her heavy dramatic presence bounced off her style of casual naturalism. Sometimes, the glances of her vulnerable girlhood, her magical ability to silently swallow her tears, her sublime portrayals of the pain of her passion—these were some of the unforgettable memories of independent India's years of adolescence. The audience has witnessed an attempt to represent the woman's point of view or to centre the narrative on a woman caught between desire and an oppressive tradition. The screen woman's melodramas are male-centred. But at the same time they raise the question of women's desire, and albeit with adequate patriarchal scaffolding, broached questions connected with the emancipation of women from the oppression of feudal orthodoxy. The contradictory attitudes to kissing (which was banned) and the erotic display of the female body as spectacle (which was widespread) in the popular Hindi film is explained by this very ideology of the public sphere. The female body as spectacle is a public representation, a putting before the public of an erotic imagery that does not violate the code that prohibits the representation of the private.

AIMS AND OBJECTIVES

This chapter has tried to enquire the status of women on trial in the representative Hindi films of the decade of 1960s and 1970s by following the documentation and archival method. It has tried to interpret the relationship between women characters, state, society, family, time, events and narratives. Besides, the chapter has also followed the method of content analysis and has tried to identify diverse kinds of problems and crisis faced by the women.

METHODOLOGY

This chapter follows the Historical Method. It tries to focus on the representative films of the decade of 1960s and 1970s. It has tried to interpret the relationship between women characters, state, society, family, times, events and narratives. The chapter mainly depends on the articles, books, magazines and also critical appreciation of the films. The chapter has analyzed the films, documents and records and has drawn inferences. The primary sources of data and information lie on the films, articles, newspapers, magazines, books etc. It has offered explanations based on thorough analysis of films. Besides, the chapter also follows the Method of Content Analysis. The chapter has selected purposefully certain films as sample of study which represents the decades.

'ARADHANA' (1969)

The story opens against the backdrop of idyllic hilly terrain with airforce officer Arun Varma (Rajesh Khanna) crooning "*Mere sapno ki rani*" atop an open jeep along with his co-worker Madan (Sujit Kumar), while Vandana (Sharmila Tagore), the daughter of a doctor Gopal Tripathi (Pahadi Sanyal) demurely sneaks glances at him from a mini train. After a brief romance, they have a secret wedding. Soon afterwards, Arun dies in an air crash leaving behind a heartbroken and pregnant Vandana. His family refuses to accept the unwed mother-to-be since her marriage with Arun is never formalized. Meanwhile, her father also dies, leaving her destitute. Vandana's son is finally born, but she is forced to let a childless couple adopt him. But determined to be a part of his life, she accepts the responsibility of becoming his nanny. The boy is named Suraj. Events take an ugly turn when her employer's brother Shyam (Manmohan) arrives and lusts for Vandana. He tries to harass her physically when no-one is around, but Suraj arrives and stabs him to death in order to save his nanny. Upon the arrival of police, Vandana confesses to the murder while Suraj runs away. Thus, Vandana is sent to jail and Suraj forgets this mishap as he grows up. Several years later, when Vandana is released from jail she is befriended by the jailer (Madan Puri) who takes her home and introduces her to his daughter Renu (Farida Jalal). Vandana comes face to face with her son Suraj (Rajesh Khanna) when she discovers that Renu is dating him. Suraj, just like how his father wished, is an air-force officer. He slowly starts remembering that he has seen Vandana somewhere, although Vandana wants to hide the truth as she feels Suraj may be embarrassed upon realizing his parent's background and history. Vandana makes herself home at the jailer's house. At one time, Suraj gets injured in an air crash just like his real father Arun, but survives. At that time, Vandana meets Madan, who knows that Suraj is Arun and Vandana's son and he wants to tell Suraj the truth. Again, Vandana denies wanting to let Suraj know that he is her son, fearing the consequences. Later when Vandana is not around, Suraj sees her diary where Arun's photo is found. Realizing that Arun and Vandana are his true parents, he however salutes Vandana's self-sacrificing attitude and accepts her as his own mother.

Shakti Samanta's 'Aradhana' based on an old Hollywood melodrama, 'To Each His Own', proved a tremendous success, with its message of patriotism and a little boost from the rumoured 'controversy' over Sharmila Tagore's appearance in a bath towel.

The intense mother-son bond not only appears repeatedly in popular film narratives, but their passion is often central to the plot along with other acts that define the hero coming into his own—becoming a man, as it were. Traditional genre divisions associated with gender—women's 'weepies', the maternal melodrama. But in Hindi film the hero is typically also motivated by a consuming desire to avenge the sins against his mother, which drives the narrative forward. 'Aradhana' (Prayer, 1969) resonates with the son's desire to redeem his mother's suffering and to fuse with the maternal figure.[1]

In maternal melodrama the mother's devotion to her son is profound. 'Aradhana' (Prayer, 1969) exemplify this.

Peter Matthews argues that the constant symbolic replay of maternal loss tells of a 'suppressed desire' that must be 'mastered'. On both sides the mother-son relationship rests on a desire for pre-oedipal oneness with the mother, as experienced by the woman with her own mother and now by her son. The mother's yearning for her son is a 'safe' investment of women's passion.[2] For the son, the mother is a pre-oedipal figure of primal love, displaced by the process of oedipal separation, she becomes a lost object who recurs in the mother-son fantasies replayed in popular films. This pre-oedipal desire is scripted in films in narratives that are retold with varied emphasis on the subject's point of view—the mother's or the son's—and tapping into a reservoir of un-resolved conflicting desire. Wider social and institutional shifts, however, are also significant in accounting for the unique fixation on the mother-son relationship, the absence of the father, and the constancy of family drama in Hindi film. In 'Aradhana', the lover dies, causing the mother to suffer social censure for bearing his child out of wedlock.

'Aradhana' spawned a virtual woman-victim subgenre in the early 1970s. The narratives recuperate all kinds of 'fallen woman', defying them and their suffering, and setting them up as objects of reverence. While representing women as abject but idolized victim's 'Aradhana'—style became the dominant mode of such women's films.

In 'Aradhana', the centrality of affect shored up by the pro-filmic masculine fantasy acknowledges patriarchal oppression and proffers reverence in the form of a grand award from the state (fusing mother/nation/state)—an awkward and phantasmic compensation.

The premarital sex openly suggested in 'Aradhana' has punitive consequences. In 'Aradhana' the nation-state applauds a mother's sacrifice for her son.

'Vandana'—The Protagonist

Shakti Samanta's 'Aradhana' faithful to the maternal melodrama tradition, is a narrative of excess—a woman's acute suffering, sacrifice and her intense love for her son. The film depicts a woman's youthful passion turning into lifelong trial and tribulation.

The film commences with trenchant arguments in court where the female protagonist, Vandana (Sharmila Tagore), is on trial. As the credits end, the viewers hear the prosecutor's concluding statements. 'Your honour', he says, 'in the eyes of the law, there is nothing more grave than the murder of a human being. And when the one who gives birth to human beings, a woman, murders a man, the crime becomes even more heinous. I therefore plead with the court that the defendant not be spared because she is a woman. She should be punished severely so that people learn from this precedent and justice is served.' As Vandana, dressed widow-like in austere white clothes, is incarcerated, the camera tilts up to the barred window, and in a protracted flashback, the story unfolds.

Its portrait of a suffering woman derives from the Indo-Anglian literary tradition developed in the shadow of Orientalist canons and Victorian norms.[3] Sexual restraint is intrinsic to this representation. While popular films absorbed principles of female chastity, 'Aradhana' was the first to explicitly associate romantic love with sexual desire. Yet harking back to chastity principles, it also shows the ruinous consequences of extramarital sex for women.

'Aradhana' breaks with the taboo on explicit sex scenes in Hindi film, where song and dance sequences function as elaborate substitutes.[4] In keeping with the location shooting trend where heroines stretch languorously across the landscape as if innocent of the camera's gaze and their own sexualized bodies, 'Aradhana's opening depicts the 'wonders of falling in love'. Yet it somewhat daringly disrupts the sexual sublimation during the couple's courtship. Caught one day in an unexpected downpour, Vandana and Arun take shelter in a motel. Vandana changes out of her drenched clothes and swathes herself in a blanket.

As the camera cuts between Arun's gaze, fixed on Vandana, and the object of his gaze, the two circle of the fire in the middle of the room, which within the mise-en-scene excessively signifies their passion (and perhaps a mock Hindu wedding). Shot against the silhouette of a couple in the neighbouring room (divided from theirs by an opaque glass door) where the man is serenading his lover, Vandana and Arun, in an unusal moment for Hindi film, grapple with the intensity of their sexual desire. At the end of the famous 'Roop Tera Mastana' (You are irresistible) number Vandana steps forward, unbuttons Arun's shirt, and the camera averts its gaze, cutting to the glowing fire. The next shot is of a sunrise. The sequence is memorable for its elegance, skillfully skirting the censor board and Hindi film's own curious prudery on matters of sexual intimacy—incessantly spoken of (or sung about) but never 'shown'.

Yet the entire film exhibits the cunning of the maternal melodrama which operates on two levels—both condemning woman's victimization and punishing her for a reckless moment of sexual passion for which men get off scot-free.[5] Bereft of a man's protection when her lover dies, Vandana distances herself from her son to avoid the ignominy of unwed motherhood, hands over her rights and recognition as a biological mother, and, worst of all, becomes easy prey to strange men.[6] Though she wards off an imminent rape, its upshot—the death of her rapist—drives the narrative forward. Through this, and her voluntary incarceration to protect her son, her severance from him is complete. Typical of the genre of melodrama there is "a constant struggle for gratification and equally constant blockages to its attainment. [The] narratives are driven by one crisis after another, crises involving severed family ties, separation and loss... Seduction, betrayal, abandonment, extortion, murder, suicide, revenge, jealousy...are... the familiar terrain of melodrama. The victim's are most often females threatened in their sexuality, their property, their very identity."[7]

In Asian melodrama desire is dealt with safely when put in terms of female romantic love.[8] Thus in 'Aradhana', Vandana's sexual affair frames her as a desiring subject who is punished, but her sacrifice and atonement as a mother are honoured by the state. Here melodrama, with its 'poetics of hyperbole', emotional intensity, excesses and extremes, illuminates 'priorities of valuation' and articulates what cannot be said—"demands inadmissible in the codes of social, psychological, or political discourse."[9] Thus in the moment of Indian social history, victim-woman melodrama is the patriarchal national-popular's acknowledgement of sexual difference, women's subjectivity, and compensatory validation for her subjugation.

'Aradhana' spawned a virtual woman-victim subgenre in the early 1970s. The self-punishing Vandana in 'Aradhana' quietly acquiesced to a twelve-year incarceration for defending herself against rape. If melodrama condenses profound public/private conflicts, at once exposing and reaffirming power relations, it is also a vivid emotional register in Hindi films.[10] In 'Aradhana', the centrality of affect shored up by the pro-filmic masculine fantasy acknowledges patriarchal oppression and proffers reverence in the form of a grand award from the state (fusing mother/nation/state)—an awkward and phantasmic compensation. The premarital sex openly suggested in 'Aradhana' has punitive consequences. In 'Aradhana' the nation-state applauds a mother's sacrifice for her son.

'ANDAZ' (1971)

This film tells the story of a widow Sheetal (Hema Malini) who is left devastated after the death of her husband Raj (Rajesh Khanna). She is left with a son to look after and teaches in a school. One of her students is the daughter of widower Ravi (Shammi Kapoor). The children become instrumental in getting the single parents to meet and fall in love with each other.

G.P. Sippy's 'Andaz' was also a 'script film' with a borrowed French narrative. It was successful, but the brief appearance of Rajesh Khanna in a flashback, singing the immensely popular '*Zindagi Ek Safar Hai Suhana*' became the highpoint of the film, obscuring the somewhat unorthodox plot involving widow remarriage.[11]

Hema's character has a gravity that makes it work. Ravi (Shammi) lives on a timber plantation which he manages for his mother (Achala Sachdev). He is a widower with a small daughter named Munni. Little Munni has a new teacher at school by the name of Sheetal (Hema Malini). Ravi meets her during a game of hide-and-seek with Munni, when Sheetal mistakes him for a blind man and tries to help him. That night there is a New Year's school charity party scheduled and Sheetal is encouraged to attend by the kindly priest Father John (Abhi Bhattacharya) who urges her to forget her sad past. Ravi flirts with Sheetal gently, and she responds shyly. Intrigued and attracted by this quiet beauty, Ravi volunteers to take little Munni to her teachers the next morning. They find Sheetal singing to a little boy—her little boy, Deepu. Ravi soon realizes, much to his discomfiture and initial disappointment. But he finds out the reason for her underlying sadness.

Sheetal confides her history to him. Sheetal was Raj's (Rajesh Khanna) fiancée. Raj and Sheetal get caught in the rain one evening and check into a hotel to dry out. The next morning Raj takes Sheetal to a temple and marries her in front of God. Raj's wealthy and proud father (Ajit) refuses to acknowledge Raj's marriage to an orphan when his son informs him about it. Raj, a fairly reckless motorcycle rider, buzzes along at top speed towards Sheetal's birthday party with his father's words ringing in his ears, dies after facing an accident. Sheetal tells Ravi that she went to Raj's parents and they turned her away. Finding herself pregnant, she tried to kill herself but was saved by a priest who took her in. That same priest sent her to Father John, who has given her the job she now has. Sheetal begins to avoid Ravi. She is not only avoiding him because she's a widow and not supposed to remarry, but she is genuinely torn between moving on with her life and not wanting to let go of Raj and his memories as well. Ravi for his part tries to respect her wishes, but finally breaks down and in a wonderful scene tells her that he loves her. But will Sheetal? Can she put Raj's memories behind her and find love with Ravi? And even if she can will it last?

'Sheetal'—A Fiancée, A Lonely Widow, A Mother

Sheetal, the character, played by Hema Malini is a character consists of blending of a fiancée, a lonely widow and a mother. She had an affair with Raj, but their romantic life did not last long. Their marriage did not receive any social stamp. She was not accepted by her in-laws despite her argument that their marriage took place in the temple and God was the only witness of it. Broken heart, Sheetal while deciding to end her life, realizes that she is pregnant. She gives birth of a boy and from there initiates the new episode of the life of the lonely widow. Sheetal now turns to be a mother. She nurtures her son Deepu keeping in memory of her beloved husband Raj. She takes a job of school teacher. Here, Ravi, a widower comes to her life who gradually comes to know the past history of Sheetal's life. The film exhibits the heartless society, family that abandon a woman, compel her to choose the path of suicide, questions the chastity of a woman and questions again the widow remarriage. The society here is portrayed like an unsympathetic institution which rely on some taboos and norms. It did not want to feel the pain and sorrow of a woman. It did not try to understand that a woman is a human being of blood and flesh. She may have some likes, dislikes, aims and aspirations. In the

1970s that witnessed a couple of Hindi romantic blockbusters Sippy's 'Andaz' tried to experiment an offbeat narrative to some extent.

'DAAG' (1973)

Yash Chopra's first independent film as a producer, that subsequently earned him the title of 'King of Romance', 'Daag' ostensibly drew inspiration from the British television movie 'The Mayor of Casterbridge' based on Thomas Hardy's classic novel by the same name. Unlike other directors, Chopra's adaptation was a roaring success, with the script full of twists and turns coupled with high-pitched dialogue and a superb performance by actor. The surprise omission was Sharmila Tagore who rendered a sterling performance, both first as an ebullient young girl and later in intense grief. In 'Daag', Sunil Kohli (Rajesh Khanna) kills his boss Dheeraj Kumar (Prem Chopra) — who attempts to rape his wife Sonia (Sharmila Tagore) while they are honeymooning. Sunil is tried for murder and sentenced to death but providentially escapes unharmed while everyone else in the jail van dies. Five years later, Sonia arrives in an unnamed town and starts working as a school teacher, bringing up their son Pinku. Sonia discovers that her husband is alive in a new avatar of would-be mayor Sudhir and married to Chandni (Raakhee), daughter of the wealthy Dewan Saheb (Manmohan Krishna). Sudhir plays father to her illegitimate child, Rinky, to escape the law. This leads to some interesting confrontation scenes between Sonia and Chandni. The situation takes a turn when Inspector Singh (Iftekhar) gets posted to the township, and instantly recognizes Sudhir as the fugitive Sunil, leading to a courtroom drama where Chandni's testimony (an unexpected twist), and the plea of the defence lawyer (Madan Puri) lead to his innocence being established.

Sonia and Chandni: The Confrontation

The film begins with Sunil and Sonia, who are young and madly, passionately in love. Sonia is an orphan living with her kindly uncle and his shrewish wife. When Sunil lands a good job, he asks her uncle for permission to marry her. Her aunt objects strenuously as she's found a rich, but ugly husband for Sonia. The lovers declare their defiance. They get married with just a priest as witness, although Sonia's uncle arrives to bless them at the end, and leave immediately for Sunil's new job at a Kapoor Industries' plantation. They are greeted on arrival by

Dheeraj Kapoor, the debauched son of the owner, who immediately has eyes for Sonia. Sunil is arrested for killing Dheeraj in order to save the honour of his wife Sonia. Sunil is convicted and on the way to the prison, the police van overturns and burns. All the occupants are declared dead and Sonia is grief-stricken. The doctor discovers that she is also pregnant. Her aunt goes ballistic. Not wanting to cause more trouble, Sonia sneaks out, leaving no word of where she is going. She gets on a train and eventually winds up at a clinic where she gives birth some months later to a baby boy. She has showed the transition from carefree, somewhat self-centred girl to a sober woman weighted with grief for her lost husband, but full of love for their little son. Anyway, she takes him far away to Himachal Pradesh where she finds a job teaching at an elementary school. Years pass and her little boy Pinku grows into a kid. Even this peaceful existence is ruined when the school committee discovers Sonia's connections to a convicted killer. The only person on the board to stand up for her is Chandni, the mother of one of Pinku's friends, Rinky but is overruled. Sonia is fired from her job. Chandni offers her a place in her home. Her husband is rarely there, and she is lonely with just her father and Rinky. She needs a companion, and could use some help with her daughter Rinky. With no other options and Pinku to think of, Sonia accepts her offer gratefully. They have been at Chandni's house for a few days when her husband Sudhir returns home. He and Sonia are stunned at the sight of each other. Reunited does not feel so good! Sonia manages to say hello and flees to her room with Pinku. Sudhir asks Chandni about her new house guest. Chandni tells him Sonia's sad tale and voices her admiration for Sonia's unswerving loyalty and devotion to her dead husband. Sonia sings a truly amazing song about betrayal—'Jab Bhi Ji Chahe'. It is full of sadness, longing, bewilderment, anger, bitterness and Sonia's face mirrors these emotions perfectly.

CONCLUSION

Mainstream Bollywood Hindi films are male dominated through the decade of sixties and seventies. The women characters were looked down upon. The birth of a female child has been regarded as a disaster in the Hindi films especially in family melodrama. There is also the disgusting practice of dowry in majority of the family films. In many other respects the representation of women was as bad as it was before. The films exhibit that most women characters do not have real freedom. In many cases, the female characters are guided by superstitions. The male dominated narratives cast women driven by remnants of feudal and medieval practices and mentality. The popular mainstream Hindi films of these decades are no separate from objectifying women for its commercial outlook. These did not show any interest to uphold the rights of the oppressed and exploited women in the society that the Hindi films of parallel and middle-stream of 1960s and 1970s have tried to address with an alternative outlook.

NOTES

1. Virdi Jyotika, (2003), *The Cinematic Imagination: Indian Popular Films as Social History*, Ranikhet: Permanent Black, 91.
2. Kaplan, *Motherhood and Representation*, 79; Mathews, "Garbo and Phallic Motherhood," 22; and Kakar, *Intimate Relations*, 135.
3. Susie Tharu, (1989), "Tracing Savitri's Pedigree", *Recasting Women: Essays in Colonial History*, (eds.) by Kumkum Sangari and Sudesh Vaid (New Delhi: Kali for Women), 255-256, 260, 265.
4. Yash Chopra's earlier 'Dhool Ka Phool' (Blossom of Dust, 1959) narrates the terrible consequences of premarital sex, which occurs off-screen.
5. Christian Viviani, "Who Is Without Sin: The Maternal Melodrama in American Film, 1930-1939," in *Imitations of Life*, (ed.) Landy, 178.
6. Viviani points out that the maternal melodrama, Madam X-style, repeatedly traces the mother's separation from the child. The mother watches the child "from afar; she cannot risk jeopardizing his fortunes by contamination with her own bad repute." Viviani, "Who Is Without Sin", 171.
7. Marcia Landy, "Introduction", in *Imitations of Life*, (ed.) Landy, 14.
8. Ann Kaplan, citing Chris Berry, calls this an "anti-individual aesthetic" in Chinese melodrama. See her "Problematising Cross-Cultural Analysis: The Case of Women in Recent Chinese Cinema", *Perspectives on Chinese Cinema* 145 and "Melodrama/Subjectivity/Ideology: Western melodrama theories and their relevance to recent Chinese cinema", in Dissanayake, *Melodrama and Asian Cinema*, 25.
9. For priorities of hyperbole and valuation see Wimal Dissanayake "Introduction", in his *Melodrama and Asian Cinema*, 2 and 4; and for inadmissible codes, Ann Kaplan citing Christine Glendhill, *Home Is Where the Heart Is* (London: BFI) 1987, 38 in Dissanayake, *Melodrama and Asian Cinema*, 10.
10. On melodrama see Glendhill, (1987), *Home Is Where the Heart Is* (London: BFI) and (ed.) Landy, *Imitations of Life*.
11. M. Madhava Prasad, (1998), *Ideology of the Hindi Film: A Historical Construction*, (New Delhi: Oxford University Press), 139.

15

Population Ageing and Demographic Transition: Indian Experience

Sidhartha Sankar Laha

INTRODUCTION

Ageing is one almost irreversible natural process. The rapidly increasing number of older people may indicate biological success for humanity, but the living conditions of elderly, especially in developing countries like India, are lagging behind those enjoyed by economically active age group. The International Plan of Action on Ageing, 1982 aimed at strengthening the capacities of governments and civil society to deal effectively with ageing population and address their developmental needs. The UN Principles for Older Persons, 1991 pointed out that such person should remain integrated in society, participate actively in the formulation and implementation of policies that directly affect their well-being and share their knowledge and skills with the younger generation.

The twenty-first century is well poised to witness a gradual transition to an ageing society the world over. The process which first started in low fertility Western societies and in Japan is now spreading to the developing countries of Asia, Africa and Latin America. Countries like China and India will not only be at the forefront in terms of absolute number of total population, but also in terms of absolute number of the elderly (60+) population. In short, the long term impact of decline in fertility and reduction in the size of family will lead to a decrease in the population of children (0-14 years), which in turn will push up the population in the working age group. Population ageing has recently become a global phenomenon with serious implications for the developing countries in particular. Consequently, governments of developing countries have to devise developing plans and programme to address the challenges being posed by ageing. The United Nations declared the year 1999 as the International Year of Older Persons. More than a decade has passed since then and it is critical that we take stock of the advancement done to improve the welfare of ageing population.

Population ageing refers to shifts in the age distribution of the population such that the relative share of persons at older ages increases and the share at younger ages decreases. This is distinct from absolute increases in the number of older persons, which can occur even if their share does not increase (Kondel, 1999). The reason behind the continuing population growth and continuous increase in the ageing of the population is due to "the combined impact of increasing life expectancy and declining fertility" (*Population Reference Bureau*, 2012). While the increasing numbers of the elderly is attributed to demographic transition, "their deteriorating condition is considered as the end result of the fast eroding traditional family system in the wake of rapid modernization and urbanization" (Rajan *et al.*, 1999).

"India's older population will increase dramatically over the next four decades (*Population Reference Bureau*, 2012). The share of India's population aged 60 and older is projected to climb from 8 per cent in 2010 to 19 per cent in 2050 (UN, 2011). Several studies indicate that all the states in India and India as a whole are well in progress in their ageing and the demographic transitions.

Recent results of the 2011 census bring out the fact that as a fast progress in their demographic transition many states (namely Andhra Pradesh, Karnataka, Kerala, West Bengal and Tamil Nadu) have experienced a decline in their population from 26 per cent of India's total population in 1951 to a figure of 21 per cent in 2011. Projected figures indicate this figure may yet decline to 16 per cent by the year 2051.

The evidence clearly indicates that different states in India are at different stages of the demographic transition, as a consequence experiencing the ageing transition at different levels. It is evident that so far no comprehensive attempt has been made by State Governments to look at both the ageing of the population and the demographic transition taking place in India and the states.

Ageing is basically the result of the interplay of two forces of population dynamics—fertility and mortality. This chapter makes an attempt to focus on comparative perspective about the ageing of the population and the demographic transition in India and the major states based on the population ageing parameters. The shift to an older age structure has important implications for the country as well as for elders and their families. Therefore, the need is to achieve synergy or to promote harmony between development and demographic change by increasing economic and social sources of support for elderly.

The chapter focuses on the demographic parameters like total fertility rate (TFR), crude birth rate (CBR), crude death rate (CDR), infant mortality rate (IMR), natural population growth rate (NGR), life expectancy, ageing index, dependency ratio etc.

The main objectives of the chapter are:

(i) To throw light on the demographic process that has brought about changes in the age structure of the population thereby making ageing an inevitable outcome.

(ii) To provide a comparative perspective of ageing transition taking place in India and its major states.

(iii) To study the present and future perspective of ageing and demographic transition in light of regional variations and ageing parameters in India.

The analysis is based on the secondary available data. Specially, the information from the United Nations publication, Sample Registration System (SRS) of the Registrar General of India, Census of India (various years) and other available secondary sources.

AGEING—A GLOBAL PHENOMENON

The projected size and growth of elderly population is of major concern among the demographers and policy-makers throughout the world. Table 15.1 outlines the global ageing scenario for the next 150 years as per the United Nations projections.

The population of the world stood at around 6.1 billion in the early twenty-first century and is projected to increase to 9.4 billion in 2050 and 10.4 billion in 2100. If we compare the global population, it can be observed that the population has doubled between 1950 and 2000 and is likely to add another 4.4 billion in

Table 15.1: Global Ageing Scenario: UN Estimates

Year	*Population (billion)*	*% of Aged 60+*	*% of Aged 65+*	*% of Aged 80+*
2000	6.0	9.9	6.8	1.1
2025	8.0	14.6	10.8	1.7
2050	9.4	20.7	15.1	3.4
2075	10.1	24.8	19.1	5.3
2100	10.4	27.7	22.0	7.1
2125	10.6	29.2	23.6	8.6
2150	10.8	30.5	24.9	9.8

Source: United Nations, 2003.

the next 100 years. However, the growth of the elderly population is much higher than the general population (UN Population Projection, 2003). The proportion of elderly aged 60 and above is expected to grow from 9.9 per cent in 2000 to 14.6 per cent, 2025 and 21 per cent in 2050. Among the elderly, the oldest (80+) is likely to increase its proportion from just 1.1 per cent in 2000 to 3.4 per cent in 2050 and 7.1 per cent in 2100. Overall, the female elderly outnumber the male elderly. This is a clear indication of feminization of ageing (Bhat, 1992).

Department of Economic and Social Affairs Population Division, United Nations (2013) estimates that the proportion of the world's population aged 60 years or over increased from 8 per cent in 1950 to 12 per cent in 2013. It will increase more rapidly in the next four decades to reach 21 per cent in 2050. The stages and speed of ageing are quite different between the less and more developed regions. Ageing in the more developed regions started many decades ago, but it is just taking off in less developed regions, while it has yet to unfold in the least developed countries.

The proportion of the population aged 60 years or over in the more developed regions was 12 per cent in 1950, it climbed to 23 per cent in 2013 and is expected to reach 32 per cent in 2050. In the less developed regions, the proportion of older persons increased slowly between 1950 and 2013, from 6 per cent to 9 per cent; however, the increase in the proportion of older persons is expected to accelerate in the coming decades, reaching 19 per cent in 2050. In the least developed countries, the proportion of older persons has remained fairly stable at about 5 per cent for many decades, but this proportion is expected to double by 2050.

DEMOGRAPHIC TRANSITION IN INDIA: A COMPARATIVE PERSPECTIVE

The theory of demographic transition, which shows how a country experiences significant changes in its mortality and birth rates leading to moderate growth rate in future was derived from the observation of a process of demographic change in Asian countries, consisting in a gradual evolution from high birth and death rates to low ones in response to the social and economic changes brought about by industrial modernization (Notestein, 1945). In simple term, the demographic transition model describes the movement from high birth and death rates to low birth and death rates in a country which is developing and where modernity and industrialization are taking place.

Although crude birth rates (CBR) and crude death rates (CDR) indicators do not reflect fertility and mortality levels accurately, they do determine the rate of natural population growth rate and reveal, to a large extent, the influence on the population age structure. Another component of demographic change is international migration, which, given its relatively marginal influence on growth and population structure and because trends are not easily foreseeable, has not been taken into account in this chapter.

Birth rates and death rates affect the population of a country. Crude birth rate (CBR) refers to the number of live births occurring during the year, per 1,000 population estimated at mid-year while crude death rate (CDR) means the number of deaths during the year, per 1000 population estimated at mid-year (Macionis, 2000). The rate of natural increase, which is equal to the rate of population change in the absence of migration, is obtained by subtracting the crude death rate from the crude birth rate. On the other hand, Infant Mortality rate (IMR) relates to the number of deaths among infants under one year of age per 1000 live births during a year.

Table 15.2 shows population and vital statistics about CBR, CDR and Natural Growth Rate (NGR). In view of the above, we have been computing vital rates by indirect methods known as survival ratio method or differencing method. Different census actuaries have used different methods and varying assumptions; hence, the rates presented from 1901-11 to 1961-71 are not strictly comparable. Data for the decade 1971-78 presented in the table are average of annual estimates obtained in SRS. CBRs and CDRs from 1981 onward included are three years moving averages.

Table 15.2: Summary of Demographic Estimates for India, 1901-2010

Decade/Year	*CBR*	*CDR*	*NGR*	*IMR*
1901-11	49.2	42.6	6.6	—
1911-21	48.1	48.6	–0.5	—
1921-31	46.2	36.3	9.9	—
1931-41	45.2	31.2	14	—
1941-51	39.9	27.4	12.5	—
1951-61	41.7	22.8	18.9	—
1961-71	41.1	18.8	22.3	—
1971-81	37.3	16	21.3	129
1981	33.8	12.3	21.5	110
1986	32.6	11.3	21.3	96
1990	30	9.9	20.1	80
1991	29.3	9.9	19.4	80
1992	29.1	9.7	19.4	79
1993	28.8	9.5	19.3	74
1994	28.5	9.2	19.3	74
1995	28.1	9.1	19	74
1996	27.7	9	18.7	72
1997	27.1	9	18.1	71
1998	26.6	9	17.6	72
1999	26.1	8.7	17.4	70
2000	25.8	8.5	17.3	68
2001	25.4	8.3	17.1	66
2002	25.1	8.2	16.9	63
2003	24.6	7.9	16.7	60
2004	24.2	7.7	16.5	58
2005	23.8	7.6	16.3	58
2006	23.5	7.5	16	57
2007	23.1	7.4	15.7	55
2008	22.8	7.4	15.4	53
2009	22.5	7.3	15.2	50
2010	22.1	7.2	14.9	47

Source: SRS Bulletin December 2011, (Latest) Registrar General of India, New Delhi.

The first stage of demographic transition (DT) in India continued till about 1920 when both birth rates and death rates were very high. The second stage of DT in the country began from the early 1920s and spread well up to early 1970s. During this period major causes of high mortality—famines and epidemics—were brought under control and, between 1921 and 1951, the country witnessed a gradual rise in population growth rates; the decline in death rates became sharper during the 1950s without any appreciable decline in birth rate resulting in higher population growth rates that continued during the 1960s.

India seems to have entered the third stage of DT since 1971 (Table 15.2 and Figure 15.1). The decline in death rate during the 1970s was almost the same as the decline in birth rate leading to a plateau in population growth rate during the 1960s and 1970s. There has been a faster decline in birth rate than decline in death rate during the 1980s and 1990s. Faster decline in birth rate than death rate has continued during the present decade as well. According to the population projections prepared by the Office of the Registrar General, India in 1996, India is expected to enter the fourth stage of DT by about 2006.

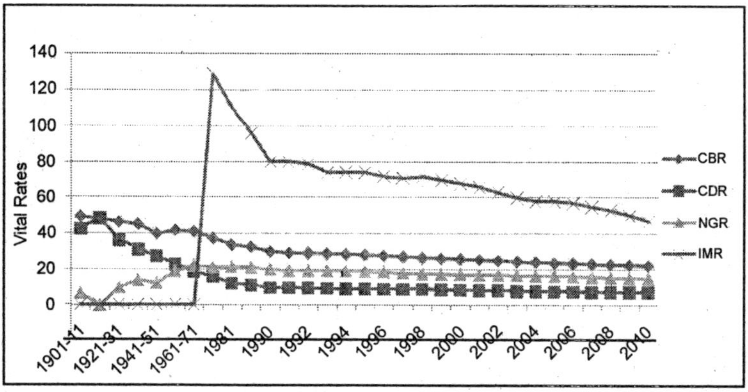

Fig. 15.1: Demographic Transition in India (DTI), 1901-2010.

The Registrar General has also worked out the likely dates when the major states would achieve total fertility rate of 2.1 (equivalent to net reproduction rate of one). Kerala and Tamil Nadu have already achieved that goal and Andhra Pradesh, Karnataka, Maharashtra and West Bengal have also achieved the same by 2006. The problem states in this respect are Bihar, Chhattisgarh, Jharkhand, Madhya Pradesh, Rajasthan, Uttar Pradesh and Uttarakhand where the goal of TFR of 2.1 is likely to be achieved by 2030 (United Nations Population Division, 2011). It is noteworthy that National Population Policy documents indicate that India's population and that in every state would be stabilised by 2040, that is, when TFR would become 2.1. This implies that birth rate would be around 20 per 1000 persons and death rate would be 6-8 per 1000 persons. It would not be the stationary stage with birth and death rates being almost equal at the lower end of demographic transition.

After a thorough examination of the literature and projected trends, it may be concluded that: (1) the four northern states of Bihar, Madhya Pradesh, Rajasthan and Uttar Pradesh are observed to be the only states which have not achieved 70 per cent of the demographic transition by the year of 2010, when compared to all major states of India and India as a whole. All the states under consideration are expected to complete about 90 per cent of their demographic transition by the year 2101, obviously led by Kerala and Tamil Nadu.

(2) While the southern states, with Kerala at the forefront, are seen well in progress in their demographic transition, the northern states, particularly Uttar Pradesh, are observed to be below India as a whole over the complete transition period considered here, that is starting from 1970s to the year 2101.

(3) Overall, while demographic transition is said to be fast in progress in all the southern states, and also in the states of Maharashtra, Punjab and West Bengal, it is said to be progressing slowly in the remaining states of India. India as a whole may be predicted to complete only 90 per cent of its demographic transition by the year 2101; until and unless some drastic changes take place in the fertility transition of the northern states of India in the near future.

The reduction in birth and mortality rates has had important consequences for the country. The fall in the mortality rate has lead to an increase in the life expectancy which has resulted in the process of an ageing population in India.

TRANSITION IN THE AGED POPULATION: AN INDIAN OVERVIEW

It is emphasized that ageing is the ultimate outcome of the completion of the demographic transition. As observed before, except the four northern states, all other states in India are seen to be well in advance of their demographic transition.

In 2008 India had 90 million older persons, the second largest in the world after China. According to the 2001 census, there were about 77 million persons aged 60 years and older, a notable increase from 25 million in 1961. The proportion of older persons rose from 5.6 per cent of the total population in 1961 to 6.6 per cent in 1991 (Rajan, *et al.*, 1999) and to 7.5 per cent in 2001 (Rajan & Aliyar, 2008). The number of persons aged 70 years or older increased from 9 million in 1961 to 29 million in 2001, representing 2.0 per cent of the total population in 1961 and 2.9 in 2001 (Table 15.3).

In 1961 Census reported 99,000 centenarians. In 2001 there were 1,39,472 centenarians, 50,139 of them males and 89,333 females. The growth of different age groups among the elderly (i.e. 60 years or older, 70 years or older and 80 years or older) during 1991-2001 was much higher than the annual growth of 2.0 per cent for the general population. About 75 per cent of older persons live in rural areas (Rajan & Aliyar, 2008).

Data indicate that men are expected to live 16 years beyond the age of 60 and 10 years beyond 70. The figures for women are 18 and 11 respectively. Urban women are expected to live two years longer than urban men (Rajan *et al.*, 2008).

Rajan and Aliyar's (2008) projections indicate the share of the elderly to be 19.1 per cent in 2051, 24.5 per cent in 2071 and 30.1 per cent in 2101; in sharp contrast to only 7.5 per cent in 2001. Their total number increases from 90 million in 2008 to 298 million in 2051 and 505 million in 2101. The number of persons above 70 years old was 9 million in 1961 and 29 million in 2001 and is expected to

Table 15.3: Distribution of the Resident Population by Selected Age Group, 1961-2101

Year	*60 years or Older*		*70 years or Oder*		*80 years or Older*	
	Million Persons	*% of Total Population*	*Million Persons*	*% of Total Population*	*Million Persons*	*% of Total Population*
1961	25.0	5.6	9.0	2.0	2.0	0.6
1971	33.0	6.0	11.0	2.1	3.0	0.6
1981	43.0	6.5	15.0	2.3	4.0	0.6
1991	57.0	6.8	21.0	2.5	6.0	0.8
2001	76.8	7.5	29.4	2.9	8.1	0.8
2011	96.5	8.1	42.4	3.5	10.9	0.9
2021	133.0	9.9	52.4	3.9	15.8	1.2
2031	184.1	12.7	74.8	5.1	19.7	1.3
2041	233.3	15.3	104.4	6.8	28.8	1.8
2051	298.2	19.1	131.3	8.3	40.5	2.5
2061	346.5	22.4	171.6	11.0	51.6	3.2
2071	377.2	24.5	195.5	12.9	69.8	4.5
2081	422.3	26.9	212.7	14.1	77.6	5.3
2091	463.6	28.7	247.8	16.1	88.8	6.1
2101	504.7	30.1	273.0	17.2	105.5	7.1

Source: 2001 Census & Rajan and Aliyar, 2008.

be 131 million in 2051 and 273 million in 2101. Similar trends hold for the age group above 80.

This shows clearly that the population in India will continue to grow older in the coming years. As a consequence, the old age dependency ratio will also rise. A growing old age dependency may mean a substantial change in both the informal and formal systems. Given the trend of elderly population in India, a National Policy for Older Persons was announced by the Government in January 1999. The ageing of population has social, medical and financial implications at the macro as well as at the household level. The larger number of elderly persons in this country will invite the need for providing social services and other related facilities for this segment of the population. An analysis of the demographic, social and economic aspects of ageing can provide a solid foundation for further analysis and intervention policies.

REGIONAL VARIATIONS IN POPULATION AGEING

Census data on older persons in India show significant variations among states. While all the states in the country showed an increasing trend from 1961 to 2001, the southern states and Punjab and Himachal Pradesh have larger increases in the proportion of elderly, with Kerala registering the greatest increase. Projections for the next 25 years demonstrate a similar pattern, with the largest proportion of elderly in the southern states; Kerala in particular, along with West Bengal, Punjab and Himachal Pradesh. Northern states, UP in particular, and eastern states have lowest proportion of elderly in the country (Fig. 15.2).

The inter-state variations in population ageing (Kerala and Tamil Nadu projected to have 18 per cent and 17 per cent of elders in by 2026 followed closely by Himachal Pradesh, Punjab, Karnataka, West Bengal and Andhra Pradesh) mean that issues such as economic dependency and elder care are much more apparent in certain states than others. However, the rising number of elders in all regions of the country, along with the various sources of vulnerability mentioned earlier, makes the ageing of the population a compelling reason for the elderly to receive focused and concerted attention at policy and programme levels.

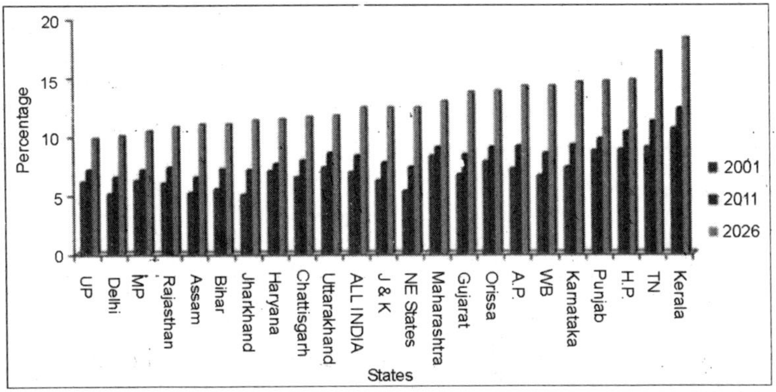

Fig. 15.2: Proportion of Elderly in India and its States, 2001, 2011 and 2026.
Source: Designed on the basis of Registrar General and Census Commissioner of India, 2006.

DEMOGRAPHIC PARAMETERS TO THE AGEING PROCESS

Fertility decline has been the primary determinant of population ageing (United Nations, 2002). In India the trend of fertility is decreasing over the last five decades. In 1950-55, the total fertility rate (TFR)[1] was 6 children per women and it became 3 children per women in 1995-2000 and it is projected that by 2050 it will be 1.85 children per women. Similarly, the crude birth rate (CBR)[2] and crude death rate (CDR)[3] is also decreasing over this period. In 1950-55, the CBR and CDR was 45.4 and 25.4 per 1000, so, the natural growth rate of population is around 2 per cent. In the following years, the trend is decreasing over the period 1950-2050. But the growth rate of older population has seen increasing trend over this period. In 1950-55, the growth rate of older persons was around 2 per cent, which is same as the growth rate of total population. Afterwards, the growth rate is higher than the growth rate of total population as shown in Table 15.4.

Not only the fertility was decreasing over the past decades, the life expectancy[4] had simultaneously increased in India. In 1950-55, it was 38.7 years whereas in 2000-05 it became 64.2 years and it is projected that by 2045-50 it will be 75.4 years in India. Similarly, life expectancy is also increasing by sex. In 1950, the life expectancy of female and male was around 38 years and 39 years respectively. But in 2000, the life expectancy of female exceeds that of male. In 2000, the life expectancy of female and male was 64.9 years and 63.6 years

Table 15.4: Total Fertility Rate (TFR) and Growth Rate of Total and Old Population over the period 1950-2050

Years	TFR (Children per women)	Growth Rate (%)	
		Total Population	Older Population
1950	6.0	2.0	2.0
1975	4.8	2.1	2.9
2000	3.0	1.5	2.7
2025	2.1	0.8	3.2
2050	1.8	0.4	2.2

Source: United Nations, 2002.

respectively. This trend will continue up to 2050, as shown in Table 15.5.

Table 15.5: The Life Expectancy at Birth and at Age 60 by Sex over the period 1950- 2050

Years	Life Expectancy (yrs) at Birth			Life Expectancy at Age 60 (yrs)		
	Male	Female	Total	Male	Female	Total
1950	39.0	38.0	38.7	—	—	—
1975	53.3	52.4	52.9	—	—	—
2000	63.6	64.9	64.2	17.9	16.1	17.6
2025	69.6	73.4	71.6	20.7	18.1	19.4
2050	73.5	77.4	75.4	22.2	19.4	20.8

Source: United Nations, 2002. '—' implies not available.

Not only the life expectancy at birth is increasing over the period but also the life expectancy at age 60 years is showing upward trend up to 2050. In 2000, the life expectancy at age 60 was 17 years whereas the female and male life expectancy at age 60 years was 17.9 years and 16.1 years respectively. The upward trend is shown up to 2050 in Table 15.5. From the above discussion it can be contended that the added lifespan plays an important role to promote the population ageing in India (Alam & Mukherjee, 2005; Alam & Agarwal, 1999; Gulati & Rajan, 1990; Prakash, 1999).

Since, female mortality rates are lower than male at older ages, the proportion of women in the older population grows substantially with advantage age (60+). Because their life expectancy is greater than men's, women comprise a significant majority of the older population. So, the ageing scenario will comprise more number of females than the number of male (Rajan *et al.*, 2000; Dinesh & Rayappa, 1983; Kumar, 1999; Knodel, 1999). Factors underlying the ageing of India's population include a falling fertility rate and increasing longevity. Life expectancy at birth rose from 38 years in 1950 to 64 years in 2010 (Fig. 15.3). While this is not nearly as high as the average in developed countries (78 years), it is similar to the average for the developing world (66 years) and is projected to rise another decade by the middle of the century.

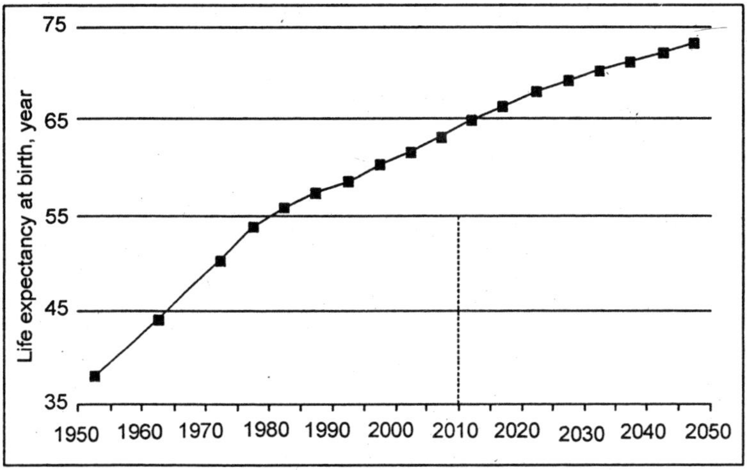

Fig. 15.3: Life Expectancy in India; the Rising Trend.

MEDIAN AGE

The median age of a population is that age that divides a population into two groups of the same size, such that half the total population is younger than this age, and the other half older.

The evolving population dynamics in India arising out of the combined effect of declining fertility and increasing longevity and consequent shifting of the population age structure cannot be ignored. The trend in the median age (in years) of the population is presented in Table 15.6 for the period from 1961 to 2026. Until recently, India, like other developing countries, had a young age structure with the median age remaining at about 20 years from 1961 to 1981, and increased marginally to 22.5 years in 2001. However, the projections suggest that the country is gradually but surely transitioning away from a young age structure with a steady increase in the median age to 31 years by 2026.

The median age for almost all the states was close to the All India average of 22.5 years in 2001, except for Kerala and Tamil Nadu which had median ages of 29.9 and 29.1 years respectively. The projections for the subsequent 25 years show an increase of more than seven years for all the states, with the median age reaching 37 years in Kerala and TN, and 35 years in Himachal Pradesh in 2026. The state with the lowest median age is Uttar Pradesh, with 27 years.

INCREASING OLD AGE DEPENDENCY

The ratio of the dependent population to that of the working age population is defined as the dependency ratio and it is an important indicator of the economic burden carried by each worker. The young age dependency ratio reflects the dependency burden from children below 15 years of age. Similarly, old age dependency is the ratio of persons aged 60 years and above to the working age population. In 2001, the total dependency ratio (from both the young and the old age-groups) was significantly high (73%), but is expected to fall to 56 by 2026. The young age dependency ratio is generally much higher than the old age dependency ratio[5], since the population age structure in India has been young. While the young age dependency ratio is expected to decrease by 25 percentage points to 36.3 by 2026, the old age dependency ratio shows an increasing trend and is expected to increase by about 7 percentage points during the same period.

POTENTIAL SUPPORT RATIO

The potential support ratio[6] is a measure of the available support base for the older population and is the inverse of the old age dependency ratio. The expected potential support ratio for the next 25 years for India (Table 15.6) shows that there were about 17.2 persons of working age for every older person in 1950, but that number is expected to decrease to about four by 2050. Thus, with increasing proportion of elders in the total population, there will be fewer and fewer working age persons to support them economically during old age.

Table 15.6: Socio-Demographic Indicators of India, 1961-2026

	1961	*1971*	*1981*	*1991*	*2001*	*2006*	*2011*	*2016*	*2021*	*2026*
Median Age (Years)	20.5	19.6	20.2	21.6	22.5	23.9	25.5	27.4	29.3	31.4
Index of Ageing (Per cent)	13.7	14.0	15.0	17.6	19.4	23.4	28.4	34.7	42.5	53.1
	Dependency Ratios (per cent)									
Young	76.6	81.6	74.4	67.0	61.4	53.2	46.4	42	39.2	36.3
Old	10.5	11.5	11.6	11.8	11.9	12.4	13.2	14.6	16.7	19.2
Total	**87.1**	**93.1**	**85.6**	**78.7**	**73.4**	**65.6**	**59.6**	**56.6**	**55.9**	**55.6**
Potential Support Ratio	1950	1975	2001	2006	2011	2016	2021	2025	2026	2050
	17.2	14.7	12.4	8.4	7.6	6.9	6.0	8.2	5.2	4.4
Parents Support Ratio	1.0	0.9	4.7	5.9	9.9	11.5	12.8	13.1	13.9	14.2

Source: Registrar General and Census Commissioner of India, 2006 and United Nations, 2002.

PARENT SUPPORT RATIO

The Parent Support Ratio is the ratio of the number of persons aged 80 years and above per 100 persons aged 50 to 59 years and is an approximate measure of the available support for older parents from their families. An increase in the ratio would imply that those who are reaching the later stages of their working lives will have more aged relatives/parents to support in the future. The parent support ratio for India in 2001 was about 5, and is expected to increase to about 14 by 2026—almost three-fold increase of older persons for every 100 persons in final years before retirement.

INDEX OF AGEING

The ageing index is calculated as the number of persons 60 years old or over per hundred persons under age 15.

$$\text{Index of Ageing} = \frac{\text{Population aged 60+year}}{\text{Population aged 0-14 year}} \times 100$$

The index of ageing is the shift in the balance between the child and older populations and is expressed as the number of persons above 60 years for every 100 children below the age of 15 years. In India, the index of ageing increased slowly between 1961 and 2001, but is expected to increase more rapidly in the following 25 years (Table 15.6). In 2001, the index of ageing was 23.4 elderly persons for every 100 children but this number is projected to increase rapidly to 53 elderly persons for every 100 children by 2026, signifying an increasing pace of ageing in the coming decades.

In 2001, the state with the highest index of ageing was Kerala, with 40 elderly persons for children below 15 years of age. The next two states were Himachal Pradesh and Punjab with an index of about 28 persons. However, in 2026 the index of ageing is over 60 for many states, including Andhra Pradesh, Himachal Pradesh, Karnataka, Kerala, Maharashtra, Odisha, Punjab, Tamil Nadu, and West Bengal. More notably, Kerala is at the forefront of the demographic transition with an ageing index of 97 persons per 100 children. Uttar Pradesh is expected to age most slowly, with 34 elderly persons for every 100 children.

CONCLUSION

In the chapter a thorough analysis of the ageing and the demographic transition taking place and the expected direction of the above transitions have been carried out using reliable data provided by the Registrar General of India and the Population Reference Bureau.

While the shift from a young to an older age structure reflects a successful and desirable outcome of health improvement, the pace of ageing and the size of the older population with varying needs and resources pose many problems and challenges. It is manifest that the percentage of elderly has increased and is expected to increase further while the percentage of the young age-group is decreasing, resulting in a slow, but sure transition to an older population structure in the country. Further, the transition away from a young age structure is not uniform across the states. Some states, particularly those in the Southern region which are more economically and socially developed, are at the vanguard of this transition.

Unprecedented growth in the elderly population raises many pointers for policy-makers, researchers and civil society. Equally important is their partnership for a more effective and sustainable care and support for senior citizens. A growing older population implies the need for a higher quantity and quality of geriatric services, arrangements of income security and improved quality of life in general. The need for social pension payments and resulting financial outlays to meet the increasing old age dependency and decreasing support base are more important for future policy consideration. Further, older persons and their families will have to deal with challenges arising out of increased longevity. Consequently, scientific studies have to be undertaken to revisit both the formal and informal care systems with a view to improve the lives of the elderly population and have to fashion effective link between development and demographic growth.

Hence, the state needs to provide suitable institutional, social motivation programmes, and other economic support to address the socio-economic needs of the elderly. There is a need to shift from the welfare approach to the rights based approach. Imperative is to identify the minimum conditions for living with dignity for the elders. There is need to formulate policies that can lead to respect, protection and fulfilment of the needs of the elderly and enable them to live in peace in the years of seniority. Both the civil society and the governments should take measures based on empowerment, equality, entitlement, dignity, justice and respect for the elderly.

While we still exist, let us make the lives of ourselves and those of the elderly fellow human beings not only longer but also livelier.

The aged should be able to live with dignity and security, free from any physical or mental abuse. Attention to and emphasis on the state of physical, mental and social well-being is necessary so that the aged enjoy better levels of health and life. Neurological and psychological researches have corroborated that experience is vital for an individual to live and work. Experience leads to rational decision-making, planning of projects and handling people and situations. And elderly persons are enriched with such crucial quality. Not surprisingly therefore, many private organizations employ retired personnel people and engage them as consultants. Thus, the elderly are still assets and not definitely liability.

NOTES

1. TFR: The Total Fertility Rate is the average number of children a woman would bear over the course of her life time if current age specific fertility rates remained constant throughout her child bearing years (15-49 years).

2. CBR: Crude Birth Rate is the number of births per 1000 population in a year.
3. CDR: Crude Death Rate is the number of deaths per 1000 population in a year.
4. Life Expectancy at Birth is the average number of years a newborn baby would live if current age-specific mortality rates were continue.
5. Old-age-dependency ratio is the ratio of the number of elderly people at an age when they are generally economically inactive (i.e. aged 65 and over), compared to the number of people of working age (i.e. 15-64 years old).
6. Potential Support Ratio is the number of persons aged 15-64 years per every person aged 65 or older.

REFERENCES

Alam, Moneer, (2004), "Aging, Old Age Income Security and Reforms: An Exploration of Indian Situation". *Economic and Political Weekly,* Vol. 39, No. 33, pp. 3731-40.

Alam, Moneer and M. Mukherjee (2005), "Ageing, Activities of Daily Living Disabilities and the Need for Public Health Initiatives: Some Evidence from a Household Survey in India". *Asia Pacific Population Journal,* Vol. 20, No. 2. pp. 47-76.

Alam, Moneer and R.N. Agarwal (1999), "Ageing, Macro-Economic Implications and Health Insurance Requirements in India". *Indian Journal of Labour Economics*, Vol. 42, No. 3, pp. 471-500.

Bhat Mari, P.N., (1992), "Changing Demography of Elderly in India's Current Scenario". *Indian Journal of Gerontology*, Vol. 63, No. 80.

Dinesh, B. Manjeshwar and P. Hanumantha Rayappa (1983), "The aged and their work status in rural areas". *Demography India,* Vol. XII, No. 1, pp. 38-51.

Gulati, S.C. and S. Irudaya Rajan, (1990), "Social and Economic Implications of Population Ageing in Kerala, India". *Demography India,* Vol. 19, No. 2, pp. 235-50.

Jai Prakash, Indira (1999), *Aging in India*, World Health Organization, Geneva.

Knodel, J., (1999), "The Demography of Asian Ageing: Past Accomplishments and Future Challenges for Asia, Population Ageing Lies Almost Entirely Ahead". *Asia-Pacific Population Journal*, Available with www.unescap.org/appj.asp.

Kumar, S. Vijay (1999), "Population ageing in India causes and consequences". *Monthly Public Opinion Surveys,* Vol. 44, No. 10, pp. 35-38.

Macionis, J. J., (2002), *Society: The Basics*, Prentice Hall, New Jersey.

NSS, (1998), *The Aged in India: A Socio-Economic Profile, 52nd Round.* New Delhi, National Sample Survey Organization, Government of India.

Notestein, F.W. (1945), "Population: The Long View". In Theodore W. Schultz (ed.). *Food for the World*. Chicago: University of Chicago Press.

Ponnapalli, K.M., (2011), *Indian Model Life Tables Based on SRS Life Tables of India*, Mimeographed, Mumbai: International Institute for Population Sciences.

Population Reference Bureau, (2012), "India's Aging Population. Today's Research on Aging. Programme and Policy Implications", *Population Reference Bureau*, 25: 1-6.

Rajan, I.S., U.S. Mishra and P.S. Sarma, (1999), *India's Elderly: Burden or Challenge?* Sage Publications, New Delhi.

Rajan, I.S., Aliyar, S., (2008), "Population Ageing in India", in S. Irudaya Rajan, C. Risseeuw; M. Perera (eds.) *Institutional provisions and care for the aged: Perspectives from Asia and Europe*, London/New York/New Delhi: Anthem Press.

Registrar General and Census Commissioner, India, (2006), *Population Projections for India and States, 2001-2026*, Report of the Technical Group on Population Projections constituted by the National Commission on Population, New Delhi.

Registrar General, India, (2011), *Maternal and Child Mortality and Total Fertility Rates*, Sample Registration System, 7th July, 2011 (PPT presentation), down-loaded from censusindia.gov.in.

United Nations, (2009), *Population Ageing and Development, 2009, Datasheet*, United Nations, Department of Economic and Social Affairs, Population Division.

United Nations Population Division (UN). (2011), *World Population Prospects: The 2010 Revision*. New York: United Nations.

United Nations, (2013), *World Population Ageing* (2013), Department of Economic and Social Affairs, Population Division.

Index

Aboriginality, 193–194
Academic Achievement scores, 213
Access sub-centres, 55–56
Access to Money (AMI), 125, 127, 130
Accessing health facilities, 56
Adivasis, 88–89, 94–95, 97–98, 181–187, 191–196
  agriculturist, 193
  communities, 91, 183–184, 191
  culture, 183
  distinctiveness, 183
  mahasabha, 183
  migrated, 194
  of Chotanagpur, 193
  parlance, 186
  protests, 182
  safeguard, 185
  unfortunate, 194–195
  uprisings, 182–183
Adivasi Socio-Educational and Cultural Association, 167–168
Adulthood, 203–204
Advancement of education, 185
Ageing, 239–242, 246, 248–251, 253–254
  index, 241, 253–254
  parameters, 241
  population, 239–240, 246
  scenario, 250
  transition, 240–241
Agencies, 6, 9, 18, 27, 76, 80, 82, 124, 131, 216
  anti-corruption, 10, 80
Aggression, 203–204, 206
Aggressive
  behaviour, 203–205
  personality pattern, 204
Agriculturalist caste, 184
Alien
  colonial policy, 185
  language, 170–171
Anaemia, 101–102, 104–106, 109, 111–113, 117, 119
ANC check-ups, 106
Anganwadi, 103, 170
Anganwadi Worker (AWW), 103–104
Animal Husbandry Scam in, 3
Antepartum period, 111–112
Anti-corruption
  agencies, 82
  campaign, 77
  convention, 11
  institution/agency, 80
  law, 9, 11, 76, 81
  movements, 64, 68, 76
  reforms, 80
Anti-development, 96
Anti-dowry movement, 15
Anti-social elements, 38
Anxiety, 95, 137, 141–142, 144, 148, 153, 205

Apathy, 31
Arcelor Mittal, 93–94
Assam, 19, 179–180, 193–195
  tea gardens of, 193–194
Associated Risk Factors, 101, 103, 105, 107, 109, 111, 113, 115, 117, 119
Attitudes, 28, 33, 36, 43, 45, 72
  index of, 40–41
  political, 37, 48–49
  radical, 46–47
Audience, 228–229
Austric communities, 180
Autonomy, 179, 184, 188
  cultural, 182
  demands, 195
Awareness, 128, 130, 132, 148

Background characteristics, 106
Bauxite, 89, 93–94
Behavioural factors, 219
Bengal, 37–38, 47, 111
Bhushan Company, 95
Birth attendants, 120
Birth rates, 243–245
Bivariate analysis, 106
Bodo Students' Union, 180
Bodoland movement, 180
Breast cancer, 137–138, 140, 142
  early-stage, 140
  maternal, 142
Bribery, 3, 7, 9, 64, 69, 80
  and Corruption Survey, 8, 10
British colonialism, 178–179
Bully, 203–204, 206–209, 212–213
  boys, 210–211, 213
  girls, 211–213
  questionnaire, 213
  score, 209–211, 213
Bullying, 203–207, 209, 211–213
  behaviour, 203, 208
  boy/girl, 204
  defined, 203, 206
  definition, 203, 206
Bureaucrats, 68, 70, 73–74, 95

Cachexia, 144
Canadian Association of Psychosocial Oncology, 153
Cancer, 64, 81, 113, 136–151, 153–154
  advanced, 139
  blood, 113
  care, 153
  colorectal, 138
  deaths, 136
  diagnosis, 136, 141
  experience of, 138, 153–154
  patients, 136–137, 146, 148, 151–152
  -related treatment, 149
  stress, 137, 141
  survivors, 136, 139, 146
  survivorship, 137
  treatments, 136, 138, 140, 154
Cancer Centre Welfare Home and Research Institute, 152
Care, 39, 91, 102, 137, 139, 141, 145, 148–152, 154–157, 219
  antenatal, 106
  antepartum, 106
  catheter, 150
  end-of-life, 156
  high-quality preventive, 155
  hygiene, 152
  medical, 148
  obstetric, 100
  poor maternity, 107
  psycho-social, 153
  sustainable, 254
Caregivers, 137, 141, 149–154, 156–157
  outcomes, 150–151
Caste factor, 128
Casterbridge, 236
Causal factors, 123, 125
Cement factories, 195
Census of India, 241

Central Board of Forests, 194
Central Bureau of Investigation (CBI), 5, 9–10, 65, 80
Central Statistical Organization (CSO), 101–102
Central Vigilance Commission, 9, 65, 71
Central-eastern India, 97
Centre for Media Studies, 1, 6
Centre for Studies in Social Sciences in Kolkata, 36
Chemotherapy, 144–145
Child health, 53
Childbirth, 102, 107, 109
Childhood, 203
Chi-square, 105, 113, 115, 117
Chotanagpur Charitable Association, 183
Christian Association, 183
Christian Missionaries, 182–183, 185
Civil Rights Act, 218
Civil society, 11, 31, 33, 64, 66, 76–77, 239, 254–255
Class exploitation, 184, 186
Clinching factor, 80
Clinical research process, 155
Coalition politics, 75
Colonial
  developmental projects, 178
  discourses, 193–194
Colonialism, 190
  internal, 191
Committee on Prevention of Corruption, 2
Component and Distribution of Women, 128
Conflict, 17, 19, 97, 177, 179–180, 188–189, 199, 204
  bloody, 97
  matrimonial, 23
  public/private, 234
  social, 87
Consciousness, 165, 190, 221
Constitution of India, 91, 98, 168, 197, 217, 224
Contemporary Bengal, 36–39, 41, 43, 45, 47, 49
Contemporary India, 21
Content analysis, 40, 229
Cooperativeness, 175, 208
Coping, 137, 141–143, 149, 153
Core elements, 156, 193
Corporate
  house-political nexus, 4
  escape, 11
Correlation, 209–212
Corrupt elements, 81
Corruption Perception Index (CPI), 7, 64–65
Corruption
  abetting, 7
  combat, 11, 81
  conceptualise, 66
  cycle of, 70, 72
  defined, 2
  destroy, 75
  extortive, 73
  fighting, 78
  forces of, 77–78
  high profile, 76
  identified, 3
  incidence of, 9, 79, 81
  level of, 7
  menace of, 1–2
  petty/retail, 69
  public, 74
  rampant, 1
  spawn, 73
  spectre of, 68, 76
  systemic, 71
Counter-development, 177, 179, 181, 183, 185, 187, 189, 191, 193, 195, 197, 199
Crime syndicates, 5–6
Criminal gangs, 5
Criminal Law Act, 9
Crude Birth Rate (CBR), 241, 243, 249

Crude death rates, 241, 243, 249
Cultural
  bond, 175
  division of labour, 189
  factors, 113
  heritage, 185

Daily life activities, 130
Death rates, 243–245
Decision-making factors, 130
Declaration of Rights of Man, 223
Deliberate cooperation, 69
Democracy, 2, 38, 66, 188, 190, 215, 222
Demographic change, 241, 243
Demographic Estimates for India, 244
Demographic Transition (DT), 239–241, 243–247, 249, 251, 253–255
Dependency ratio
  old age, 248, 252
  young age, 252
Depression, 137, 144, 148, 153, 205
Deprivation, 25, 181, 190, 194, 198, 225
Development/Developmental, 6, 20, 27, 66, 86–89, 91, 93, 95–97, 124, 139, 149, 177, 181–183, 185–193, 195–199
  activities, 197, 199
  changes, 174
  educational formal, 162
  efforts, 190
  endeavours, 188, 190
  hegemonic, 197, 198
  historical, 182
  infrastructural, 63
  intellectual, 163
  model, 87
  modern, 88
  patterns, 204
  planned, 87
  planners, 87
  process, 174, 190, 192, 196–198
  programmes, 192
  rural, 184
  socioeconomic, 27
Diabetes, 104, 140
Disadvantaged majority, 198
Disparities, 219–220
Displacement, 86, 88, 90–91, 94–95, 97–98, 196
Distinctiveness, 172, 175, 177
Domestic violence, 13–19, 21, 23–31, 33–34
Dowry, 14–19, 21, 23–24, 27, 33–34, 237
  death, 14–15, 17–19, 23
Dowry Prohibition Act, 14, 17, 21
Drinking water, 59, 61

Eclampsia, 104, 111, 113, 117, 119
Eclamptic fit, 109
Economic
  attainment, 219, 221–222
  crisis, 194–195
  deprivation of women, 220
  development, 90, 191
  factors, 123–124
  freedom, 124
  growth, 86–87
  liberalization, 87–88
  participation, 219–220
  violence, 24–25
Educational policy, 174
Educational system, 38
E-governance, 76, 79
Elementary schools, 206, 237
Emergency Obstetric Care (EmOC), 100
Emotional Stability (ES), 208
Empowerment Index (EI), 125–127, 130–131
Empowerment, 78, 123–125, 127 128, 130–132, 255
  determinants of, 125–126
  level of, 125, 128, 130–131
  political, 219, 222, 224
Ethnic conflict, 177, 179, 188–191

Ethnic discontents, 177, 179
Ethnic identity formation, 185–187
  process of, 185–186
Ethnic mobilization, 179, 181–182, 184–185, 187–188, 198
Ethnic movements, 179–182
Ethnic separation theory, 188
Ethnic solidarity, 165, 189–190
Ethnicity, 178, 182, 184, 186–190, 198
Extortions, 79–80, 233

Family caregivers, 149–152, 157
Family Income, 42
Fatigue, 139, 143–144, 151
Fertiliser factory, 195
Fertility, 124, 138, 239–240, 243, 249
Field Survey, 56–57, 59–60, 209–212
First Information Report (FIRs), 23
Food insecurity, 91–92
Food trolley, 144–145
Forced displacement, 91–92
Foreign Direct Investment (FDI), 93
Forest Rights Act, 98
Forestland, 96

Gender analysis, 206
Gender gap ranking, 220
Globalization, 42, 86–89, 91, 93, 95, 97, 177
Government of India Act, 1
Green vegetables, 107
Group identity, 164, 177

Haemorrhage, 102, 105, 109, 111, 113, 117, 119
Health
  care services, 119
  care team, 149–152
  centres, 58, 62
  education, 52–53, 155
  facilities, 53–55, 103, 107, 125
  hazards, 152
  indicators, 52–53
  institutions, 51, 54–55
  personnels, 58, 61
  problems, 52–53, 62, 105
  services, 1, 53, 61–62, 100
  situation, 51, 53
  workers, 105–106
Health Administrative Unit's (HAU), 103
Healthcare, 55, 61–62, 104, 106, 113, 125, 157
Heavy Engineering Corporation, 95
Hepatitis, 102, 112, 117
Home delivery, 112, 117, 119
Honorary Health Worker (HHW), 103–104

Illicit financial flows, 8
Indian condition, 31, 217
Indian democracy, 199
Indian Penal Code (IPC), 9, 14, 17, 19, 24–25, 30
Indian Population Project VIII, 103
Indian Premier League, 65
Indo-Hungarian Educational Exchange Programme, 37
Inequality, 75, 97, 190, 215–216, 219, 221
Infant Mortality Rate (IMR), 52, 54, 241, 243
Inhabitants, 181
Inheritance, 15, 185
Integrated Child Development Services (ICDS), 103, 170
Intelligentsia, 178
Inter-correlations, 211, 213
Interrelated factors, 68
Intra-partum periods, 111

Jharkhand Movement, 167, 177, 180–182, 186, 188, 192, 198
Jharkhand Party, 183
Judicial decisions, 29
Judiciary, 21, 23, 29, 97

Kolkata Metropolitan Area (KMA), 100, 102–103, 105, 108–109, 112

Land alienation, 90, 193
Lawyers Collective Women's Rights Initiative, 28
Left Front, 36–38, 43, 48
Liberalism, 39, 47
Libido, 138–139
Life expectancy, 241, 246, 249–251
  of female, 249
Literacy Rate in India, 222
Little Munni School, 234
Lok Sabha, 168–169, 224
Lokpal Bill, 10
LPG Development Model, 87, 97

MacMillan Cancer Support Survey, 146
Mafia, 2, 5–6
Mainstreaming, 123
Malpahari families, 55–56
Marginalized people, 96–97, 190
Maternal
  age, 113
  death, 100–107, 109, 111, 113, 117, 119–120
  health, 101, 117, 119
  melodrama, 231, 233
  mortality, 100–105, 113, 119–120
  mortality ratio, 101–102, 119
Matrimonial
  families, 18, 33
  home, 14, 17–18, 25, 30–33
Matrimonial Homes Act, 32
Mazdoor Kisan Shakti Sangathan (MKSS), 77–78
Mega-corruptions, 77
Migrated tea plantation worker, 194
Millennium Development Goals (MDG), 101
Mineral-based Industries, 86
Mineral Policy, 96
Mining industries, 93–94
Mobility freedom, 125–126, 130
Mobilization, 179, 187
Modernist paradigm, 188
Modernization, 72–73, 165, 188–190
Morbidities, 105, 109, 111–112
  maternal, 105
  threatening, 111
Mortality rates, 112, 246
Mother tongue, 163, 166–167, 169–171
Mother-son relationship, 231
Multinational Corporations, 89
Multivariate analysis, 106
Munda community, 56, 58
Munda-Oraon Education Conference, 183

Narcotics trade, 6
Natal families, 28
National Crime Record Bureau of Government of India, 13
National Human Rights Commission (NHRC), 65
National Hydroelectric Corporation, 95
National Population Policy (NPP), 101
National Rural Health Mission (NRHM), 1, 100
Nationalism, 178
Natural Growth Rate (NGR), 241, 243, 249
Natural resources, 81, 87–88, 90, 94, 97–98, 172, 181, 192, 196–197
Nausea, 143–144, 151
Nepotism, 71, 75
Niyamgiri hill Vedanta Company, 93
Nodal Centre, 6
Non-adivasis, 184, 186–187
Non-tribal
  families, 91
  students, 171
North-eastern India, 180
North-western India, 180
Nuclear families, 91, 130–131
Nutrient intake pattern, 225
Nutrition, 103, 143–144, 150
  adequate, 143–144

education, 144
parenteral, 145
Nutritional anaemia, 57

Ol-Chiki movement, 163–164, 167
Oncology professionals, 150–151
Oraon families, 55

Palliative care, 154–156
Panchayat Election, 224
Paramilitary forces, 97
Personal hygiene, 52–53
PESA Act, 89–91
Physical violence, 24
Planning Commission, 87
Pohang Iron and Steel Company, 93
Political corruption, 2–5, 69, 72
Political integration, 178
Political participation, 38–39, 46, 48
Positive entitlements, 25–26
Post-development theorists, 197
Post-natal cares, 120
Post-partum periods, 105, 107, 111–112, 119–120
Potential support ratio, 252
Poverty, 52–53, 61, 73, 75, 92, 97, 173, 196, 226
Pregnancy, 102, 104–107, 109, 111–113, 117, 119
Pre-independence era, 162
Prevention of Corruption Act, 9, 81
Private nursing homes, 62
Pro-social scores, 209–213
Protection of Civil Rights Act, 218
Protection of Women from Domestic Violence Act, 14, 25, 32
Protection Orders, 29–31
Psycho-educational approaches, 156
Psychological factors, 144
Psychosocial oncology, 153
Public domain, 79, 81
Public services, 7–8, 80

Quality education, 174

Race, 51, 217
Radicalism, 37, 39–40, 43–47
Radicals, 39–41, 45–46, 48–49
Rank by Rate (RR), 19
Red tape, 73
Regression analysis, 125
logistic, 117
multiple, 126
Residential schools, 172
Right to Equality, 215, 217, 219, 221, 223, 225
history of, 216
Right to Information (RTI), 78
Risk factors, 104, 113, 117
Roman Catholic Cooperative Society, 183
Routine Household Decisions (RHDI), 125–127, 130
Rural agricultural folk, 195
Rural students, 43, 49

Sample Registration System (SRS), 226, 241, 243
Sanitary toilets, 60
Sanitation, 53, 59–60
Santal
children, 169, 173
education, 165
families, 55
identity, 163, 165
women, 165
language, 166–169
Scheduled Areas, 90
School achievement, 206
School bullying, 206
Script movement, 167, 169
Self-confidence, 130, 132, 204
Sex-ratio, 126, 219, 226
Sexual
activity, 138–139
intercourse, 140
Sexuality, 16, 139, 154, 233
Social changes, 39, 43, 87
Social development, 3, 86, 98, 206

Social factors, 124
Social identity theory, 164, 174–175
Social structure, 4, 178
Socialist society, 40
Socio-Demographic Indicators, 253
Socio-economic
  factors, 119, 125–126, 128
  features, 127
  groups, 52–53
Sociological
  analysis, 152
  paradigm, 187–188
South Eastern Coalfields Ltd. (SECL), 96
Special and Local Laws (SLL), 19, 22
State Bureau of Health Intelligence, 111
Statistical analysis, 105
Stringent law, 9, 23
Student Federation of India (SFI), 37, 39
Student leaders, 38–39
Student movement, 36–38, 40, 48
Student politics, 39, 48
Student radicalism, 36–39, 41, 43, 45–47, 49
Student union elections, 38–39, 48
Supreme Court, 22–23, 32, 75, 97, 218

Tata Steel, 95
Tax evasion, 7–8
Tea gardens, 193–194
Tetanus Toxoid (TT), 106
Third World, 221, 225
Tolerance, 71
Torture, 14, 18–20, 194
Total Fertility Rate (TFR), 241, 245, 249–250
Traditional Birth Attendants (TBAs), 101–102, 107, 117, 119
Traditional caste hierarchy, 183
Transparency, 2–3, 48, 73, 76–77, 79
Transparency International (TI), 64–65, 67, 77
Tribal
  communities, 52–53, 88–89, 91–93
  development, 162
  families, 55, 59–60
  health scenario, 51, 61
  villages, 54, 59, 61, 94
  world, 174
Tube wells, 59, 61
Tumour, 145

UGC Major Research Project, 36–37
UK Bribery Act, 11
UN Convention Against Corruption (UNCAC), 11
Unhygienic water sources, 59, 61
UNICEF, 100
United Nations Development Programme Report, 86
United Nations, 240–242, 249
United States, 4–5
Universal Declaration of Human Rights, 216–217
Untouchability, 217–218
Untrained Dais, 107, 117, 119

Verbal autopsy, 104
Victimization, 204, 206
Viral Hepatitis (VH), 101, 104–105, 112–113, 117, 119
Vohra Committee, 5–6
Vote-banks, 75

Water sources, 94–95
Water tables, 59, 61
Western principle of nationalism, 178
Whistleblower's Bill, 10
Widow remarriage, 234–235
Women
  backward castes, 129, 131
  divorced, 28
  employed, 126
  empowerment, 123–125, 128–131
  exploited, 238
  illiterate, 117, 126

pregnant, 102, 107, 112
representation, 222, 224, 237
resourceful, 33
single, 25
suppress, 21
tribal, 52–53
World Economic Forum, 3, 219
World Health Organization, 51, 109, 225

Youth dormitories, 162

Zend Avesta, 216